Advance Praise for *The Accidental Project Manager*

"I found much to admire in *The Accidental Project Manager*, Patricia Ensworth's book of useful and always gentle advice for the novice manager."

—Tom DeMarco
Author, *Slack: Getting Past Burnout,
Busywork, and the Myth of Total Efficiency*

"In an engaging style, Ensworth poses hundreds of thought-provoking questions that will help both new and seasoned project managers get a solid grip on the myriad aspects of a complex software project. The book includes a wealth of sound recommendations drawn from software development best practices, combined with the experience of a savvy manager who understands both the technical and the human aspects of success project leadership."

—Karl Wiegers
Process Impact

"Her book fills a gap between books like *Winning at Project Management* and other introductory management tomes that focus heavily on the technical aspects of generic project management and books like *Software Project Survival Guide* that focus on key practices and processes of software development projects. I commend her focus on team dynamics and intergroup politics—the hardest topics and the ones that get less ink than they deserve—along with the practical, from-the-trenches introduction to the software development experience from the project manager's point of view. While management styles will differ for seasoned pros, the overwhelmed new manager can use her book as a point of departure. More importantly, fresh managers can use Ms. Ensworth's advice to avoid finding themselves "Peter Principled" on their first projects. I wish I'd had this book when I started as a project manager 15 years ago, and I can think of some project managers on recent engagements that could have used this book to lessen the pain and, in one case, avoid some of the fatal pitfalls Ms. Ensworth describes well in her book."

—Rex Black
President and Principal Consultant,
Rex Black Consulting Services
Author, *Managing the Testing Process*

"An excellent buffet of practical and proven tools and techniques for newly appointed software project managers, and a compact refresher course for veterans. Patricia Ensworth cuts to the heart and gets you up the learning curve fast."

—Doug DeCarlo
Principal, The Doug DeCarlo Group

The Accidental Project Manager:

Surviving the Transition from Techie to Manager

Patricia Ensworth

Wiley Computer Publishing

John Wiley & Sons, Inc.

NEW YORK · CHICHESTER · WEINHEIM · BRISBANE · SINGAPORE · TORONTO

For Mike

Publisher: Robert Ipsen
Editor: Theresa Hudson
Development Editor: Kathryn A. Malm
Managing Editor: Angela Smith
Associate New Media Editor: Brian Snapp
Text Design & Composition: Publisher's Design @ Print Services

Designations used by companies to distinguish their products are often claimed as trademarks. In all instances where John Wiley & Sons, Inc., is aware of a claim, the product names appear in initial capital or ALL CAPITAL LETTERS. Readers, however, should contact the appropriate companies for more complete information regarding trademarks and registration.

Forms reproduced herein with the permission of Moody's Investors Service, Inc.

This book is printed on acid-free paper. ∞

This publication is designed to provide accurate and authoritative information in regard to the subject matter covered. It is sold with the understanding that the publisher is not engaged in professional services. If professional advice or other expert assistance is required, the services of a competent professional person should be sought.

Library of Congress Cataloging-in-Publication Data:

Ensworth, Patricia.
　　The accidental project manager : surviving the transition from techie to manager / Patricia Ensworth.
　　　p. cm.
　　Includes index.
　　ISBN 0-471-41011-X (pbk. : alk. paper)
　　1. Project management. I. Title.

HD69.P75 E57 2001
658.4'04—dc21
2001026757

Printed in the United States of America.

10 9 8 7 6 5 4 3 2 1

Contents

About the Author

Patricia Ensworth is a Vice President of Systems Development and manager of software quality assurance at Moody's Investors Service. Over the course of her 20-year career in software development, she has worked as a project manager, systems analyst, system administrator, product manager, developer, tester, technical writer, and trainer. She has participated in development projects for products ranging from mainframe applications to Internet e-commerce systems. She holds a master's degree in anthropology from Columbia University and specializes in cultural issues affecting usability design and the globalization of technology. Her articles about software engineering and other subjects have appeared in many technical publications and popular magazines.

Acknowledgments

I'm very grateful to many people for helping me with this project. Some helped with the book itself, and some helped my family and me cope while it was being written.

First and foremost, thanks to Kathryn Malm of John Wiley & Sons for recognizing the potential appeal of this guide. I appreciated her editorial advice on the manuscript's structure and her thought-provoking queries on the content. During the past year she has labored many long hours; her talent, skills, and commitment have taken a rough nugget and turned it into a gem.

XML expert Bob DuCharme was a mentor during the early stages of the project, explaining methods of market research, reviewing the proposal, and offering guidance and encouragement. Patrick Forbes showed me the tools and methods he used to improve his team's performance and obtain a CMM Level 3 certification. Supreet Kaur Anand typed most of the first draft of the manuscript.

I am indebted to Joe Sniado, Managing Director of Systems Development at Moody's Investors Service, for his support, understanding, and open-mindedness during the past six years. Within the inevitable limits imposed by resources and deadlines, he has continually endorsed my efforts to improve software development processes and project management practices within our own organization. He is an astute manager of project managers, and I have learned a great deal from him.

Other colleagues at Moody's have also contributed to this book. Russ Le Blang provided the inspiration for most of the advice contained in the chapters describing the roles of the Entrepreneur and Team Captain. As far as I can tell, Nancy To is pretty much the ideal Technology Partner; she also taught me everything I know about enterprise databases. An outstanding team of quality assurance engineers—Bazil Clyne, Winfield Eng, Maggie Gilliam, Colin Grimes, Mila Guz, Ana Jaicks, Linda Joe, Jorge Lee, and Alex Shifrin —influenced the sections on software testing and reviewed early drafts of the QA documentation templates.

During the course of my career, several people have opened important doors for me, particularly Humberto Castellanos, Nancy Gleason, and Bill Rosenblatt. During the writing of this book, I received a great deal of aid and comfort from Maryann Bird, Gerrie Nachman, and Marjorie Saltzberg.

A special acknowledgment is reserved for my father, who taught me how to write and how to manage projects.

Finally—most importantly—my husband, Mike McDonnell, and my son, Terry McDonnell, have been cheering me on and enduring my workaholic binges for a long time now. No wife or mother could ask for better emotional and tactical support from her family. Their contributions to this book may not be visible or quantifiable, but they're enormous.

Introduction

Your manager shakes your hand and wishes you good luck. You walk back to your desk in a daze, excited and pleased, but also apprehensive. You've been asked to manage a software development project.

Congratulations . . . or condolences?

You've never done anything like this before. You might have a lot of experience in programming or testing—or you might be a business analyst or a "power user" of an important application. Yet managing an entire project, supervising and coordinating the development process from beginning to end, is something you've never tried. But you're smart and hard-working, and the fact that you've been given this assignment proves that management has confidence in you. How difficult could it be?

So you open a new word processing document and a blank spreadsheet and get to work. You think about what the product is supposed to do and who is going to use it. You speculate on various state-of-the-art designs and tools you might employ to build it. You envision a virtual community of contented, productive users who have nothing but praise for your product.

After a while you pause, dismayed. Several troubling thoughts have occurred to you:

- Nobody is going to tell you how to do this job.
- You will have to depend on many other people to get the job done.
- Other people are going to be depending on you to tell them what to do.

Often the first challenge a novice project manager faces is understanding the role. You're not following detailed instructions to perform specific tasks. You don't have creative control over the work. Yet somehow you're supposed to provide leadership—and you know you're going to be held accountable for the results. How, then, should you proceed?

Furthermore, you now find yourself with a staff to manage and a lot of decisions to make on issues about which (you soon realize) you understand very little. You know there is a right way to do things, but you don't have time to go back to school to learn it—or to read through weighty textbooks that seem designed for project managers at large, complex, zero-defect facilities like nuclear power plants or air traffic control centers.

Hang in there, new project manager. This book will be your "cheat sheet." It will give you enough good advice so that you can act as if you know exactly what you're doing, even as you're learning on the job and figuring out what works in your organization.

No doubt you have heard about software development standards such as ISO 2001, 6-Sigma, and the Capability Maturity Model. This book incorporates many of their principles. However, most people who have ever tried to apply these standards to software project management in a real-world organization have encountered two major obstacles:

- The ideal software development group envisioned by the models is part of an organization where the structure, culture, and leadership remain stable.
- The senior management of the model organization makes a long-term commitment of substantial resources to an initiative that for several years produces little tangible return on investment.

In today's information technology environment where mergers and reorganizations and outsourcing happen all the time, and where senior management focuses on quarterly results, life doesn't always follow the recommended procedures.

Using these models as your guide for software project management is like trying to dock a boat by referring to the diagrams in a Coast Guard manual. Theoretically the process should work smoothly as described; you, on the other hand, are standing on a rolling deck in the rain, fighting the wind and the waves.

But you can benefit from reviewing the industry's best practices and implementing them wherever possible on your own turf. This book will outline them for you briefly, with minimal jargon and maximum common sense.

How This Book Is Organized

The plot unfolds sequentially. You (the hero/heroine) manage the development of a software product from conception through release, with many adventures along the way. You travel a well-worn path, through a series of challenging and sometimes treacherous escapades.

Accompanying you is a hardy band of stalwart, worthy companions on whose skills and efforts you depend. Your project might be large enough that you have one person to do each job, or your team members might take on several functions simultaneously. In addition to the project manager, these roles are as follows:

Client. The project's sponsor or the manager designated by the sponsors to supervise the project. Typically a senior manager within your user community. Ultimate authority on design and usability issues. The person who signs off on the user acceptance test, who approves or rejects your work.

Product manager. Your users' primary representative. The contact person you call for routine research on what your users need and want. The expert your users contact with their questions, suggestions, and complaints. Sets priorities for product requirements, especially future enhancements. Normally appointed by the client. A patient, caring, cheerful person with excellent communication skills and attention to detail.

Development manager. The architect of the system. A skilled artisan capable of selecting and customizing appropriate development tools, evaluating alternative designs, and following exemplary software engineering practices. Supervises the

Research ⇒ Analysis ⇒ Design ⇒ Construction ⇒ Deployment ⇒ Assimilation ⇒ Maintenance

Figure I.1   The path of a project manager can be challenging and treacherous.

work of other developers, both staff members and consultants. Prioritizes development tasks. Provides estimates of time and resources required to accomplish specific programming goals. Divides the work into manageable tasks and tracks progress, notifying the project manager of any problems or delays. Monitors the development environment.

Quality assurance manager. The author of the product's test plan. An experienced systems analyst capable of selecting and customizing appropriate quality assurance tools for such tasks as change management, version control, automated functional testing, automated performance testing, configuration management, monitoring, and documentation management. Supervises the work of product testers, both staff members and consultants. Negotiates schedule of versions and length of test cycles with the development manager. Provides estimates of time and resources required to accomplish specific testing tasks. In case of time or resource shortages (i.e., always), evaluates risks associated with alternative testing strategies. Divides the work into manageable tasks and tracks progress, notifying the project manager of any problems or delays. Supervises the change management database. Monitors the testing environment.

Technical writer. The creator of the user manuals and online Help. Experienced in graphic design and layout of publications. Organizes information from the user's point of view.

Trainer. The creator of tutorials and classroom instructional material for different groups of users based on their daily tasks, security level, educational background, location, and technological proficiency. Conducts classes, demos, and videoconferences.

Distribution coordinator. The developer or tester responsible for the logistics of moving the product from the development environment into the production environment. Supervises database installations on the mainframe or server. Monitors automated delivery of programs. Confirms users' access rights, security levels, and login permissions.

Support coordinator. The developer or tester responsible for making sure the users' questions are answered accurately and their problems addressed expeditiously.

Documentation coordinator. The developer or tester responsible for organizing, auditing, and maintaining all the documentation necessary for project management, system development, and testing. Supervises the documentation library database.

Configuration/version coordinator. The developer or tester responsible for making sure that the hardware and software the project team members use are compatible with each other and with the rest of the organization. Supervises the configuration management database and the version control database.

Procedures coordinator. The developer or tester responsible for organizing, auditing, and maintaining the project's procedures guide.

Mascot. A soft, fuzzy stuffed animal either small enough to play catch with or large enough to use as a punching bag.

(Don't worry if some of the concepts or terms in this description are unfamiliar to you at this point—they'll all be discussed in greater detail later.)

During your journey you will need to assume various disguises. Actually they're all aspects of your project manager role, but at first they may feel as unfamiliar and artificial as if you were putting on a costume and speaking in a funny voice. The character you will portray will depend on whom you're dealing with:

Entrepreneur. Your project team is like your own small business, and you are in charge of marketing your product. Your users are your customers; it's up to you to find out what they want, provide it to them at a price they can afford, and make sure it continues to function reliably for them. You'll have to get funding from somewhere—probably not just once, but repeatedly. You'll need to draft proposals and make sales pitches and justify expenses and manage expectations. Sometimes you're P.T. Barnum, sometimes you're Machiavelli.

Technology Partner. Your product is only one of many development projects being undertaken by your Information Technology (IT) department on behalf of your user community. You are therefore only one among many project managers, all of whom have their own requirements and priorities. In addition, to deploy your product and keep it running you will need assistance from a number of IT services. You'll have to find out what each service entails and establish relationships with all the service managers. You're the new kid on the block; you've got to get along with the rest of the gang and stand up for yourself.

Figure I.2   Sometimes you're P.T. Barnum, sometimes you're Machiavelli.

Team Captain. Technology professionals are notoriously difficult to manage. Effective teamwork and communication among project participants who have vastly different specialized knowledge don't just happen. You'll need to evaluate people's strengths and weaknesses, set goals, devise procedures, inspire confidence, referee disputes. This aspect of the job demands the toughness of a football coach and the empathy of a psychotherapist.

The book is divided into four sections that correspond to the four major phases of a software development project. Within each section one chapter is devoted to each of the project manager's roles.

Section I —**Before Coding Begins** (Research and Analysis)
    Chapter 1— *Exploring the Elephant*
        Role: Entrepreneur
        Topics: Learning about your user community, understanding the political forces affecting your project, investigating your organization's technology environment.
    Chapter 2—*On Blueprints and Leaps of Faith*
        Role: Technology Partner
        Topics: Gathering requirements, creating a project plan, negotiating an agreement with your client.
    Chapter 3—*Who's on First*
        Role: Team Captain
        Topics: Recruiting staff, providing training, building a strong team.

This method of presenting the different roles might make you wonder at first whether an aptitude for project management has a lot in common with a tendency toward schizophrenia. Rest assured, it's mostly a narrative device. At the beginning of your project you'll probably be conscious of the behavior whenever you're switching roles to suit the occasion, and you might even find the shift a bit awkward. Yet with practice, as the project progresses, the different perspectives will gradually fuse together into a more integrated project manager outlook. Once you've gotten the knack of it, you'll make the transitions effortlessly and instinctively, with no more awareness than when you drive and talk and listen to music all at once.

Who Should Read This Book

You will find this book useful if you're a new project manager at an organization whose primary purpose is not commercial software development. Large or small, private sector or public sector, for-profit or nonprofit, it's an organization where an array of home-made and customized off-the-shelf software products are installed to serve specific organizational purposes.

The book assumes that prior to becoming a project manager you were a "techie"—most likely a software engineer—and the material in it was selected to bridge the gap between techie knowledge and project manager knowledge. Nonetheless, people in other types of jobs also sometimes find themselves suddenly promoted to project manager. If you were a business analyst, a product manager, or a "power user" of a legacy application that is being replaced, you'll find this book a good introduction to the bewildering assortment of technical issues you now face.

In many organizations, the software quality assurance (QA) group is responsible not only for testing products, but also for maintaining development standards across project teams and educating project managers and developers on the recommended practices. If you're a QA engineer, this book will provide you with an overview of the software development process you can use for your audits and training sessions.

Nowadays the managers of software project managers are not always technology professionals. In an attempt to improve the planning and budgeting process, or to build software products that are better suited to the organization's needs, a Manager of Information Technology or a Chief Information Officer may be appointed whose previous career might have been spent in finance, administration, or some other mission-critical area of the organization. If you're in this position, the technology learning curve looks like Mt. Everest. This book can help you evaluate whether the project managers who report to you are doing a good job.

The advice contained in this book should generally be relevant no matter on what type of platform, architecture, or hardware your product will run. The book does assume that your product will have an important front-end component and a workflow with significant interaction between the system and the end users. If your project is a back-end database migration or an automated data feed from one system to another, this is probably not a book for you.

The model project team on which the examples and suggestions in this book are based has 12 staff members: a client, a product manager, a project manager, four developers, three testers, a documentation writer, and a trainer. These participants' activities, however, are treated as roles rather than discrete jobs. You could apply the same principles to a much smaller team with only a project manager, one developer, and one tester or to a much larger team supplemented by consultants and vendors.

What's on the Web Site

The companion Web site is located at www.wiley.com/compbooks/ensworth and provides checklists and documentation templates that the novice project manager can use to get started. They are intended to offer guidance, not to impose a rigid order. Every organization, project, and team has unique, dynamic requirements and processes. If you adopt any of these tools, you should expect to modify them within the first month.

Milestone Marker

This book is a beginner's guide. It describes the essential activities of a software project manager and the typical situations you can expect to encounter. Software projects, though, are unpredictable. Events will occur for which the specific advice presented herein may not be adequate or valid. Yet most of the general principles and strategies recommended are based on decades of experience in many different types of organizations. If you find yourself in a unique crisis, you should be able to draw on the examples in these pages to point you in the right direction.

Your career may have taken a surprising turn when you were elevated to project manager. You may not be sure yet whether you're going to like the job. The goal of this book is to help you apply the skills and knowledge you already possess and to show you the path when you venture into new territory. Whatever measures your organization employs to evaluate you, you'll know you have succeeded if your project team creates a software product that makes your users glad to turn on their computers.

Exploring the Elephant

At the beginning of a project the most important fact to acknowledge is that everyone has a different idea about what is going to happen. It's like the parable of the three blind men and the elephant. When asked to identify what they were touching, the blind men came up with three different answers depending on their location. The man feeling the trunk thought it was a fire hose; the man sitting beside the leg guessed a tree; the man standing in the middle thought it was a large warm pillow.

In the early stages, your product is the elephant, and everyone involved in creating, distributing, maintaining, and using it are the blind men. Your role as an Entrepreneur is to find out who they are, what they perceive, and why. Before you can comprehend the requirements for the product, you must learn about your user community. Before you can count on receiving the necessary approvals and funding, you'll have to acquaint yourself with the political forces affecting your project. Before you can expect to be taken seriously as a software project manager in your organization, you'll be obliged to demonstrate an understanding of the technology environment.

Know the Users

So you're going to build a software product. Who is going to use it? Often novice project managers answer this question in vague, general terms: The Purchasing Department. Branch office managers. Cashiers at sporting goods stores. Yes . . . but who *exactly* are these people? Male or female? How old? What is their educational background?

Figure 1.1   The shape of your project isn't always clear at the beginning.

How comfortable are they using computers? What language do they speak primarily? What is their work environment like?

This can be a tricky issue if the client commissioning your system is the manager of your users. It's fairly common for the Vice President of Widget Production to try to appoint himself as the ultimate authority on the work processes of widget makers on the assembly line. If you listen only to the manager when you are building your product, you will almost certainly overlook some critical step or data element, an omission that will make your users' life miserable later.

To better understand the needs of all your users, examine your assumptions, conduct thorough research, and form a committee of experts.

Assumptions

It's much quicker and easier to develop a software product based on assumptions about the users than on verifiable facts. Here are some common assumptions, which are nearly always false:

   The users are like me. One thing you can be sure of: your users are not going to resemble you, your developers, or your testers. If your developers design a product based on their own knowledge, habits, and tastes, your users are going to be baffled.

   The users are all the same. Your users probably will not resemble each other. Even if your product is a small application that performs one simple function and the members of your user community share the same job title, you should not assume that everyone thinks and acts alike. From the outside, a task may appear simple or a group homogeneous. Once you get to know the details, however, the reality is usually more nuanced.

The users' work environment is like my work environment. Software development is a unique activity. Although there are different opinions about the ideal physical layout of development teams' workspace, nearly everyone agrees that engineers need a lot of peace and quiet for unbroken concentration, plus occasional encounters with colleagues to exchange ideas. In contrast, your users may spend most of their time interacting face-to-face with people outside your organization or answering 15 phone calls per hour. They may log on to your system remotely via modem from a hotel room in the middle of the night, stupefied by jet lag. If the product you give them is perfectly suited to your development environment, chances are your users will find it awkward.

It can be very enlightening for you and your team to write down your assumptions about your users before you actually meet them. By becoming aware of the influence of your own imagination and your unconscious expectations, you're more likely to see the users as they really are on their own terms. You could make it an entertaining, non-competitive game: ask every member of your team to submit three paragraphs to you anonymously describing who your typical user will be as an individual, who your user community will be as a group, and what your users' work environment will be like. Put the submissions aside until after you've done your fieldwork, then read them aloud at a staff meeting. The person who was most wrong in his or her assumptions—and admits it—should get a token prize.

Figure 1.2   Getting to know your users.

Fieldwork

There's really only one way for your project team to get to know the users, and that's by getting to know the users. Personally.

Many engineers are not gregarious by nature, and they would therefore prefer to forgo this process. Many project managers feel that developers are supposed to write code and testers are supposed to break code, and they would therefore prefer to delegate this research to a business analyst. But no matter how grumpy or disheveled your staff might be, no matter how talented and efficient the business analyst, direct human contact ultimately yields the best results. At the beginning of your project, you should send every member of your team out into the field at least once.

Site Visits

Try to visit every location where your product will be installed—every department, every floor, every branch office. If this is impossible due to the large number of locations or the small size of your travel budget, consult with your client and come up with a representative sample of locations. During your visit, look around carefully. Listen to the sounds in the room. Make notes and take photos. Create a paper form so that you observe the same factors in each location. Your observation should answer the following questions:

- How is the space arranged? Do people work in isolation or in groups?
- How much privacy do people have? Can everyone see what is displayed on people's screens or hear what they say on the phone?
- How bright is the space? Is there a great deal of sunlight?
- How crowded is the space?
- How noisy is it?
- Do people work standing up or sitting down?
- Do people share computers or have their own? Do they have more than one computer on their desks? Do they share printers?
- When they talk on the phone, do they use headsets? Are both of their hands usually free?
- When people do work on their computers, how often are they interrupted? Can they control the pace of their work and the times during which they might be interrupted?

After you've completed your site visits, gather the forms in a file folder and store them until you're ready to analyze the data.

Interviews

Ask your client for a list of all the major tasks your users perform. Next ask for a list identifying at least two or three users who perform each task in every location where your product will be installed. Then ask your client to notify all the people on the list that you will be contacting them to arrange an interview and to request their cooperation.

The interview should cover not only the person's job functions and information requirements, but also the more subjective factors that affect your product. Take pictures or make a videotape of each person in his or her work environment. Create a form for the interview so that you remember to ask everyone the same questions. Among the questions you might include are these:

- How long have you worked at the organization?
- What do you do? (Be prepared for facetious answers. When interviewing managers, expect that they will respond by telling you their title.)
- Can you describe a typical day at the office? (Don't bother to take extensive notes on this question—listen instead for general patterns, such as "lots of meetings with production staff" or "research and analysis of industry trends" or "call 12–20 sales contacts per hour.")
- Where do you look up the information you need to do your job? What publications? What computer systems or online resources? (Ask for samples to take with you and contacts to obtain access.)
- Whom do you speak to in person or on the phone to get the information you need to do your job?
- What information are you expected to provide to other people? Do you regularly fill out any forms or logs, update any lists, produce any reports? Which of these are paper documents? Which are inputs to computer systems? Are there any other formats, such as phone consultations or e-mail messages? (Ask for samples to take with you.)
- Do you type and print out your own documents and input your own data into the computer? If not, who does it for you?
- Who are your managers?
- Whom do you manage?
- Where are you from originally?
- Where did you go to school? What did you study? (Ask about high school, college, and graduate or technical school.)
- What languages do you speak?
- Do you have a computer at home? What kind? What do you use it for? When you have problems with it, whom do you call?
- Do you like to read books and magazines? What have you read during the past month?
- Do you like to watch movies and TV? What are some of your favorite films and shows?
- What do you enjoy most about your job? What aspect is the most stressful?

Although you should not ask these questions directly, the form you use for the interview should also record the person's gender, approximate age, and any important physical characteristics or disabilities. There should also be a section where the interviewer can make personal, subjective notes, such as: "Very friendly and helpful," "Piles of paper all over the office," "Star Trek fan," "Arrogant and obnoxious," and so on. Finally, the interviewer should inquire whether the person would be willing to serve on a committee of users who help design, test, or support the product.

Template 1.1 is a sample form that you can use when you conduct these interviews. You may also download this template from the Web site. As with the information from the site surveys, you should gather your interview forms and notes in a file folder in preparation for data analysis.

User Survey

USER NAME: _____

AGE: ___ [don't ask—estimate] _____

GENDER: _____

LENGTH OF EMPLOYMENT: _____

POSITION/TITLE: _____

MANAGER: _____

DIRECT REPORTS: _____

Interview Questions

- What do you do?

  _____
  _____
  _____

- Can you describe a typical day at the office?

  _____
  _____
  _____

- Where do you look up the information you need to do your job? What publications? What computer systems or online resources?

  _____
  _____
  _____

- Whom do you speak to in person or on the phone to get the information you need to do your job?

  _____
  _____
  _____

- What information are you expected to provide to other people? Do you regularly fill out any forms or logs, update any lists, produce any reports? Which of these are paper documents? Which are inputs to computer systems? Are there any other formats, such as phone consultations or e-mail messages?

  _____
  _____
  _____

- Do you type and print out your own documents and input your own data into the computer? If not, who does it for you?

  _____
  _____
  _____

Template 1.1　　User Survey

Personal Information

- Where are you from originally?

  _____
  _____
  _____

- Where did you go to school? What did you study? (Ask about high school, college, and graduate or technical school.)

  _____
  _____
  _____

- What languages do you speak?

  _____
  _____
  _____

- Do you have a computer at home? What kind? What do you use it for? When you have problems with it, whom do you call?

  _____
  _____
  _____

- Do you like to read books and magazines? What have you read during the past month?

  _____
  _____
  _____

- Do you like to watch movies and TV? What are some of your favorite films and shows?

  _____
  _____
  _____

- What do you enjoy most about your job? What aspect is the most stressful?

  _____
  _____
  _____

- Would you be willing to serve on a committee of users who help design, test, or support the product?

  _____
  _____
  _____

Notes/Observations

_____
_____
_____

Template 1.1   (*Continued*)

On-the-Job Training

Anthropologists who do fieldwork soon learn that what people tell you about their behavior is often quite different from how they actually behave. Yet your subjects are probably not intentionally lying. It's more likely that they don't consciously keep track of their own actions. They do know how they're supposed to behave, and when asked by an outsider they overestimate their own virtue. As a result, your project team can't completely rely on the interviewers' accounts.

If your user community provides formal training for new hires, ask your client to enroll your team members in the class. This will give everyone an understanding of the ideal process under normal conditions. Then select several cooperative, articulate users whom you got along well with during the interviews and arrange with your client for your team members to become their trainees. If possible, the users chosen should perform a variety of the tasks included on your client's original list. Your team members should first sit next to the users and observe them performing their jobs. After a while, the users should begin teaching your team members to do their jobs and letting them try to perform routine tasks. Gradually your team members will become aware of how the users modify the ideal process to suit their own requirements and how they handle unusual conditions and exceptional data.

As they receive their on-the-job training, your team members should keep written notes about their lessons. They should type up and submit to you any procedures they encounter that will affect the data model encoded in your product—particularly if these procedures are undocumented or if they deviate from the ideal presented in the official training course. Gather the notes and the documents in a file folder for data analysis; they will also be helpful later, during development, when you create use cases.

Data Analysis

After your finish your fieldwork, you'll have amassed folders of notes and documents and boxes of pictures and videos. You'll have met some interesting people and learned more than you ever wanted to know about whatever it is your users do. No doubt your team members will be eager to get on with the project. But what you have at this point is only a collection of anecdotes. You'll need to analyze the information you gathered to derive any useful knowledge from it.

Site profiles. Based on the notes and photos you took and the forms you filled out during your site visits, write a description of your users' various workspaces. Include the size of the space, the number of people who work there, and the layout of the offices, cubicles, counters, and open areas. List equipment and devices that are shared. Describe the physical relationship between the people and their machines. Attempt to convey the "look and feel" of the place.

User profiles. Review the forms you filled out during your interviews. Can the users be grouped by any distinguishing characteristic, such as language, educational background, job description, or computer experience? Write a composite description of a typical user for each category you can identify. The number of profiles you'll need will vary depending on the nature of your product and your user community. If your product will provide an automated workflow that links many types of tasks, then you will probably require more profiles than if your product will automate the functions within a single task. If your users will be located in many branch offices or in different countries, more profiles will be necessary than if they all occupy the same floor at the home office.

Procedures profile. Read through the research notes your team members took and the procedures documents they submitted during their on-the-job training. Try to determine how consistent your users are in following a defined process. There will always be variations in how people do things; what you're interested in is a high-level view of their behavior. Within the workflow your product will model, identify those activities in which your users all adhere to standard procedures and those in which they improvise.

Present these profiles at a staff meeting, and encourage your team members to discuss them. (If you decided to play the "Worst Assumptions" game, now would be the time to read the entries and award the prize.) You'll find that the results of your analysis will have both a direct effect on your product's design and an indirect influence on your staff's relationship with your user community.

Your team members who are responsible for building the product's user interface will translate the information into guidelines shaping their design decisions. For example:

- If people work in groups or have very little privacy, the data elements you present on the screen might be different than if each individual user works in seclusion.
- If people are interrupted often, the search function should display a verification screen before executing the query in case the user turns away to deal with another matter and forgets what he or she has asked for.
- If people work standing up, the speed of the program should be an important issue because when the users have to wait a long time for a response they will become aware that their feet hurt.
- If many people's primary language is not the language of the product, the interface should either be translated or employ icons to convey messages to the users.
- If people are technophobic, the product's workflow should incorporate wizards with lots of explanatory text.
- If people share a common educational background in a particular field, your messages to users can include jargon from that occupation.
- If people in different locations around the world assign roles to users of different seniority, your rules for permissions and data access should make provisions for this flexibility.
- If people spend all day wearing telephone headsets and typing data, you should give your users shortcuts and avoid making them reach for the mouse.

You don't have to be a user interface designer to benefit from first-hand knowledge of the user community. Developers of portions of the system such as the database and any middle-tier components will communicate better with the front-end developers when they understand why the UI is constructed in a particular way to suit the users' characteristics and work environment. Testers will invent more effective and more realistic methods of breaking the product when they're aware of your users' blind spots, areas of ignorance, procedural workarounds, and stress points. Documentation writers and trainers will adjust their style and content more appropriately when they know in detail who their audience will be. During the development and testing of your product when usability issues inevitably arise, everyone on the team will be better prepared to fathom the users' underlying concerns.

When you finish your data analysis, post the pictures you took of your users on a project bulletin board. Their faces will help your team remember that your product will become part of the lives of actual human beings.

Advisory Groups

Throughout the development of your product, and after its initial release when you're working on changes and enhancements, there will be times when you'll need to ask the users for advice. Whether it's a question about the rules encoded in the system, or about the layout of the forms, or about the priority of requested features, you won't be able to guess what they want, and if you try you'll probably be wrong.

Novice project managers frequently decide that the easiest way to obtain answers is to ask the client who commissioned the product. This approach may be easy at first, but it rarely serves the purpose for more than a few weeks. If your team members are doing their jobs well, they will always have a lot of questions. Sooner or later the client's patience will wear thin, and your urgent messages will go unanswered for so long that the project will slow down.

Busy clients customarily appoint a product manager from the user community to serve as a liaison with the project team. But even a designated product manager is only one person with a single point of view. Few product managers possess the research skills to survey, report on, and accurately represent a large and diverse population.

The solution is a user committee—or several. At different times during the development process you will need users to perform different roles:

Usability consultants review design specifications, prototypes, and versions-in-progress. They provide their opinions on the accuracy of the program rules, the suitability of the workflow, the clarity of the user interface, and many other look-and-feel issues. These users must be articulate and relatively sociable. They should understand the abstract model of the process that your product attempts to emulate. They should have enough patience to evaluate rough drafts and enough diplomacy to offer criticism and suggestions without offending the developers. They should not mind sitting through lots of meetings.

Beta testers review the final draft version of the product and try to find as many flaws as they can. They should be detail-oriented, methodical, and well organized. It helps if they are able to follow instructions carefully and keep accurate records. Rather than attending endless meetings, they will have to endure the boredom of performing repetitive tasks.

Point people help support the product after it has been released. They are the "power users" and gurus who explain its more esoteric functions to their colleagues. They gather complaints and suggestions from their colleagues and convey them to the product manager or directly to the project team. They should be capable teachers and respected leaders.

These three distinct sets of people will undoubtedly overlap to some degree, and certain people might do an excellent job as both usability consultants and beta testers or as usability consultants and point people. You won't be able to discern their talents until you get to know them, however. During your interviews you asked each person if he or she would be willing to participate in a user group, so you already have a few volunteers with whom to start. Because your ultimate goal is to create a group with representatives from each job category, each step in the workflow, and each location, you may need to ask your client to appoint some additional delegates. Begin to meet with the group as a whole as early as possible. Explain the tasks they can perform, the roles they can play, and the benefits they can provide to the project. As the development proceeds, you will soon learn who can make the most valuable contributions in each area.

Know the Management

It would be nice if the success of a software product depended solely on its intrinsic quality. Software that was developed for commercial sale is judged by its revenues and its reviews—not a perfect measure of quality, but a reasonable barometer nonetheless. Yet software built by an organization for its own use typically is viewed through a distorting lens: politics.

When you become a project manager, you enter a political arena where the rules of the game are somewhat different from the rules you've played by so far. Diplomacy and salesmanship are more important. The ability to devise a long-term strategy and to estimate the strength of your own position is a crucial skill. Novice project managers sometimes recoil from such activities, arguing that the skills have nothing to do with building a good product and are fundamentally cynical and manipulative. After a while you come to realize that politics is what makes building the product possible in the first place and that the game can be played with integrity.

At the heart of every political conflict are people with unique perspectives and opinions. From your point of view, the people who matter most are your client and other leaders within your user community, and the senior management of the technology group. The more you learn about these people, their values, and their fears, the better prepared you will be to advance the cause of your own project.

User Community

Start with the client who commissioned your product. Who is this person? Without actually conducting a structured interview, make sure you find out the answers to all the questions on the user interview form. In the process, try to determine what your sponsor has to gain personally from backing your project. Why this project, and why now? What will be the consequences for your client if the project is delayed or if the product fails to deliver the benefits the users expect?

During your discussions with your client, you will no doubt hear other names mentioned repeatedly. Within your user community there are other leaders, some of whom may be your sponsor's allies, and some of whom may be rivals. Each will have his or her own agenda that may, in some way, affect your project. In addition, depending on the structure of your organization, your client may have allies and rivals in other departments. There may be friendly leaders in other organizational groups who think your project is a great idea and are begging your client to expand the scope to include them. There may be hostile leaders who think your project is a waste of resources or a threat to their group's existence and are just waiting for a chance to prove that your client is incompetent. Without taking any of it personally, you should determine the range of opinions about your project and identify the sources of support or opposition. This sort of inquiry is best conducted openly, without any clandestine encounters or espionage: if you ask people frankly what they think and seem unfazed by their doubts or criticism, most of the time you'll hear at least part of the truth.

Even more important than the personal agendas of your client and other individual leaders are the long-term goals and priorities of your user community as a whole. Your project is probably among the major initiatives they've decided to undertake, but you can be sure that it's not the only one. Find out if the managers of your user community have participated in any strategic planning sessions for the coming year. If they have, try to obtain copies of any documents they discussed or produced, such as operating plans, project lists, or marketing presentations. If they haven't, try to attend a few staff meetings of managers at your client's level. By reading and listening you should be able to figure out where your project fits into their overall strategy. You'll also develop a better sense of which functions in your product are most crucial for them to achieve their objectives. Finally, because there are competing factions in every group, you'll gain insight into the forces shaping your users' future.

IT Department

To anyone who works with computers, "IT" usually stands for Information Technology. There are other possible acronyms, such as MIS (Management Information Systems) and ITS (Information and Technology Services), but basically they all mean the same thing: the techies. For the purposes of this book, we are assuming that your organization has an IT department and that you are part of it. Our hypothetical IT department is responsible for the entire technological infrastructure of the organization: the servers, the networks, the telecommunications, the desktop computers, the portable computers, the wireless information devices, the data security, the database administration, the distribution of software, and the routine end-user support. Our IT department also employs business analysts, programmers, testers, technical writers, trainers, and project managers to develop and support software products; it hires consultants to augment its regular staff; and it outsources certain activities and services to specialized vendors.

While the politics of your user community may have an influence on what your product does, the politics of your IT department will certainly have an influence on how your project gets done.

Consider the person at the top of the IT organization chart. The position goes by different names in different organizations: Chief Information Officer (CIO), Chief Technology Officer (CTO), or even Chief Administrative Officer (CAO). Whatever he or she is called, this leader is ultimately responsible for determining the standard hardware and software everyone will use and the standard technology processes everyone will follow. If you don't already know, do some research and find out about the person's background. Is she a 15-year veteran of the organization who rose through the ranks of mainframe programmers and is now re-educating herself on the architectures, tools, and methodologies of Internet development? Is he a former VP of Finance who was transferred to IT because the last CIO couldn't fill out a budget worksheet accurately and somehow lost track of two million dollars? Does she have a graduate degree in library science? Did he once publish a book on UNIX shell scripts? These details may help you to create a more persuasive presentation when you need senior management support for purchasing a new piece of equipment or introducing a new tier to the architecture.

In larger organizations, the various services of the IT department are usually divided among several managers. When planning your deployment, for example, you might need to coordinate your activities with the regular schedules and assignments of an operations group, a database administration group, a network support group, a desktop support group, a Help Desk, and so forth. As soon as you become a project manager, find out how many service managers you'll have to deal with on a regular basis and introduce yourself to each one. Be nice to them. Ask their advice. Treat them like powerful chieftains with whom you would like to establish a trading relationship.

The role of project manager is sometimes akin to joining a club. If there are other software project managers in your IT department or your organization, they probably all know each other and have their own informal network. They may go out to lunch together in pairs or in small groups and compare notes or give each other advice. For the sake of your project and your career, make an effort to join them. From their discussions you will learn how to navigate around obstacles and determine the true criteria for a product's success. Don't expect to be welcomed or even accepted right away: you'll need to prove yourself first. As a newcomer you should take your time, watch, and listen—and be a good sport if any harmless practical jokes are played on you.

Cultural Issues

Becoming acquainted with the decision-makers within your user community and your IT department will make you aware of the personalities and the motives behind the episodes of human drama that occur at your organization. You'll understand better how to approach certain people and why others always seem to give you a hard time.

After the faces and the idiosyncrasies have grown familiar, you'll begin to look at your organization in a new way. Based on the knowledge you've acquired about and from management, you'll discern the patterns of influence and the dynamics of change. All organizations exist in a state of continuous evolution, with unpredictable forces pulling them in unexpected directions. The more accurately you assess the tension between those forces, the more astutely you'll be able to plan your project. For example, senior managers today often find themselves in the middle of a cultural tug-of-war on several vital issues:

> **Technology versus enterprise.** All organizations are engaged in some sort of enterprise and employ some kind of technology—even if it's just adding machines and typewriters—but the balance between the two varies greatly. Does your organization equip the staff with the latest-and-greatest devices to stay ahead of the competition, or does it make do with older models and invest only enough to get the essential jobs done? Does it fund long-term projects to upgrade complex systems and integrate

standalone applications, or does it always treat those budget items as less important than initiatives that directly support the immediate goals of the enterprise?

Engineering versus marketing. When the marketers decide they want to sell a new product or offer a new service, do they consult with the software engineers to determine the impact on existing systems, or do they just go ahead and announce it and set a launch date of their own fabrication? If the two groups do discuss the matter, does the marketing group adjust its schedule and its pricing to give the development group a chance to do a reasonably good job, or are the developers always working under the gun in a crisis atmosphere? Does the marketing group understand enough about system development and software project management to factor in the cost of good practices, or is it ignorant of any measure of software quality other than revenues and delivery dates?

Central control versus local initiative. Does the IT department build, manage, and/or control every software product in use throughout the organization, or do different departments or offices create their own independent applications? If there is strict central control, how do enterprise managers obtain the resources to build new products quickly enough to take advantage of new opportunities—and how do they restrain the more technologically sophisticated members of their staff from seizing the initiative and building something on the sly? If there is support for decentralized development activities, then how does the IT department maintain standards of software quality, engineering process, and data security which are high enough and consistent enough for the organization to pass its inspection by financial auditors? How does the legal department ensure that the independent project teams negotiate similar contracts with consultants and service-level agreements with vendors, or that they comply with local laws in the states and countries in which their software is used, or that their products meet the organization's requirements for displaying the company logo and follow other style guidelines? If the nature of the project requires a mixture of central control and local development, what are the criteria for deciding who manages the project?

Staffing versus outsourcing. Every software development group seems to have more projects to do than it can handle. Assuming yours is no exception, how does your organization deal with the overload? Does it hire as many new permanent staff members as it can and try to build a corps of loyal, long-term employees who know the enterprise well? Does it instead resort to short-term temporary workers who can be recruited and dismissed based on fluctuating project needs? Does it maintain permanent relationships with consulting firms for particular services such as user interface design, testing, or documentation? Does it outsource entire projects to external vendors or application service providers (ASPs)? Who on the permanent staff is responsible for overseeing the temps, consultants, and vendors? Are there standard contracts and service-level agreements that must be negotiated? How is knowledge transferred from internal staff to external participants, and vice versa? Are external participants treated like full team members, with the same access to the organization's resources and facilities as the internal staff, or are they treated like second-class citizens with no cafeteria or parking privileges and desks in the dustiest, dingiest corner of the building? Are there any formal procedures for enabling a temp or consultant to join the full-time staff?

The politics of software project management can seem daunting and unpleasant at first—a necessary evil. Yet as you become better acquainted with the leaders of your organization and the issues they face, your perspective may change. You may come to regard those senior managers as ordinary people with the usual range of eccentricities and foibles. After a while you may find that you yourself care about those issues and have well-informed opinions on the course the organization should follow. You'll see your project in the context of a larger strategy and develop a sense of when you should speak up. Eventually you may be surprised to discover that you've acquired your own political influence.

Know the Environment

At the conceptual stage, your product has limitless possibilities. As far as your users are concerned, you can build it out of fairy dust as long as it does what they want. Your IT department, on the other hand, has very little interest in what the project does as long as you can build it with the available materials.

Moving a project out of the realm of ideas and into three-dimensional reality is not always easy. It's much more fun to daydream about what the product might do than to tackle the hard work of coding those features into existence—and less risky, too. Although many novice project managers know in the back of their minds that their ability to achieve their ambitious visions is limited by the tools, methods, and resources of their organization, they linger far too long in the fantasy phase and make far too many rash promises. It's very tempting to indulge in this sort of behavior when you're spending a lot of time getting to know the users and the managers because you naturally want to appear confident and create a good impression.

You can avoid this trap by thoroughly educating yourself as soon as possible about your organization's technology environment. Even if you are already considered an expert in a particular area, as a project manager you will need to concern yourself with a far wider range of issues. The more familiar you become with the infrastructure, tools, standards, and procedures, the more realistic your daydreams will turn out to be. You can still collectively fantasize with the users and the managers about the amazing things your product will do, but in the end you'll impress them even more when the visions you conjure actually take shape before their eyes.

So paste on your entrepreneur's smile and get ready to schedule more interviews. Create a technology environment survey with separate sections for hardware, software, tools, administration, and support. You can use the Technology Environment Survey in Template 1.2 as a starting point. Find out who the managers and/or experts are for each area and go ask them questions—or deputize your team members to help.

Hardware Configurations

Software project managers are always constrained by the physical equipment on which their products will run. Back in the days of the first moon landing, one had to schedule time on the CPU and take care not to overload the processing memory. Twenty-first-century machines are bigger and faster, but they still have their limits. Investigate your organization's resources in the following areas:

Technology Environment Survey

HARDWARE CONFIGURATIONS

Servers: _____

Network: _____

Telecommunications: _____

Front end: _____

SOFTWARE STANDARDS

Database: _____

Middle tier: _____

Operating system: _____

Directory structure: _____

Office functions: _____

Customized applications: _____

Web browser: _____

TOOLS

Computer-Aided Software
Engineering (CASE): _____

Modeling language: _____

Code generators: _____

Programming languages: _____

Configuration management: _____

Version control: _____

Test environment: _____

Automated functional testing: _____

Automated performance testing: _____

Monitoring: _____

Change management: _____

Documentation library: _____

Project management: _____

ADMINISTRATION

Operations: _____

Change control: _____

Quality assurance: _____

Process adjustment: _____

USER SUPPORT

Documentation: _____

Training: _____

Help Desk: _____

Template 1.2   Technology Environment Survey

Servers. What types of servers will host your product? How large are they? How much free space do they have? Whose responsibility is it to monitor, maintain, and configure them? Will you need a database server, a Web server, a messaging server, and/or a file server? Will you be obliged to share any servers with any other projects? Are any of the servers maintained by a vendor? Where are they located? Is there a firewall to protect them?

Network. What type of local area network (LAN) connects the equipment in your offices? What type of wide area network (WAN) connects your offices with each other and with your off-site data centers? What is the bandwidth of the connections? How fully utilized is the bandwidth at present? Whose job is it to monitor, maintain, and configure the network?

Telecommunications. What type of phones, faxes, modems, pagers, earth stations, satellite links, and other telecom devices does your organization use? If your organization has many branch offices, is there a standard type of equipment? Who is responsible for the installation and maintenance? To what extent will your product depend on telecommunications services?

Front-end devices. What type of desktop, laptop, and wireless mobile equipment do your users possess? Are all the machines supplied by your organization, or will some of your users have purchased their own? Is there a standard? How much memory does each kind of device have for storage and processing? How fast is the processing speed? What are the display characteristics? Who configures and maintains the equipment and keeps track of the inventory for the users?

This information about your organization's hardware will help determine your range of options when you begin to design your system architecture.

Software Standards

The proliferation of software that is available for industrial, commercial, and personal applications is both a blessing and a curse. On the positive side, it's much more likely that you'll find exactly the right tool for a particular job. Unfortunately, the likelihood of conflicts between incompatible programs is also much greater.

If you are lucky, your organization already has a configuration management group that polices your users' machines zealously. If your organization is closer to the statistical norm, you probably have an official policy that outlines the standard configuration—but then your users install their own modems, sound cards, joysticks, and copies of Doom, Wedding Planner, and Tax Cheat.

Each device or application loads its own versions of the standard shared programs that communicate with the hardware, operating systems, memory, and databases. Newer versions of the shared programs are supposedly backward compatible, but depending on what you're installing you might overwrite your newer version with an older one. This problem gets even thornier when different developers or development groups within an organization create their own customized libraries of shared functions.

The resulting chaos is known with fear and loathing industry-wide as "DLL Hell."

Obviously, you can't promise that your product will work perfectly with every combination of hardware and software installed anywhere in your organization. On the other hand, your users expect you to deliver a system that functions reliably and coexists peacefully with its electronic neighbors.

So get to know the neighborhood. Ask your IT department's configuration management group for the specifications on the standard approved combinations of hardware and software, plus the major exceptions to the rule, and the most common applications running on your users' computers. Develop your product to perform well in this environment no matter how many of the other programs are running simultaneously or which one the user opens first. A complete set of specifications would include the following:

Database. Does your organization mandate development for Oracle, Sybase, Microsoft SQL, or some other type of enterprise-scale database, or does it tolerate a mixed environment? Are all the databases running the same software version? Are they all configured identically for such localized features as date and time format, character sets, and sort order? Who is responsible for operations, maintenance, and administration? If there are different databases in use, is one group responsible for all of them, or are there different groups for Oracle and Sybase? Who creates logon IDs and permissions? Who controls access to the databases and arbitrates disputes over ownership of the data?

Middle tier. What standards has your organization adopted for elements in the data architecture that provide a layer of processing functions between the front end and the database? Do other products employ COM objects or Java scripts or workflow programs? Is there a long-range strategy, or does every project make its own decisions? Who is responsible for collecting, organizing, and distributing information about architecture among the various project teams?

Operating system. How many different operating systems will your product need to run on? For those operating systems, how many different versions exist with which your product must be compatible? Is there a standard configuration? Are there localized settings in the international offices? Who is responsible for changes to the operating system?

Directory structure. Does your organization impose a standard directory structure on the users' PCs and require that all internally developed software install itself in a specified location? Are there naming conventions for files? Is there a designated location for .DLL files, .OCX files, ODBC drivers, and other shared resources? Are there rules about updating shared resources? Who sets the policy for management of the users' PCs? Is compliance actively monitored? How is the monitoring performed?

Office functions. Do all of your users have the same tools for creating word processing documents, spreadsheets, presentations, small databases, and e-mail messages? Are they all the same version? Are they all in the same language, or does each international office install the interface in its own native language? Do they all have the same configuration settings, or does each office choose its own format for date and time, currency, numerical separators, and other localized preferences? Who is responsible for installing, maintaining, and upgrading the office productivity tools? Who sets the standards and distributes the information to the organization?

Customized applications. What other internally developed software products will your users run? How is the software distributed? Who maintains the inventory of the software products each user receives? Who tests the products for compatibility with each other and with the rest of the environment? Is there a list that describes all of your organization's internally developed software products and identifies the project manager for each one? Are you on it yet?

Web browser. Which Web browser will your users have? Is there a standard configuration? Who is responsible for setting the standard? Who installs, maintains, and upgrades the browser versions?

Software standards can seem like a pain in the you-know-what . . . until the moment comes when somebody else wants to distribute a file that would break your product. The earlier your team is aware of the standards—and the restrictions placed thereby on their unfettered design creativity—the more cheerfully they will work within the necessary limits.

Tools

Whatever type of work you do, a tool becomes an extension of your thought processes and your physical strength. Chefs are very opinionated about the knives they use; jewelers know exactly which set of tiny tweezers and screwdrivers will suit a particular job. Software development could not occur without specialized tools, and the creation of new, improved, more adaptable, and cheaper tools is a major growth industry.

The challenge software project managers face is that the variety of tools is too wide, and the utility of each one too specific, for any single person to become an expert on all of them—or even on most of the important categories. To cope with this phenomenon and to save money on volume discounts and training costs, many organizations strongly recommend an approved set of tools. At other organizations, IT management gives up in despair and leaves the choice of tools to individual project managers.

You'll need to find out where your organization falls on this spectrum and how much or how little influence you have on the selection of your tools. Talk to other project managers: Ask what their teams are using, how they arrived at the decision, and whether they're satisfied. Among the tools you're likely to consider are these:

Project planning. Is there a standard tool for project management? Are there templates for project plans, status reports, and staff time sheets? Does the tool provide automated PERT and GANTT charts to help you forecast project duration, account for dependencies, and allocate resources to tasks?

Computer-aided software engineering (CASE). Are your developers already familiar with CASE tools to map the database structure and data flow, or would they need training before they could get started? How well would the tool represent your architecture?

Modeling language. Has your organization adopted a standard modeling format? Will your developers be able to produce the amount of detailed documentation this approach requires?

Code generators. Will an automated code generator speed up your development process, or will the code it produces need so much modification and customization that you might as well have written it out manually? Will it work with your programming language and data model?

Programming languages. What will determine your choice of programming language? Does the organization have a strategy that takes into account the ongoing maintainability of software products?

Configuration management. How does your organization keep track of the hardware and software that is installed for every user? How does it deploy upgrades and new releases?

Version control. Where is the source code stored for your organization's software products? Where do projects archive their documentation? Who manages the process and administers the database? How do developers who work on the same project ensure that they are not overwriting each other's changes?

Monitoring. How does your organization keep track of whether its information systems are running properly? Is there a standard tool that alerts people when production servers crash or networks disconnect?

Test environment. Does your organization maintain a central software test lab, or is each project responsible for setting up its own test environment? How will you establish separate but identical hardware configurations for development, testing, and production?

Automated functional testing. Is there a standard tool for automating repetitive tests of a product's user interface, workflow navigation, and data quality?

Automated performance testing. Is there a standard tool for automating repetitive tests of a product's behavior with a varying number of users and a varying volume of data?

Change management. How do software projects keep track of user requirements, design changes, enhancements, and problem reports? Do all projects employ a standard tool, or does every project invent its own system? Is there one central database or many? Who maintains and customizes the database(s)?

Documentation library. Where do software projects store the current documentation that team members use to keep track of their work and collaborate with each other? Is there a central public database that is accessible to the entire IT department, or does each project make its own arrangements to share information among the team members? How much documentation is required by the organization, and how much is optional?

Veteran project managers know that every one of these tools serves an important function and contributes to the professionalism of a software development effort. Your research on tools for the technology environment survey will probably be very educational. It may disclose gaps in your own knowledge and cause you to ponder your management strategy. The choice of suitable tools and the methods of implementing and customizing the tools you've chosen are among a software project manager's most critical decisions. Take as much time as you can, explore contrasting opinions, and be sure to consult with the members of your own team.

Administration

In any organization there are a lot of unwritten rules. Often you don't know they exist until you break one!

Procedures manuals only go so far in describing how things actually get done, and by the time a procedure is written down it may actually be out of date because someone has thought of a better way to do things. Changes in organizational behavior can happen very fast and very unpredictably—even in centuries-old organizations that claim to revere tradition.

As a project manager, you need to find out about as many of the IT department's unwritten rules as you can and to stay alert for changes. Watch, read, listen, and ask questions of people in all types of positions. If there is a documentation library or any other public database that contains archived material from different projects, browse through it and read between the lines.

Your project will be affected by the official and unofficial administrative procedures in several important areas:

Operations. Who is in charge of the technology infrastructure? Who restarts the servers? Who backs up the databases? Who fixes a broken router on the network? Who loads software on a newly purchased PC? What is the chain of command, both at headquarters and the remote offices? How can you get in touch with these people during business hours and at other times?

Change control. How do people in the IT department and elsewhere in the organization notify each other of changes in the technology environment? Is there a Change Control Board that reviews and approves changes in the hardware infrastructure? Is there a Project Office that reviews and approves changes in software products? What happens when the hardware is reconfigured or upgraded? Is there a process that enables software project managers to announce their plans—to describe their product's architecture in detail—so that other developers can evaluate whether the proposed design will affect shared resources? Does anyone maintain a log that records all environment changes? Is the change control process linked to the configuration management database or the version control database? Is there an e-mail distribution list for change control notices, and if there is how do you get on it? How does the organization resolve conflicts between project teams over control of shared resources?

Quality assurance. Does your IT department have a central software quality assurance (QA) group that provides services to the various project teams, or is each project expected to make its own arrangements? If there is a QA group, does it perform only certain types of testing, such as performance tests and localization tests, or can it design and execute all kinds of tests based on the requirements of the projects? Does the QA group supervise the test lab? Does it manage a central change management database used by all projects for keeping track of user requirements, enhancement requests, and the problem reports? Does it establish standards for documentation? Does it audit the software development process employed by all the project teams?

Process adjustment. How does the IT department evaluate its own performance and recognize that it needs to change the way things are done? Are there regular staff meetings where project managers and service managers can raise issues of general concern? Are managers expected to record quantitative data about their projects or services? Is the data from different groups compared and discussed publicly?

The answers to these questions will determine much of your communication with your IT department colleagues and with the members of your project team. In the end, your performance as a project manager will be evaluated not merely on the quality of your product, but also according to the manner in which you fulfilled your administrative duties.

User Support

If your IT department were a hotel and your end users were the guests, how would they describe their accommodations? Organizations vary enormously in the amount of coddling and the type of amenities they provide. Some pamper their executives with five-star luxury suites while relegating everyone else to a campground. Some give everyone the same franchise motel treatment, with a combination of basic necessities and self-service indulgences.

Whatever your own tastes or inclinations might be, as a project manager you'll have to adopt the prevailing standard of the department. So before you set goals for your own project, do some research and find out about your users' expectations for product documentation, training, and technical assistance.

Documentation. What kind of documentation do users customarily receive? Are there printed manuals, online manuals that can be printed in whole or in part, or indexed Help files? How is the documentation distributed? How often is it updated? Is there a central documentation group staffed by technical writers who work on many projects simultaneously, or is each project responsible for creating its own documentation?

Training. How do the users generally learn about new products? Are there demos or formal classes where a teacher leads the students in preplanned exercises, or both? What about users in remote offices? Do most products provide an online tutorial? Who develops the training material, performs the demos, and teaches the classes? Does the IT department have a specialized group that produces and coordinates the training, or is every project on its own?

Help Desk. After a product is released, who answers users' questions and investigates their complaints? When a user's screen goes blank, who determines whether a specific application caused the computer to crash or the user simply kicked the power cord out of the wall? Is there a Help Desk to provide primary support and filter legitimate questions, suggestions, and problems to the appropriate project team? Are there technicians who make house calls to users' desks to diagnose problems? If not, what is the extent of the troubleshooting and problem-solving each project team is obliged to offer?

If you give your users much more support than they are accustomed to, for your next project your budget in that area may be criticized as too extravagant. If you fail to assist them when they expect you to, your software product itself may acquire a bad reputation. If you understand the normal and customary organizational behavior, you'll allocate your resources wisely and provide a level of support that satisfies both demanding users and parsimonious managers.

The technology environment survey you and your team compile will probably turn out to be a bunch of long, handwritten, messy, inconsistently formatted documents. Yet it will contain vital information of use to everyone involved in the project. As with the site survey and the user survey, it's worth the trouble to consolidate, edit, and reformat the data into a technology environment profile. Of all the documents you create for the project, the technology environment profile is likely to have the largest circulation. If you kept it in your desk under lock and key and charged everyone a dollar whenever they wanted to consult it, you'd soon earn enough to treat your entire team to dinner.

Milestone Marker

Good project managers tend to be decisive, hands-on kinds of people. Doing research is often less appealing as an activity than jumping into the midst of a chaotic situation, organizing the resources, setting the priorities, and getting the job done. By taking the time to inform yourself about the ideas and customs of the people who will play an important role in your project, you will be a better entrepreneur. You will avoid many errors of misconception, misjudgment, and miscommunication. You will be able to tell everyone that, based on your more comprehensive understanding of the situation, you know what they perceive is actually not a snake or a tree or a rock, but an elephant.

Nonetheless, at this stage it is still a theoretical elephant. In the next chapter, we'll examine the process by which you distill this abstraction out of everyone's brains and represent it on paper so that you can show what the animal you create will actually look like and calculate how long it will take you to perform this feat.

On Blueprints and Leaps of Faith

Research is a great boon to procrastinators. As long as you're doing research, you have an excuse for not accomplishing anything else.

Novice project managers usually wonder when they can be sure that they are done with their research. The answer is: never. The process of exploration is ongoing. Throughout the project you'll continue to discover new facets of your users, your managers, and your colleagues, new complexities in the procedures you follow, and new insights into the way technology both serves and controls people.

Time and money, though, have a way of setting arbitrary limits. Sooner or later you'll be obliged to take that first step on the road to deployment. If all your questions haven't been answered yet, don't worry—you'll gather the information along the way.

Planning and designing are, at best, a dialectical process. Time and again, the participants reach a consensus and draft a blueprint for whatever you'll work on next. Everyone gets busy accomplishing their tasks—and then inevitably you arrive at a point where the blueprint doesn't tell you what to do and nobody really knows. So you guess. You use your imagination. You take a leap of faith and keep on going until you've achieved the agreed-upon goals. When you're done, the original group reconvenes and examines the results. Questions are asked, ideas are debated, modifications are proposed, another consensus is reached. The project moves forward, and eventually the product gets built.

This constant lurching from certainty to uncertainty can be disorienting for a novice project manager. It's especially difficult when other people are looking to you for leadership. In your Technology Partner role, you're expected to demonstrate expertise and act with authority. You'll find it much easier if you structure the process around the creation of four specific documents. Different organizations have different names for them; we'll call them the product definition, the project requirements, the project plan, and the project proposal.

Define the Product

Let's say you've just received your project assignment. Usually these assignments are somewhat vague—for example, your boss will tell you that the Widget Department needs a new inventory system and you've been selected to manage the project. What do you do next (after thanking your boss for this great opportunity, of course)? Do you read through all your computer magazines in search of the perfect architecture? Do you seek out your organization's most talented developers and try to persuade them to join your team? Do you call your mother?

No. You do not do any of those things, at least not immediately. . . well, maybe you can call Mom. Here is what you do instead:

GET IT IN WRITING.

The most effective first step you can take as a software project manager in dealing with your user community is to insist that you have clear, unambiguous, officially authorized instructions for everything you work on. As early as possible, convey the impression that your project team is an independent enterprise and that it will treat your user community collectively as a paying customer. To establish this relationship on both sides, the client should submit a project request and the project team should perform a feasibility study. The product definition should be a joint effort, yielding a document similar to a signed contract.

Project Request

The *project request* is a short summary of one or two pages that describes your client's initial ideas about the product. It should include the following:

Sponsorship. Who is commissioning the work? Is more than one manager or department involved? If so, who will be designated as the client and have authority to determine the necessary features and to approve or reject the final product?

User community. Who will use the product? How many users will there be? What types of jobs do they perform? Where are they located?

Functions. What will the product do? What purpose will it serve? What organizational goals will it promote? Will it be an entirely new product, or will it replace an existing system or systems?

Media. What hardware devices will the product run on? Will it be a Web site, a CD-ROM, a client/server application?

Deadline. When must the product be ready for release?

Budget. Who is paying for the product? Is the funding allocated yet? Will the project span more than one budget cycle? Has a maximum amount already been determined?

These are all very basic questions, and you should be able to get answers even when the project is still in the conceptual stage. You might have to write a draft of the project request yourself and ask the appropriate managers to sign off on it or send you an e-mail that indicates their approval, but they should make some form of commitment in writing. If different managers among your users can't agree with each other, or if they can't bring themselves to officially submit the project request, go back to your boss and explain to him or her that you can't begin the project until they figure out what they want and cooperate with the development process.

Feasibility Study

Once you have a project request, it's up to your project team to determine how realistic your client's initial ideas might be. Now is the time to begin your interviews and to consider alternative designs, methods, and tools. Depending on the scope of the project and the size of the user community, the feasibility study might take days or weeks. Your team members will need to schedule meetings, transcribe their notes, and discuss their findings. Technically you have not started building the product yet, so before you get going make sure there is an understanding about who will be authorizing and funding the effort.

Among the questions a feasibility study might explore are these:

Prior experience. Has anyone on your team or in the IT department ever done a project like this before? How many people are familiar with the media and technology under consideration?

Current infrastructure. How well would the proposed product fit into your present environment? Could you build it using the tools and methods you already have available?

System dependencies. To what extent would the product interact with other systems in your organization? Would those other systems need to be modified before the proposed product could be deployed? Are there questions about data ownership?

Resource estimates. Based on your organization's prior experience with similar projects in the current infrastructure, is it reasonable to assume that the proposed product can be built within the deadline and budget constraints specified? If the type of project or technology is unfamiliar to your organization, how will you acquire the knowledge you need to create reasonable assumptions?

Resource availability. Does your organization already have staff members who are capable of building the product? Are they available to work on the project? If not, how difficult, costly, and/or time-consuming will it be to find and hire people?

Unless the project you've been assigned is a very ordinary, routine development effort, it's likely that your feasibility study will uncover some flaws in the client's initial ideas—or, at the very least, some issues that require clarification.

Your goal is to engage your client in a discussion so that you can jointly explore alternative approaches and solutions. Therefore, the best format for presenting a feasibility study is not simply a word processing document e-mailed to all interested parties. Many people who receive such documents postpone dealing with the complex matters raised therein until "things calm down"—or they respond in great detail and start separate e-mail threads, which get crossed and tangled. To avoid these delays, prepare the document but then distill the main points into a presentation and call a meeting to deliver it. Invite all the members of your project team who worked on the study, your client, other members of the user community who have articulated important points, and any IT department colleagues whose experiences or responsibilities may be relevant.

You'll know the process is working well if the participants acknowledge your concerns and begin to evaluate compromises and adjustments. Assign someone on your team to take minutes so that you have a record of the options considered and the various points of view. Be prepared for the entire project to be canceled or postponed indefinitely—for the sake of your team and your own career, it's better if you abandon a leaky ship before it leaves the dock than after you've sailed out of the harbor. But also be prepared if the discussion veers off course or goes around in circles to stand up and insist that the questions get answered and the issues get resolved before any further work on the project is undertaken. It might take several meetings, and you might need to call on your manager to back you up. A consensus between your project team and your client on the feasibility of the overall effort is essential before you move on to the product definition.

Product Definition

The *product definition document* is an expanded, more detailed version of the project request. The sections that describe the product's functions and media are longer and more comprehensive, and they reflect the decisions made during the feasibility study discussions. The deadline and budget sections are also usually adjusted based on the participants' more realistic expectations. Template 2.1 is an example of a product definition document. You can use this from as a starting point for your document.

In addition, there should be three new sections:

Feasibility study review. Describe how the feasibility study was constructed. List the people you interviewed. Summarize the questions, concerns, and issues that were raised.

Contributors. Mention everyone who participated in the feasibility study meetings and discussions.

Approvals. Indicate that you are going to sign and date this document and that you expect your client to do so as well. If the project will be funded out of several managers' budgets or will depend on the cooperation of participants in several managers' groups, make sure they sign the document, too. It doesn't have to be a pen-and-ink signature on a piece of paper; electronic approvals are fine as long as they can be recorded, filed, and retrieved.

Beware of clients and other managers who hesitate to commit themselves to a documented product definition. They might say something like, "We don't know exactly what we want yet. Just build a prototype, and we'll let you know what we think." Or they might say, "Why are you slowing things down with all this bureaucracy? You ought to be coding already."

Product Definition Document

PROJECT REQUEST	
Sponsorship:	
User community:	
Functions:	
Media:	
Deadline:	
Budget:	

FEASIBILITY STUDY	
Prior experience:	
Current infrastructure:	
System dependencies:	

Template 2.1   Product Definition Document

Product Definition Document (*continued*)

Resource estimates:	
Resource availability:	
Feasibility study review:	
Contributors:	

APPROVALS

_____   _____
Name   Date

_____   _____
Name   Date

_____   _____
Name   Date

Template 2.1   (*Continued*)

Many novice project managers make the mistake of giving in to these ploys. In their joy at being appointed to the position and their eagerness to create a good impression, they become overly responsive to their client. They interpret their performance objectives as an open-ended mandate to make their client happy. All goes well for a while . . . but eventually, after many iterations of prototypes built for ambiguous, shifting, undocumented functions, no one can agree anymore on whether the project's goals are being met, and the schedule and budget balloon out of control.

Commitment

Being firm at the outset can help avert this disaster. Remind your client that your project team is being hired to perform a service for the user community, and it is your job to negotiate the extent, the limits, and the specific criteria of that service. Use analogies: When the client employs a contractor to replace the windows in his house, doesn't he sign an agreement that states exactly what work will be done, what materials will be used, and how much it will cost? When the client asks a caterer to prepare and serve food at a party, doesn't she indicate on her order how many hours they will work and what dishes they will offer?

If you are cheerful and patient and professional in your demeanor, most clients eventually will be persuaded by your reasoning—and the relationship will be off to a good start. If, however, you find yourself confronted with a truly headstrong or slippery character, don't hesitate to bring the problem to the attention of your management. Your client may have ulterior motives for not wanting to make commitments in writing. There may be political forces behind the scenes working against the project. If you are obliged to manage a project under these circumstances, play a defensive game. Prepare all the documents and schedule all the meetings as if your client were cooperative. When the cooperation is not forthcoming, record that fact, notify your management, and move forward with the project.

The product definition document is really not so much a technical blueprint as an artist's sketch. But you're not ready yet to start writing code based on a mere sketch. The next step is an analysis of your implementation strategy.

Analyze the Requirements

Your client has placed an order. In a general way, your team understands what you're expected to deliver and when. Exactly how you'll accomplish this feat is still vague, but everyone is looking to you for guidance, and when you get nervous, your first instinct is to prod the developers to start writing code so that people can see that your team is *really productive*!

Resist the impulse. If necessary, hang up a picture of someone frowning accusingly and paste the letters WAYCY (for "Why Aren't You Coding Yet?") in a thought bubble above the person's head. Whenever you feel anxious about your team's productivity during the analysis phase, throw spitballs at the picture.

Creating the project requirements document is a productive activity for your team because it enables them to figure out for themselves how they're going to get from Point A (the product definition) to Point B (the product launch). It also gives them an opportunity to talk about how they could complete this journey more easily and more successfully by working together. You might think that as project manager it is your sole responsibility to draft the requirements document—but you would be mistaken. After all, you are only one person with one set of experiences to draw on for wisdom and insight. The more you listen to your team members' ideas and suggestions, the more likely you are to produce a requirements document that accurately predicts what it will take to get the job done.

If you are still in the process of recruiting your team or if your team members include many junior staff, new hires, or consultants, don't try to fill in the blanks in your own knowledge by taking wild guesses. Interview other project managers and IT colleagues, and ask about any difficulties they've experienced. If you plan to introduce any new technologies or tools or methods, arrange consulting and advisory sessions with experts outside the organization now, prior to the purchase or setup, so that you're sure about what you're getting into.

Ultimately, you'll submit the requirements document to your client for approval. Your client, however, will probably not have the expertise to evaluate many of the decisions your project team has made. Assuming that your team members have actively participated in determining the project requirements, most of them should be able to provide a convincing explanation.

Design

There is a magic moment in the early stages of any software project when a manager contemplates all the possible ways in which to build a new product. You put your feet up on your desk and daydream. What if . . . we built a Web site that was so amazing it won an award? What if . . . we made all the screens look like MS-DOS applications circa 1985? What if . . . we incorporated voice recognition software?

Sooner or later the phone rings, and you come back down to Earth long enough to consider your real alternatives. No matter what purpose your product will serve, you'll need to evaluate various strategies in a number of areas:

Off-the-shelf products. Are there off-the-shelf products that can accomplish your client's goals? With the budget for the project, is it reasonable to consider them? How much customization would be required? How well established is the vendor? How easy will it be to stay in sync with the vendor's new versions? Is the product being used elsewhere in the organization? If you implement only a part of the product, do you need to install all of it? Are there testing or support issues involving the parts you don't use?

Components and applets. Can you buy components and applets that save you the effort of developing certain functions, such as workflow rules or a chat room for a Web site? If you choose to incorporate them into your product design, will you need to ask permission from any central IT strategy coordinator? Is there a library of components and applets already being used by other projects within the organization? How reliable are they? How thoroughly do they need to be tested, both independently and as a part of your product?

System architecture. What architecture will best serve your purposes? Will your project team be in control of and responsible for every part of the architecture, or will you depend on input from sources you do not manage? Must your product output data in a format acceptable to other systems? Will you have a middle tier of components or objects you share with other products?

User interface. To what extent can you design your own user interface? Do you have complete control over the look and feel, or does the organization impose style guidelines?

Testability. How testable is your system? How many layers of architecture need to be tested independently? How many components and applets need to be tested? How many off-the-shelf products need to be tested? Will it be possible to verify data as it passes through every segment of the architecture, or are there "black box" areas where the parameters and criteria are unknown?

Performance. To what degree should processing speed and response time influence your design? If you are considering several alternative architectural models, can you compare their performance before making a decision? Are there systems you can experiment with in your organization? If not, can you obtain studies and statistics from other sources?

Scalability. Will the size of your user community remain constant? If you expect that it may increase, can you control the timing and the rate—for example, by rolling out the product to new departments or branch offices on a schedule—or will the growth be less predictable? What are the maximum number of users and the maximum amount of data traffic your system architecture can support before it needs to be reengineered?

Every project comes up with different answers to these questions. Put together the strategies you choose from the first draft of your product's design specifications. As you proceed with the development, you'll fill in the details at an ever higher level of resolution—and your users won't be interested in the nuts and bolts of the implementation. For now, though, they need to understand your basic approach to these issues, so you should include the design specifications in the project requirements document.

Infrastructure

Defining the infrastructure requirements for your project puts everyone in a much more practical frame of mind. You can design a fabulous architecture, but it won't do you much good if you don't have enough server capacity to support it. And if you're hoping to spend a large chunk of your project's budget on some expensive new hardware, you'd better be certain the purchase will be approved before you make it the cornerstone of your system.

With regard to infrastructure, the most important requirement a project manager must insist on is separate facilities for development, testing, and production. At the beginning of the project you won't need a production environment, but you should plan ahead and install one so that when your product is launched you don't suddenly find yourself without adequate equipment to test the enhancements in version 1.1. Your test environment should provide at least two distinct configurations: a clone of your production environment, so that you can investigate the effect of IT infrastructure changes on your product, and a clone of the development environment, so that you can verify the functionality of the product itself. In addition, automated functional testing usually depends on a third static configuration where baseline data sets can be maintained. Every testing configuration should enable you to perform end-to-end validation of your system, accepting all manual and electronic data inputs, executing all processing functions, and generating all output displays, reports, files, and data feeds.

Keeping in mind that establishing and maintaining three environments is at least three times more expensive than only one, review your design and create a wish list of all the hardware and software you will need. For example:

Servers. What kind of servers will your architecture require—data, Internet, application, file, messaging, or all of the above? Can you share any existing servers with other projects, or will you have to buy your own? Can you set up your development, testing, and production environments on a single server and still have room to grow, or should you plan to store them on separate servers from the beginning? Will all of your servers be maintained and your databases be administered by a service group within the IT department, or must you account for time and resources devoted to those activities within your own budget?

Network and telecommunications. Does your system design create a need for three separate network and telecom configurations to support the development, testing, and production environments, or will you be able to establish and operate all three environments independently using the existing configuration? Is there enough bandwidth available to provide adequate performance for your product at all locations where it will be installed?

Front-end devices. What kind of PCs, peripherals, and wireless devices must your product support? How many possible configurations will there be? Do you need to have all of them installed permanently in your development, testing, and production environments, or can you borrow some when the need arises?

Software. With which operating systems, Web browsers, and office applications must your product be compatible? How many versions of each exist? How many possible combinations does this add up to? Is it feasible to install multiple combinations on a single machine by partitioning the disk? To reduce costs, can your client specify a limited number of approved combinations?

External interfaces. Can the settings on incoming data feeds be easily modified to point to the development, testing, or production environment, or will you need to build a temporary storage facility that captures the data flow and redirects it? If your product will export or transmit data automatically, do the systems that receive the data have a testing environment where you can verify your product's output without affecting their live operations? If not, how will your project and the downstream systems manage that gateway to minimize the risk of inaccurate data being released into production?

External services. Will your production databases be stored off-site on servers maintained by another division of your organization or by an outside vendor? Will your production Web site be hosted by an independent Internet Service Provider (ISP)? Will these external service providers also be responsible for setting up and maintaining your development and testing environment? How much effort will it take to manage these remote services, from both you and other team members? Can you negotiate a service-level agreement to document your expectations and provide remedies for delays and failures?

Initially clients tend to skim through this section of the project requirements document. If they were commissioning an architect to design and build a new house, it would be about as fascinating to them as the parts list for the plumbing fixtures. Yet the choices you make will have an impact on your budget—and that's when your client will wake up and scrutinize each item line by line.

Tools

By the time you draft the project requirements, your research and your interviews with IT colleagues should have briefed you about the development, quality assurance (QA), and project management tools in use at your organization. You also should have formed a clear idea of how much freedom you have to make your own decisions regarding the choice of tools.

Start with a checklist of the tools you'll need (see Chapter 1). For each tool, review the options available and analyze whether they provide appropriate functionality for your project. Ask your team members for their advice on tools that serve purposes you are unfamiliar with. Be aware that the selection, preparation, and ongoing maintenance of tools are challenging and time-consuming activities, and at some point you may have to account for them and justify them to a baffled, unsympathetic client.

Most debates over tools focus on certain recurring themes:

Licensing. The tools you need aren't sold in shrink-wrapped boxes at the software store in the mall. Typically an organization purchases a package of licenses directly from the vendor. How many licenses will you need? Will they be fixed (one constant user per machine) or floating (many users on different machines at different times)? Will you also sign up for technical support?

Customization. To what degree can you modify the tool to add input forms, pick lists, search criteria, and reports customized for your project? Will someone on your team have to be trained to adapt the tool to suit your project's procedures? If every project is free to select its own tools, how much effort will it take to find the right tools, implement them, and support them?

Audits. Who will second-guess any choices you will make? To what extent will you be obliged to explain your decisions and document the effort you invested? To what standards are you expected to adhere? Who will perform inspections and how often?

As with the part about infrastructure, the section on tools is included in the project requirements document mainly to provide supporting evidence when the budget is discussed. Tools can be expensive, and the effort required for installation, maintenance, and customization can be substantial. It's best to bring these factors to your client's attention as early as possible and to call in expert witnesses from the IT department to endorse your recommendations if necessary.

IT Services

As you prepare the requirements document, it's essential to know exactly how much your project team will have to do for yourselves and how much you can rely on others. Among the services you might expect to receive from other groups within the IT department are the following:

- Server operations
- Database administration
- Network operations
- Telecommunications operations
- Backup and security of data
- Configuration management
- Version control administration
- Software deployment
- Help Desk support for users
- Technician support for users
- Documentation
- Training

Your research and interviews should have given you an indication of the customary arrangements within your organization. But don't assume that just because the project manager in the next office receives certain services that you'll be entitled to the same. Schedule a meeting with the manager of each service and confirm the procedures. Be sure to discuss these points:

Boundaries. Exactly what is your project team responsible for? Who sets the standards? Who will be the liaison with your project team?

Documentation. Are there any procedures guides you can distribute to your staff? What kind of documentation does the service manager expect you to provide about your project?

Service-level agreements. What levels of service can your project expect? Are there any organization-wide standards (for example, the Help Desk should respond to support calls within six hours or the database administrators should create logons for approved new users within three days)?

Conflict resolution. If your project team is not satisfied with the service you receive from any IT group, what recourse do you have? What are the escalation procedures? What is the approved method of communicating to your client that the problems are not being caused by your product team? Is this issue insignificant, or should you include it in your requirements document?

Charge-back. Are IT department services charged back to individual projects? If so, how is the expense calculated?

The purpose of the IT services section in the project requirements document is to establish for your user community the roles and functions or your team. This is important not only for accountability, but also for scheduling and budgeting. If your team members are obliged to perform many of these services for your own project, it can turn into a significant hidden cost.

Administration

Arranging the administrative support for your project is like putting "laundry" on your personal to-do list: unglamorous but necessary. Your team should feel that you're looking after them, providing the environment and resources for them to do their best work. Senior management is well aware that a capable project manager does not neglect the mundane details. Be a good boss to your staff and include administrative support in your requirements document. Among the logistics, chores, and expenses you should consider are the following:

Office space. Where will your project team work? Can they all be together in the same area? How many offices and/or cubicles can you reserve for them? How much freedom do you have to rearrange the furniture to suit their tastes? Can they bring in their own personal items and hang their own decorations? Is the space quiet and private enough for concentrated thinking? Is there also space available for meetings? If any of your team members will telecommute, what special arrangements must be made? Does the IT department provide technology support for telecommuters, or will you have to drop everything and become Mr./Ms. Fixit whenever one of your telecommuters has a problem?

Equipment and supplies. How will you obtain the equipment you need for your project—the servers, PCs, laptops, wireless devices, cell phones, pagers, printers, and so forth? How will you acquire your software, both the off-the-shelf applications and the licenses for databases, programming languages, and tools? Will you also purchase the vendor support packages? What about the office supplies, such as paper, printer cartridges, extension cords, power strips, pens and markers, staples and tape? Is there an IT department coordinator who handles these tasks, or will you be obliged to do all the procurement and purchasing yourself? Who on your team will be responsible for filling out invoices and tracking orders? How much time will it take?

Secretarial tasks. Will your project team have access to any secretarial support? Can anyone help schedule your appointments and group meetings? Can you ask anyone to make multiple copies of large paper documents and distribute them? Is there anyone who could take minutes at meetings and transcribe them? What about filling out expense reports, handling petty cash, tracking attendance, ordering equipment and supplies, placing maintenance calls?

Charge-backs. To what extent are individual projects charged for the office space they occupy, the equipment and supplies they use, the secretarial support they request?

Surprisingly, clients often pounce on the Administration section when they read through the project requirements document. *At last*, they think, *here's something I can understand!* More importantly, it's often something they can help you with. They might be able to lend you some of their own resources—or lobby the IT department to give you your fair share.

Revisions

The project requirements document is usually rather long—Template 2.2 is a blank sample of what yours may look like. It is the sort of document that makes a client doze off quickly. If you send it to your client as an attachment to an e-mail message, you may never get a response. When you send a follow-up message, your client's reply might be, "Looks great. Get on with the project." This is normal behavior for clients, so don't take it personally.

As with the feasibility study, the best way to focus your client's attention on the requirements document is to present it at a meeting. The number of participants can be smaller: yourself, your development manager, your QA manager, your client, and your product manager. Be brief; limit yourself to five minutes on each of the document's main categories. Identify any unresolved issues or areas of concern that could adversely affect the product definition, the schedule, or the budget. Give your client and product manager an opportunity to ask as many questions as they wish and as basic questions as necessary to give them a clear understanding of your intentions. Emphasize to your team members that they must not speak in techno-jargon or act condescending. Convey your team's willingness to reevaluate your decisions and change the project requirements if the discussion with your client reveals any major obstacles.

Even if your team members grumble about making revisions after they've put so much effort into the document, reassure them that it's in everyone's best interests. Arriving at a consensus on the requirements is essential before you proceed to the project plan.

Create the Plan

A project plan is a work of fiction. No matter what tool or format you use, the premise is the same: you imagine the actions your team members will take, and you figure out the timing, prerequisites, dependencies, and costs. The scale can be large, with milestones at intervals of weeks or months, or small, with "inch-pebbles" every few days.

Many project managers get writer's block when it is time to create their first project plan. They stare at the blank screen and wonder how they're supposed to predict the future. After all, you're only a manager, not an oracle. Yet a project plan is usually not a binding legal document. Most project plans are revised and updated periodically to take unexpected events into account.

Still, you've got to start somewhere. A project plan normally consists of a schedule and a budget. Although it's easier to figure out how much your office space and software licenses will cost, begin with the schedule. Staff wages and consultant fees are typically the largest expenditure in the budget, and until you estimate how long various tasks are going to take you won't have the vaguest idea whether you're close to the target. Ultimately the schedule trumps the budget. If your schedule is wrong, your budget will be wrong, too.

Avoid the temptation to sit alone in your office and invent numbers that add up to the desired amount. Consult with your staff. Ask them how long they think specific tasks will take. As the project progresses, reward people who tend to estimate accurately. If possible, obtain copies of the project plans for other software development projects your organization has successfully undertaken and compare their format and content.

Project Requirements

Project Name: _____

Project Manager: _____

DESIGN

Off-the-shelf products: _____

Components and applets: _____

System architecture: _____

User interface: _____

Testability: _____

Performance: _____

Scalability: _____

INFRASTRUCTURE

Servers: _____

Network / telecommunications: _____

Front-end devices: _____

Software: _____

External interfaces: _____

External services: _____

TOOLS

Licenses: _____

Customization: _____

IT SERVICES

Server operations: _____

Database administration: _____

Network operations: _____

Telecommunications operations: _____

Backup and security of data: _____

Configuration management : _____

Version control administration: _____

Software deployment: _____

Help Desk support for users: _____

Technician support for users: _____

Documentation: _____

Training: _____

ADMINISTRATION

Office space: _____

Equipment and supplies: _____

Secretarial tasks: _____

Template 2.2   Project Requirements Document

Before you create either the schedule or the budget, you'll need to formulate certain procedures your project team will follow and familiarize yourself with certain tried-and-true industry conventions. You'll want to define the development methodology and establish the development process. You should understand how to break down a large project into smaller tasks and how to calculate your team's productivity. To help you quantify prerequisites and dependencies, you ought to be aware of the average proportion of effort each development activity requires.

Methodology

Your client doesn't care what kind of development methodology you use as long as you deliver a good product. In their day-to-day interactions, your team members probably won't consciously adhere to a particular methodology: they'll evolve their own goals and behavior patterns that best suit the group, the project, and the organization.

The choice of a methodology matters most for long-term planning purposes because you'll need to clarify when during the development process you are going to set particular priorities and allocate specific resources. It also helps you sound more knowledgeable in your conversations with other project managers, some of whom will no doubt argue passionately in favor of one methodology or another with the zeal of religious fanatics. With apologies to all the scholars, teachers, and developers who have been publishing insightful works on this subject for the past 30 years, described *very* briefly are several of the most popular methodologies in use today:

Waterfall. The waterfall method is derived from traditional engineering practices in other industries. It assumes that the entire product moves from stage to stage all at once. System and test documentation are created during the design phase, and the design is reviewed on paper before it is implemented in code. This approach works well for large-scale projects, for projects that must produce very thorough documentation to meet regulatory requirements, and for products whose users have a low tolerance for defects. Release cycles tend to be slow, and innovative technology is more difficult to introduce.

Spiral/iterative/rapid application development (RAD). While the waterfall method dates back to mainframe systems, RAD first appeared in the era when client/server architecture was beginning to proliferate. This approach follows more of a spiral pattern, with shorter, iterative development cycles. Instead of being built from the ground up one stage at a time, software grows more organically in clusters of functions. Developers employ prototypes to work more closely with users to design features piece by piece. Although it is not an inherent flaw in the method, the practice of RAD in many organizations has focused so intensely on informal communication between developers and users that documentation has been dangerously neglected. When data models and design specifications exist only in a developer's head, the testing process becomes less reliable and the hidden costs of staff turnover become very high. A well-managed RAD project team always creates and updates documentation after every release.

Extreme programming (XP). Just as the client/server architecture inspired a new method, the Internet has encouraged a fresh round of experimentation. XP has emerged as one of the more coherent and systematic approaches to building software in an e-commerce environment. Several factors have changed: development cycles are even shorter, collaboration between clients and developers is even closer, system architectures are more complex and interdependent, and developers are less likely to be trained in traditional engineering disciplines or practices. The theories of XP are still evolving, but a few ideas have begun to influence software project managers. For example, XP relies very heavily on the use of automated functional testing. For every feature they implement or every change they make, developers are supposed to begin by creating test cases to verify the procedure. After the code has been written, the tests are executed—and so are many of the tests created to verify other functions in the system. The goal is to be able to change the product rapidly and with minimal risk. Inevitably, there are some drawbacks, and XP project managers need to compensate for them in their planning. Like RAD, XP encourages developers to skimp on documentation; the automated tests are often written and formatted in a manner incomprehensible to anyone who has not been trained in the testing tool. Placing the responsibility for testing within the development team ignores the need for an independent evaluation of the product. Although it does an excellent job of testing individual functions (unit testing), it makes little provision for testing the flow of data through the entire product or the interaction among components (integration testing). The setup and maintenance costs of automated functional testing can also be quite substantial.

RAD Method

Waterfall Method **XP Method**

Figure 2.1 Methodolgy mania.

Whatever methodology you decide is most suitable for your project, don't let yourself be influenced by a client or an IT manager who wants you to do things sloppily because you're developing in "Internet time." Ask yourself: If my organization were in the oil business, would my project be to drill exploratory wells or to build a facility that pumps reliably every day? If your project is a speculative venture, then speed may in fact be more important than good practices. But if your users are expecting to depend on your product for years to come, bear in mind that every methodology includes activities and priorities that slow the project down but deliver a better product in the long run. A quick-and-dirty implementation of any methodology will nearly always lead to problems of scalability and higher maintenance costs.

A methodology should provide guidelines, not rules. When you face a difficult decision in preparing your schedule or budget, remember that all models of software development agree on certain principles:

- The software you build should be as easy to maintain as possible.
- The procedures you establish should be repeatable and trainable no matter who is on your team.
- The effort your team members expend on your project should be measurable for their current tasks and predictable for their future assignments.

If your planning is based on these concepts, your methodology will unify your team and help you establish a workable process.

Process

A project management proverb: The road to technology hell is paved with abandoned processes.

Simply stated, a process is a series of steps that you can repeat. If your software development follows a well-understood, well-documented process, your successful projects will not be isolated miracles of good luck and heroic performance. You will have a pattern to follow. You will be able to plan, estimate, and predict.

It is tempting, when budgets get tight and deadlines loom, to pretend that your process isn't important and to sprint for the finish line. Like most temptations, this can feel good in the short term but have unfortunate lingering effects.

Your process will ultimately depend on the scope of your project and the staff you have available, and it will be influenced by the methodology you select. For your first release—before you have the experience to know which steps you can rearrange or shortcuts you can take without compromising the quality of the product—you might try the following.

1. **Functional specifications.** In a document with diagrams, summarize your understanding of product should do. Include as much detail as you can at this early stage.
2. **Usability review.** Show your functional specifications to your client and product manager. Revise and expand the document based on their comments.
3. **Use cases.** Write scenarios describing how the users will employ the product to perform important tasks.

4. **Paper prototype.** Create a preliminary design. Lay out the screens, and diagram the data flow. Take screen shots, and paste them into a word processing document. Don't bother to build the data tables yet; once they're built you're already too committed to the design.

5. **Usability review.** Show your paper prototype to your client, your project manager, your users, your testers, and your documentation writers. The prototype should be regarded as a rough draft: if your reviewers don't criticize it ruthlessly, they're probably not committed enough to the project. Be prepared to go back to the drawing board for major design revisions. Take notes on the discussion and distribute a summary to the participants afterward.

6. **Design specifications.** Create the database architecture. Build the workflow. Document the business rules. Finalize the features list.

7. **Screen prototype.** Construct a working prototype to demonstrate the workflow and the most important functions.

8. **Usability review.** Show your design specifications and screen prototype to the same group as before, and distribute the same type of meeting summary. At this stage, make it clear that the only major change requests you will consider are those prompted by your developers' errors and omissions. Begin entering change requests into your change management database.

9. **Coding.** The tasks and goals at each phase of coding will vary according to the methodology you have selected.

10. **Peer review.** Ask each developer to show his or her work to a peer for comments and suggestions. Do not plan to be present or to examine the results, but do set a deadline.

11. **Coding.** The tasks and goals at each phase of coding will vary according to the methodology you have selected.

12. **Unit testing.** Test functions of the program, modules of code, and elements of the architecture independently of each other.

13. **Coding.** The tasks and goals at each phase of coding will vary according to the methodology you have selected.

14. **Integration testing.** Test the passage of data through the workflow, the interaction between functions, the state changes among the architectural components, the error handling, and the product's performance with various numbers of users.

15. **Usability review.** Reconvene the same group as before in your first usability review and repeat the process.

16. **Coding.** The tasks and goals at each phase of coding will vary according to the methodology you have selected.

17. **System testing.** Review your testing environment. Update it so that the hardware and software are as close to the production environment as possible. Run your integration test again.

18. **Coding.** The tasks and goals at each phase of coding will vary according to the methodology you have selected.

19. **Beta test.** Distribute the product to the beta testers you have selected from you user community, and expect them to find new problems.

20. **Coding.** The tasks and goals at each phase of coding will vary according to the methodology you have selected.

21. **Installation and regression testing.** Make sure the installation and setup work properly for all supported configurations, and give the system a final check. Provide a demo for trainers, Help Desk staff, and support technicians.

22. **Coding.** The tasks and goals at each phase of coding will vary according to the methodology you have selected.

23. **User acceptance testing.** Distribute the product via the installation and setup program you've tested to selected users. If you're replacing an old application, migrate a subset of the data in the test environment and run both the old system and your product simultaneously for a specified period of time.

24. **Coding.** The tasks and goals at each phase of coding will vary according to the methodology you have selected.

25. **Product deployment.** Distribute the product to your entire user community. Shut down legacy systems and migrate data to the new production environment.

Many of these steps can have multiple iterations. You might go through more usability reviews before you are ready to agree on a final design. Unit and system testing often require several rounds of back-and-forth between developers and testers. Except for the design and coding steps, which depend to a great extent on the system architecture and programming language, the specific activities within each step are described in greater detail later in this book.

At first, insisting on a process can seem bureaucratic and inflexible. Once you get used to it, it becomes second nature, and your team will understand clearly what to expect of each other—and when.

Task Breakdown

A structured development process serves as a large-scale itinerary for the project, but for planning on a week-to-week and day-to-day basis you'll need to subdivide each of the stages into smaller components. Making assignments and tracking progress is easier if you adopt certain conventions for the task breakdown:

Time limit. Assume that no single task should take longer than 80 hours.

Accountability. Decide whether tasks will normally be assigned to individuals or teams.

Deliverables. Define each task to produce a specific deliverable: a document, a program function, a test case, a presentation.

Preparing the task list is a collaborative effort because no project manager could possibly be aware of all the specialized activities involved in development, testing, and documentation. At the beginning of a project it also requires a great deal of guesswork—it's like a strategy game where you can see only the area immediately in front of you and the rest of the map is hidden until you get there. Until you possess final, approved design specifications, you should reassure your team members that any analyses or estimates they offer are to be regarded as preliminary and hypothetical. You can, however, gauge the general reliability of their forecasts by comparing them with standard metrics on software development.

Industry Statistics

As the commercials warn, your mileage may vary. The growth of the software industry over the past two decades has nourished a symbiotic proliferation of academic research on how the industry operates. At conventions and conferences, in journals and textbooks, and in the studies of consulting firms, there is a wealth of information about the track records of all types of software development projects. You probably won't be too far off if you refer to a few well-accepted averages when calculating the proportion of total work effort for each type of activity:

- Project management: 15%
- Administration: 10%
- System and test documentation: 10–20%
- Testing and quality assurance: 33% (client/server environment)–66% (e-commerce environment)
- User documentation: 25%

Having selected a methodology, established a process, created a task breakdown, and evaluated the reasonableness of your estimates in relation to industry averages, you're now ready to open up your calendar and start attaching dates to your project plan.

Productivity Factors

Suppose your client has asked for a certain function in your product, and you've determined that implementing it will require four separate tasks assigned to three different team members for a total of 350 work hours. How much actual time will elapse before this job is done?

Translating estimated work hours into a daily schedule is a major challenge for novice project managers. It's tempting just to pick an arbitrary delivery date that you know will please your client and then push your team as hard as you can to meet it. This approach reflects despotism rather than skillful project management. You'll build a more cohesive and loyal team, and acquire a better reputation for keeping your promises, if you apply some tried-and-true formulas in your estimation:

Length of work day. Assume your staff works eight-hour days.

Length of work year. Assume your staff works 10 months per year. With holidays, vacations, personal days, sick days, and other excused absences, this is reasonably accurate for U.S. employees. Staff members and consultants in other countries may have shorter or longer work years—be sure to check their holiday and vacation schedules if you are expecting to include participants from around the world on your team.

Distractions during the work day. For short projects, you can ask your team members to clear their calendars and focus exclusively on their assigned tasks all day.

For projects longer than a few weeks, you will need to make allowances for all the distractions of organizational life. There will be departmental meetings, Human Resources briefings on the new benefits package, birthday parties during office hours, training sessions, and so on. For long projects, assume your staff works productively five to six hours per day.

Individuality. Be realistic about your team members' circumstances and commitments. You may employ some people who live alone, have no dependents or social life outside the office, and are happy to work 100 hours per week. You may employ other, equally talented people who have young children or elderly parents to care for, are active in political or charitable work, or are amateur musicians. As a manager you should support both lifestyles. Take people's relative availability into account when formulating their schedules.

After you've assigned each task a start date and a duration on the calendar, the final step is to calculate the budget. Add up the salaries for all the staff members working on the project for as many weeks as you forecast until the deployment of version 1.0. In a different category, add up all the fees for the consultants and vendors. Separately add up the cost of all the hardware, software, and tools you plan to buy. In the last section add up all the charge-backs you anticipate for services provided by your IT department or by other areas of your organization. The result is your consolidated budget.

If you're like most novice project managers, the first thing you do when you've finished your project plan is one of the following:

a. Faint
b. Slap your head and yell "D'oh!" like Homer Simpson
c. Consult the online employment ads

This is because your scheduled tasks take at least twice as long as the time you have available, and your budget is at least twice as large as the allocated funds.

You can adjust and trim and redesign here and there, but in all likelihood you'll reach a point where you need to discuss compromises with your client. When you and your team have done all you can to create an efficient, workable project plan based on the requirements, then it's time to put together the project proposal.

Present the Proposal

The project proposal incorporates all the essential documents created thus far, and it appends new material on goals and procedures governing the future relationship between the users and the project team. The presentation of the proposal (and any subsequent meetings at which modifications are made) resembles a contract negotiation. It helps if you regard it more as a prenuptial agreement than a treaty between warring nations.

Participants

You'll want to keep the group at the table as small as possible. You, your client, your product manager, your development manager, and your quality assurance (QA) manager should form a quorum: enough people with authority to make decisions, and enough people with expertise to provide the background information on which the decisions must be based. As always, someone in attendance should be assigned to take notes and distribute the minutes.

The presentation and discussion of the proposal take time. If possible, schedule a two-hour meeting. Anything shorter usually leaves too many open items on the agenda; anything longer tends to result in rash decisions based on crankiness and impatience. Hold the meeting in a comfortable room where you will not be interrupted. At the beginning ask everyone to turn off their mobile phones and pagers. Without being pompous, strive for an atmosphere of seriousness and calm deliberation.

Contents

For reference, the proposal should contain copies of the important documents you've already reviewed with your client:

- Product definition
- Project requirements

It should include your latest effort:

- Project plan

There should also be several sections describing goals, procedures, and expectations:

Deliverables list. Besides the software, what does your client want you to provide? What kind of user documentation and training materials? What level of technical support does your client believe your team should furnish? Are you responsible for ongoing monitoring of data quality?

Summary of roles and responsibilities. What sort of participation will you expect from your client, your product manager, your usability consultants, your beta testers, and your point people? What do they expect from members of your project team? What services do you expect your colleagues in other areas of the IT department and the organization to provide, but over which you have no direct control?

Change management procedures. In what manner should your users communicate with your project team to report problems, suggest enhancements, or request design modifications? Will users have access to your change management database? Who will prioritize change requests? Who will review changes made to the product to determine whether they accomplish the intended goals? Who will be responsible for closing items that have been resolved?

User acceptance criteria. What must version 1.0 of the product contain before it can be released? Are there speed or performance standards? Who determines whether the criteria have been met? By what method will the approval or rejection be communicated and to whom?

Because the project proposal is an important and lengthy document, you should devote some thought to its appearance, organization, and sturdiness. A three-ring binder with tabs separating the sections is a classic but still effective form of packaging.

Spiral- or tape-bound volumes are less expensive and still keep the pages in the right order. Whatever format you select, give your user interface designer a chance to flex his or her creative muscles by creating an attractive project cover and/or title page.

Negotiation

At the presentation, you won't have to spend much time going over the product definition and the project requirements because they should be familiar to the participants. The project plan, however, will call for a thorough, line-by-line explication. You should also read through and elaborate on the new material you've added about deliverables, roles and responsibilities, change management, and user acceptance.

Inevitably, there will be controversy. Be prepared for it, and prepare your team members for it, too. Your discussions about the product definition and project requirements were more abstract; now the issues are time, money, and mutual commitment, so it's only natural that the conflicts should be more intense. Through your earlier debates you've already established relationships and evolved productive methods of communication. Remember the theatrical cliché about a disastrous dress rehearsal guaranteeing a triumphant opening night? Similarly, a stormy proposal negotiation can lead to a far more placid development effort. Although it might take a few drafts before you come up with a document everyone can endorse, the process of considering assumptions and risks and trade-offs will help forge a better understanding and a stronger trust between your product's users and your project team.

In the end, the proposal is your team's blueprint for success, and your users will have faith that you can make their wishes come true.

Milestone Marker

When you hold an approved project proposal in your hands, you should feel a small thrill of victory. You've survived a kind of initiation as a project manager: all those rough drafts, all those meetings, all those debates, and all those compromises may have left you a bit battle-scarred, but now you've learned how the planning and designing process works. The proposal document in itself is a major accomplishment, and as you page through it you should think back over the project request, the feasibility study, the product definition, the project requirements, and the project plan and realize how far the project has come since your first theoretical discussions.

In the preceding chapter we mentioned the various members of your project team and described some of the activities they engage in, but we haven't devoted much attention to the workings of the team as a whole. Team dynamics have a significant effect on the outcome of any project. Before we proceed any further along the development road, let's consider your traveling companions.

CHAPTER 3

Who's on First

Televised sports broadcasts give fans the opportunity to watch great managers in action. As captain of your project team, you can learn a great deal from them. Whether they are as impassive as the Sphinx or apoplectically excitable, their leadership—even more than the talents of individual players or the luck of weather, injuries, and umpire calls—is the most important factor in creating a championship team.

When you first become a manager, your initial preoccupation is your project goal. Visions of your future achievement fill your mind, and the logistics of accomplishing it fill your schedule. But this stage doesn't last long. Although you never lose your commitment to your goal, soon you find yourself devoting an increasing amount of time and energy to issues involving the people you manage. For example: How can you help a certain developer and tester get along better and communicate about program changes without insulting each other? What can you do to persuade your star programmer to stop flouting the rules on version control and system documentation? How can you arrange family leave for your automated testing expert whose husband just had a heart attack, and who else on your team can fill in to do that job for the next few weeks?

For the purpose of management training, it's too bad the television cameras don't follow the team into the locker room and the front office. In general, the human component of project management is harder to teach than any other because there are fewer absolute rules or unambiguous cause-and-effect scenarios. Over time, by trial and error, every project manager develops his or her personal management style to suit the team and the organization. There are a few pointers that veteran project managers can offer

Figure 3.1   The team captain's dilemma.

about such universal matters as picking your players, creating your lineup, organizing your training, and building team spirit.

Form the Team

Finding and hiring the right people are major challenges for any manager. Every computer magazine publishes articles offering hints and war stories; like dating, hiring can be an emotionally intense process with long-term consequences for your sanity. Your own experience will be influenced primarily by several factors: your organization's procedures, your Human Resources department's training program (or lack thereof), and your own manager's habits and prejudices.

These elements are completely out of your control, so there's no point in worrying about them—for example, the rule that you have to use a particular headhunter, or the mock interview that you must stage with the HR staff member before you're allowed to talk to any real candidates, or the fact that your boss won't approve any Ivy League graduates. Nor is there any magic spell you can conjure to improve the number or quality of your job applicants. Focus instead on the practices and behaviors over which you do have control, and make the best of it.

Many novice project managers soon discover that they enjoy the recruitment process. It's fun to meet new people and talk about interests you have in common—and, unlike dating, if a person to whom you make an offer turns you down, you can be fairly sure that the rejection has nothing to do with you personally. On the other hand, interviewing tends to crowd your schedule and preoccupy you with novelistic issues of character analysis, and it's easy to be distracted from your project goals. Your efforts will be more productive if you first devise a strategy and adopt a methodical approach.

Team Profile

In theory, the number of people on your team should be determined by the scope of your project and the size of your budget. In reality, there's probably not a project manager alive who feels that his or her project is adequately staffed, at least in relation to the demands of the client. During your discussion of the project proposal, you no doubt debated with your client over the relative merits of various trade-offs involving head count, feature list, budget, and schedule—and this debate will be reenacted periodically throughout your development process. For now, though, you've come to terms, and you're ready to start recruiting.

Because you already are anxious that there's more work to be done than the staff you've budgeted for could ever accomplish, your first instinct is to seek out the most talented, experienced professionals you can find. You will be able to afford only a small number of them, but you hope their brilliance and their productivity will enable you to deliver on your promises and meet your deadlines.

Unfortunately, heroes are in very short supply. Typically they don't find the idea of signing on with a brand-new project manager very appealing. When this realization dawns on you, perhaps after many fruitless phone calls, you may be initially stumped. You're not sure who you want on your team, what they're going to do, or how you're going to match up people and skills and funds.

At this point it helps if you can forget about the budget and schedule for a while and try to imagine your project as a movie. You are both the screenwriter and the director: it's up to you to create the characters and cast the parts. Envision the entire development process. Who do you see building the various parts of the system? Who will test the product? Who will write the documentation? Consider different possibilities based on different skill levels among the participants. What would the team look like if all the members were outstandingly good at their jobs? How about if there were one experienced leader in each area and some novices and minor leaguers as followers? What if you had to forge ahead in spite of the fact that the best team you could assemble had merely average abilities?

Based on the characters and the plot you've imagined, write a team profile. This document describes in general terms each role and activity you foresee. It serves to record your goals and assumptions, to organize your planning efforts, and to provide a checklist so that you don't overlook any crucial skill when you get busy with the actual recruitment. Unlike the other documents you've created, you should keep the team profile private.

Next, review the document and categorize every participant's contribution in terms of the skills required and the relationship to the project:

> **Staff.** Is the participant's presence necessary from the beginning to the end, and indefinitely through future releases? Will knowledge of the organization help the

participant perform his or her tasks? Will the participant work collaboratively with the other team members? Are there any current staff members in the organization who could be retrained to assume this participant's role in the project?

Consultant. Is the participant's principal function to provide a specific service or expertise? Is the need for his or her contribution sporadic rather than constant? Can the participant's work be done off-site? Is the demand for the participant's skill so high in the marketplace that people who possess the skill tend to change jobs frequently?

Borrowed resources. Are there any participants whose contributions could be divided into smaller, independent tasks and distributed among existing IT department staff or members of other project teams? Do project managers in your organization normally barter resources? If you commit yourself to this practice, can you trust your trading partner to provide you with the resources you need when you need them? What can you offer to trade in return, and how will your resource debt affect your project plan?

As you analyze the team profile, you'll notice that there are patterns to the participants' contributions over time. In sports, different groups of players are rotated into and out of a game depending on the skills required at the moment. Software development projects can benefit from this strategy, too.

Resource Time Line

Depending on the methodology you've chosen, there may be periods of relative calm or intense activity in particular areas. For example, if you have a project with a waterfall methodology, a long development cycle, and little automated testing, you won't need a great deal of effort from performance testers or documentation writers during the project requirements stage. On the other hand, if you follow an XP methodology, have short development cycles, and rely on automated testing, you may want to hire at least one experienced person for each role from the very beginning of the project and then add to the staff in every area as the product grows in size and complexity.

A resource time line enables you to plan what kind of skills you're going to require, when you're going to need them, and how many skilled workers it would take to finish the task as quickly as possible. Generally speaking, regardless of methodology, there are three ways of staffing a project:

Big bang. Hire everyone you need as soon as possible.

Expansion/contraction. Hire a core of regular staff members and then add consultants and borrowed resources when necessary for as long as necessary.

Incremental. Start with a small team and add people as the need arises.

Using the resource time line, you can create several alternative scenarios for assembling your team and calculating the effect of different arrangements on your schedule and your budget. Some project management tools offer this feature as an automated function, but you can also write formulas to perform the calculations in a spreadsheet.

With the team profile to remind you of who you want to hire and why, and with the resource time line to remind you of when you need them and for how long, you should be able to go back to your schedule and budget and figure out how close you've come to reconciling your imaginary team with the realities of deadlines and funding. Don't worry if you're far off the first time—just go back and try again. It's a skill that improves with practice. You may even be obliged to hold another meeting to revise your project proposal. Eventually, however, your numbers will more or less add up, and you'll have a fairly good idea of who will do what on your project. As soon as you figure it out, before you interview your first candidate, write down your thoughts on every team member's responsibilities.

Job Descriptions

The Human Resources department in many organizations requires managers to document each team member's job description. Even if your organization doesn't impose such an obligation, it's a good idea for one simple reason: if you don't, you'll forget. As anyone who has ever looked for a job can attest, hiring managers sometimes say bizarre things and make outlandish promises during job interviews. You don't want to be one of those flaky managers, but if you're recruiting for several positions at once it's easy to lose track of what you've said to whom. Before you embark on a recruitment drive, write down a few key facts about each open position:

Assigned tasks. What exactly will the person be expected to do? How will his or her performance and productivity be evaluated?

Required skills. What skills are necessary to succeed in the position? How can the candidate demonstrate that he or she has mastered those skills? If you have created a position that requires several different skills, is the combination realistic? For each position, which skills are most important?

Seniority. How much experience would you like an applicant to have? How rapidly could you train a more junior person? How well would a more senior person fit in with the team?

A job description doesn't need to be long. Usually a few paragraphs will suffice. Although at first it might seem like unnecessary paperwork, in the long run it will save you time in several ways. First, when you interview candidates having a job description will ensure that you provide the same information to each applicant. This can be very important in some organizations where equal opportunity and workplace diversity are clear priorities. Second, it will enable other team members to participate in the recruitment process and evaluate candidates based on consistent criteria. Finally, when you've hired your staff and got your project underway, the job descriptions will become the basis of your performance reviews so that you can evaluate your team members' accomplishments in light of their original instructions.

Interviews

Except for politicians and journalists, most people aren't comfortable in an interview situation. It's bad enough when you're the person being interviewed for a job, but then when you become a manager you discover that it's almost as hard to be on the other side of the desk. Nearly every manager has at least one disturbing memory of a time when he inadvertently misrepresented the organization or when she asked an indiscreet question. With some preparation, you ought to be able to proceed with confidence. Here are a few things you can do to get ready:

Training. Does your organization offer any training in interviewing techniques? A novice project manager often needs practice in listening without interrupting, evaluating body language, asking evocative questions, and taking notes while conversing. If you've never hired anyone to work for you before, sign up—or find an outside course.

Standard form. Do you have a standard interview form to ensure that you ask all the applicants the same questions about their background and give them the same information about your project? If your organization doesn't provide one, create your own.

Peer reviews. Do you give the current members of your team an opportunity to interview their potential new colleague? Do you provide them with the standard form to guide their evaluation? Do you make arrangements for an applicant's technical expertise to be probed in depth either by a member of your team or a qualified colleague in the IT department? Set up these peer reviews ahead of time for the same day the candidate meets with you.

Response time. When you identify a potential candidate, how soon can you arrange to bring the person in for interviews? After the interviews, how long does it take for you to reach a decision? How quickly can your Human Resources department process the paperwork to make an offer? Let candidates know your organization's timetable.

Salesmanship. Do you and your team members realize that you need to persuade people to come work with you? Have you identified the characteristics of your project or your organization that might make it attractive to applicants? If you are having a bad day, are you able to put aside your negative feelings and describe the more rewarding aspects of your job during an interview? Remind yourself and your staff to project a positive outlook.

During the recruitment process, keep in mind one fundamental principle: The people on your team have to get along with each other, and with you. Pay attention to communication styles and interpersonal dynamics. Try to create as diverse a group as possible, with different backgrounds and skills and areas of expertise. Remember that you're all going to be working closely together for quite a while. A good manager strives not for uniformity, but for harmony. When the team troops back to the locker room after a tough game, you want to hear conversation and laughter.

Provide Training

Two hundred years ago the British Navy ruled the seas with ships whose crews had basically been kidnapped from other boats and from waterfront bars. Although this recruiting method yielded a number of intelligent, able-bodied workers from all over the world, it also dredged up quite a few sorry specimens of humanity. Yet there were methodical, effective procedures for whipping the new recruits into shape (sometimes literally, which is of course no longer recommended).

Fortunately, your applicant pool is much more promising. You also don't have to teach seasick landlubbers how to furl an ice-covered sail hanging from a yardarm a hundred feet in the air during a howling gale in the 20-foot seas around Cape Horn. So it should be relatively easy for you to establish procedures and train your team to follow them . . . although in your organization you may still need to keep an eye out for sharks.

Does the following scenario sound familiar? When a new recruit shows up for work the first day, the manager spends a few minutes explaining whatever issues are most pressing and then turns him or her over to a veteran staff member for further guidance and mentoring. Subsequently, the manager might stop by now and then to say hello and see how things are going, but by and large the person's training is an informal, unstructured process. The new recruit asks a question whenever he thinks of one; the mentor and other colleagues initiate her into the group, telling stories and offering advice whenever they see fit. It's like a preliterate tribe welcoming someone from another village who has married into their clan: customs and traditions are passed along orally.

You'd think that by now in the Information Age managers would have learned that there are better ways to train new team members. Yet tribal instincts remain strong. Although this approach may work well enough for a sales force or an accounting department where many peers perform essentially the same job, for a software development project it will not produce a winning team. Every member of a software development team accomplishes different tasks and possesses different skills and knowledge—but they all have to work together and fit the pieces they build into a working whole. On the football field a quarterback and a wide receiver might run in different directions and serve different purposes, yet both of them need to have memorized the plays.

As project manager, it's your responsibility to create the play book: your project procedures guide.

Background Information

Every new recruit to your project will go through the same learning process that you did in the beginning. By the time you reach the project proposal stage, you will probably have forgotten how much effort it took for you to educate yourself so that you felt confident you understood your assignment.

You could assume that your team members are smart enough and motivated enough to make this journey of exploration on their own. But you'd certainly prefer that they focus on building the product instead. You can give them the orientation they need by preparing a brief travelogue chronicling your own discoveries. Your account should include the following:

> **Organization.** In a paragraph describe what your organization does: the products it makes or sells and the services it provides. Include information on its size, such as the annual operating budget, the number of employees, the number and location of the offices. Relate the highlights of its history, and identify its principal

Figure 3.2 Better adapt your strategy.

competitors. Explain where to find more detailed information and how to access important internal Web sites and obtain brochures and other publications.

User community. Present a profile of your future users. Summarize the nature of their work, the structure of their department(s), their goals and priorities. Describe their work environment, and include data on all the branch offices. Plagiarize your site profiles and user profiles.

Management. Explain how the organization is subdivided and what purpose each division serves. Identify senior managers, the managers of your user community, and the IT department managers. Provide a one- or two-sentence biography of each. Attach a complete organization chart.

Technology environment. Create an abridged version of your technology environment profile. Describe the hardware infrastructure and the software standards. Summarize the IT department services, and list the name, phone number, and e-mail address of each service manager.

For the sections about your organization as a whole, you may be able to incorporate or adapt material that is already available. If your organization has a Communications Department, ask a staff member for the standard press kit. You could also check with your Human Resources department to see if it has any recruitment brochures or presentations from briefing sessions for new hires.

Development Strategy

Many aspects of your development strategy will evolve from ongoing discussion and experimentation among your team, so you should expect to revise this section frequently. Each new recruit will bring different talents and perspectives to the project, and you should adapt your strategy in the same manner that a sports coach adapts the plays according to the unique capabilities of the athletes. The procedures guide should furnish an up-to-date description of the decisions you've made and the practices you adhere to in the following areas:

System architecture. Outline the components of your system, and show where each one resides or will reside within the organization's hardware infrastructure. Attach a data flow diagram and a data dictionary.

Product design. Present the most recent versions of the product definition, prototype, and design specifications. If it's very early in the planning stage, include the project request and whatever notes you've made so far.

Methodology. Identify the development methodology you've chosen, and explain why it's most suitable for this project.

Process. Summarize the steps in your development process. Describe what each team member should do during each step. Indicate whether there are entrance or exit criteria for each step—for example, if the code must be frozen before a version can be moved from the development environment to the test environment or if testers must check 90 percent of the program changes submitted to them before they can compile their statistics and send the version back to the developers.

Procedures. Describe the procedures team members are expected to follow for version control, change management, system and test documentation, project workflow, and communication between developers and testers.

Standards. Explain the standards to which team members are expected to adhere when they document requirements and design specifications, write code, record comments in the code, perform tests, create system and test documentation, document and track change requests, record the details of communications with users, and keep track of the hours they spend on their assigned tasks. Attach sample templates and input forms.

As you compile this section, bear in mind that the people who will read it will probably know a great deal about their own jobs but very little about your organization. Thus you should not need to define concepts like unit testing or version control, but you will need to furnish detailed instructions about how these processes occur in your environment.

Project Tracking

When it comes to project tracking, you call the shots. Your team members may dislike your procedures and complain about the burden of pointless bureaucracy, but only you know what sort of information you need to monitor progress and produce suitable reports for your management. As your team grows and as your project moves forward though the development process, you will probably want to make some modifications. As Ralph Waldo Emerson noted, "A foolish consistency is the hobgoblin of small minds." To be wise, be flexible.

Of all the procedures you want your team members to follow, project tracking intrudes the most into their daily routines. In fact, new hires will probably read this section of the guide first to find out how much like Big Brother you are going to behave. Try to be as specific and as realistic as you can about your expectations in such matters as these:

> **Status reports.** Indicate how often you would like your team members to submit written status reports and how much detail they should contain. If several team members are working on a task together, provide advice on how the collective effort should be accounted for and who should act as spokesperson. Attach a sample template. You can use Template 3.1 as a starting point.

> **Time sheets.** Explain how your organization employs time sheets and who reviews them. Show the manner in which work effort is allocated to activities, tasks, or project goals. Attach sample templates for different job categories.

> **Estimates.** Describe the method by which you expect team members to predict the work effort required for their assigned tasks. Explain any formulas or guidelines employed by other IT projects in your organization. Attach a sample template or spreadsheet.

> **Status meetings.** Indicate how often you would like to convene project team meetings. Describe the preparations team members are expected to make before the meetings and the types of issues normally discussed.

To a novice project manager, this might seem like a lot of material to include in a guide—a very large documentation effort for a very small audience. Why bother writing everything down when a reasonably intelligent new recruit would probably pick up the same knowledge in bits and pieces along the way?

The problem arises when it's not just one new recruit joining your team, but many. Pretty soon you have vital information being conveyed by recent arrivals who are only half-trained themselves. It's like the children's game of Telephone: by the time the message is passed orally to the end of the chain, it's completely garbled. As project manager, you wind up spending more time undoing the damage caused by ignorant mistakes and miscommunication than if you would have originally needed to put the guide together.

Then there's the question of turnover. As time goes by, how often do you want to make the same training speech to the replacement hires, revolving-door consultants, and borrowed resources who sign on to your project temporarily? Do you have confidence that you would provide exactly the same instructions on every occasion? If you delegate the training to other team members, how much faith do you have in their consistency?

Assembling the play book for your team is undeniably a major endeavor. It has a large initial start-up cost, but over the life of the project the cost is repaid exponentially by improvements in coordination and communication. Once you've finalized the first version, you can assign the responsibility for revisions to the newest team member as a training exercise.

When you present a new team member with a procedures guide, you demonstrate not only your own professionalism but also your acknowledgment that he or she deserves to be treated as a professional. It conveys high expectations and a serious approach to the project goals. Yet there's one component of the job that neither a procedures guide, a formal training program, nor even informal mentoring by more senior

Status Report

NAME: _____	WEEK ENDING: _____

TASKS THIS WEEK

Project	Category	Task	% Complete	Hours

Issues/Obstacles/Dependencies

First Issue	
Second Issue	

MEETINGS THIS WEEK

Project	Category	Meeting	Hours

FUTURE TASKS

Project	Category	Task	% Complete	Est. Hours

Issues/Obstacles/Dependencies

First Issue	
Second Issue	

CATEGORIES

Project management	PM
Analysis	ANL
Design	DES
Coding	CDG
Testing	TST
Documentation	DOC
Training	TRN
Maintenance	MNT
Administrative	ADM
Personal	PRS

Template 3.1   Sample Status Report

colleagues can explain: every new recruit needs to be accepted into the group. The project manager must figure out how to get a bunch of independent, creative, cerebral, and idiosyncratic people to work together.

Foster Collegiality

Developing and testing computer software are solitary activities. Developers and testers resemble artists, writers, and musicians in the way they depend on "flow" states of consciousness to translate the model in their imaginations into a tangible reality. Cultivating this flow state requires a vastly different set of attitudes and habits than does cultivating a wide social network. It's no wonder that the more sociable, herd-oriented members of the human species tend to stereotype technology professionals as loners and oddballs.

You may have fit this stereotype yourself. Your social skills were evidently strong enough, though, for you to be considered a good bet for project manager. Maybe you were aware of this, or maybe you figured it was your technical skills that earned you the promotion. Whatever your manager's motives might have been, you now occupy a position in which you must devote much more thought to human relations. Project management is first and foremost people management.

Let's assume that, thanks to the vagaries of the labor market, you assemble a project team that bears no more than a slight resemblance to the lineup of superheroes you originally envisioned, but at least it includes a few interesting individuals, and as a group they seem rather promising. You'd like to get to know them all better, and you hope they'll enjoy working for you. They still act reticent around each other, however, and are more inclined to come to you if they have a question rather than to resolve the matter among themselves. Something is necessary to break the ice.

Social Activities

Even if in your private life you hate parties, as a project manager you should learn how to organize and host them. Depending on the customs of your organization, a party could be anything from a late-night, hard-drinking nightclub bash to a sedate luncheon at a vegetarian restaurant. Consider spending an afternoon bowling or touring an art museum. The main point is to get the entire team out of the office into an environment where they can relax and talk about something besides the project.

It's a good idea to schedule parties to celebrate milestones: the approval of the project proposal, the transition of your first build into system testing, the resolution of the first 100 change requests, the beginning of the beta test. Some of these events are obviously more momentous than others. If you can't justify a long lunch for the entire group, or if team members' family commitments make it difficult for them to spend an evening with the gang from work, you can at least have pizza and sandwiches in the conference room and give everyone a chance to hang out together.

Educational programs provide another excellent opportunity for team members to relate to each other away from the day-to-day demands of the project. You might hire a speaker to address the group on a technical issue related to your development strategy, or you might sign everyone up for training on a particular method or tool. Tell your team members that you're open to suggestions on subject matter for these sessions. Occasionally you might waste a couple of hours of everyone's time, but overall you'll profit from their awareness that you're willing to listen to them and let them take chances.

Interproject mixers have become popular as a means of promoting communication across organizational lines. Fueled by drinks and hors d'oeuvres, these gatherings enable members of different project teams to mingle informally during or immediately after work hours with IT department colleagues. In this atmosphere questions can be asked and ideas can be exchanged by anyone about anything—often with better results than could be obtained through regular meetings. Especially if members of your project team are having difficulty obtaining information or cooperation from other areas of the IT department, you should consider hosting or proposing a mixer.

Group Assignments

The coding cowboy's day is done. There was a time when everyone admired the brilliant programmer who worked in self-imposed isolation, creating powerful functions and elegant user interfaces, ingratiating himself with the user community while ignoring his colleagues and his project manager. He had the panache of a rock star and the vanity of a prima donna. Unfortunately, when he rode off into the sunset his code turned out to be undocumented, unextendable, and unmaintainable.

Most IT departments have at least one legendary and/or infamous coding cowboy in their past. It's a lesson nearly every organization seems to learn the hard way. Clients are often captivated by the obvious talent, the bravado, the flair for self-promotion—but, of course, they rarely see the consequences behind the scenes. Depending on the scope of the coding cowboy's mission, it can take an IT department years to disentangle the errant product from other systems and reestablish a dependable environment.

The golden age of the coding cowboy was in the early days of the client/server architecture and the Windows operating system. At that time, it was just possible for a single individual to design, build, test, deploy, and support a standalone, mission-critical application. Since then, the interconnection of software products' workflow and data has made the standalone application virtually extinct.

Nowadays every member of the project team must understand the interdependence of roles and functions, not only in technical terms but also in human ones. It's not enough for a developer to acknowledge the importance of testing in the abstract: he or she must be able to sit down with a tester and collaborate on the design of the test cases. It's not enough for an artistically gifted user interface designer to vaguely comprehend the activities of a more mathematically oriented database designer. The two of them need to seek each other out to discuss the best location for program logic, the architecture of intermediate components and tiers, the mechanics of input validation and security, and many other important issues.

Business schools do a good job of training students to work as team members by assigning many projects to groups. Technology educators, for the most part, have not yet realized the importance of this skill in the workplace, and thus they still emphasize solo performance and competition among individuals. One encouraging trend is the growth of group projects in the mathematics curriculum at many elementary schools, where students are taught to listen to their peers and evaluate alternate methods before deciding on the solution to the problem.

You won't be able to reeducate your staff to be better team members, but you can create conditions that will encourage the skill. Whenever it's appropriate, assign tasks to more than one person. Avoid publicly comparing people with each other or ranking people's abilities. Praise the group rather than individuals.

In the beginning some of your staff members might find this behavior peculiar. If they comment on it, explain what you are doing and why. Sooner or later, they will make the discovery that a collegial atmosphere is far more pleasant than a competitive one.

Attitude

During your career as a project manager you will inevitably have to cope with a certain amount of adversity and disappointment. Sometimes things will not work out the way you planned; sometimes people will let you down. That's life. The difference is that as a project manager your reactions to setbacks will be closely watched by your project team—and their reactions to setbacks will often be acted out under your observation.

No matter what happens, no matter how you feel, it's vital that you always display a positive attitude. If you don't believe in the project's eventual success, neither will your team.

Likewise, you should insist that your team members maintain their positive attitudes, at least in your presence. Nothing destroys collegiality faster than cynicism. Nothing undermines productivity more than a gloom-and-doom outlook. Make it clear from the outset that you will tolerate honest mistakes, inadvertent offenses, or temporary lapses of judgment, but that you will not tolerate overt pessimism and negativity. Regardless of the obstacles along the way or the eventual outcome, you want everyone to act as though he or she believes the project is a worthwhile endeavor. As the team solidifies and the product evolves, they won't have to act: it will become one.

Milestone Marker

In software development utopia, every new product would be launched by exactly the same team members as the ones who began building it from the original requirements. In most organizations, the reality is more like major league baseball teams: the roster changes constantly. As Team Captain, you will probably have to cope with some turnover between the day you receive your official project request and the day you roll out your product. When this happens, remember that every arrival or departure or rotation of positions changes the team dynamics to some degree. Allow for at least a two-week period of transition and adjustment. Rather than forging ahead relentlessly with your project plan, take some time out to evaluate the impact on your team. Update your team profile, focus on training, and schedule activities that reinforce collegiality. Although doing so might feel like an interruption, in the long run you'll sacrifice less progress than if you ignore the issue and assume your team members can work everything out by themselves.

We've now come to the end of the first phase of the project. You've had a chance to become accustomed to all of your different project manager roles. You've got to know

Figure 3.3   Your team roster may change—be prepared

your users, the managers who have influence over your project, and your IT department colleagues—and they've got to know you. You've created your first project plan. You've negotiated an agreement with your client on a proposal containing detailed requirements, specifications, and commitments. You're recruited your team, trained them, and encouraged them to work together harmoniously.

Time to roll up your collective sleeves and start building.

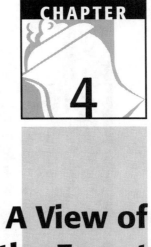

CHAPTER 4

A View of the Forest

As the development effort gets underway, you'll become preoccupied with technical concerns and team management issues. It's only natural: these problems erupt right under your nose. Your users, your management, and the rest of the organization will tend to fade into the background, obscured by the crises and dramas that plant themselves in front of your desk and demand your attention every morning.

The Entrepreneur in you should resist this tendency. During development it's important to stay in touch. If you and your project team withdraw into creative seclusion, you'll miss out on important events and fail to adapt to changed circumstances and requirements. Your product will suffer. You'll focus so intently on particular trees that you'll lose track of where you are in the forest.

You can avoid this problem by establishing three clear priorities during the development phase: involving the users in the evolution of the product, meeting regularly with management so that everyone can catch up on the news, and starting early on the task of creating your user documentation.

Confer with Users

Once your users have signed off on the requirements for the project, their natural instinct is to forget about you. They probably spent a lot of their time arguing and negotiating with each other so that they could agree on the specifications—now they want

Figure 4.1 What communication issue?

to get back to their real jobs. They've placed their order, and they assume you'll let them know when it's ready.

Without becoming a nuisance, you have to overcome the users' lack of interest and keep them involved. As the project progresses, you'll need their collaboration and cooperation to ensure that they'll be satisfied with the product you build. Based on your interviews, you've already identified a few volunteers who are willing to serve as usability consultants, beta testers, or point people. As questions arise about specific functions in your product, you'll recruit other users (some voluntarily, some not) who can provide your project team with answers and guidance. The principal activities where your users' participation will make a noticeable difference in the quality of the product are user interface design, testing, and process adjustment.

User Interface Design

The user interface (UI) of your product encompasses every component your users see, hear, or touch (and maybe someday also smell and taste): screens, windows, Web pages, printed reports, video segments, audio segments, dialog boxes, message boxes. It also includes the workflow, determining how users move from one activity to the next. A good UI makes communication between human beings and your product seem effortless. A bad UI dramatically increases stress.

The art and science of user interface design is an expertise unto itself, and there are many excellent books and courses available to teach you the basics. Besides familiarizing yourself with the fundamental principles of good design, the most important step you can take to ensure the viability of your product's UI is to get the users themselves to help you create it. This can be accomplished through use cases, usability reviews, and workflow analysis.

Use Cases

A use case describes the goals and behavior of people interacting directly or indirectly with your product. It is generally written as a text narrative, with fictional characters performing real tasks. A use case can also be presented as a diagram in the format of a standard modeling language. Depending on the task(s) involved, its length can range from a single paragraph to several pages.

Use cases vary in their focus. Several common types include the following:

Game show. A series of cases documents the range of choices available to a single actor at a particular point in the workflow and the consequences of each choice.

Historical novel. A very long case documents the actors and actions necessary to move a data element through the entire workflow.

Soap opera. A case documents the most extreme, unusual actions permitted by the program rules for a single actor.

To create use cases, first ask your client to identify and prioritize the essential tasks your product should perform. Then find out from your client or product manager who among your users actually performs those tasks now, either manually or by means of an existing computer application. If any of the users has already been interviewed by members of your project team and has volunteered to help you, you're in luck. If not, your client or product manager will need to contact the appropriate people, explain what you want, request their cooperation, and perhaps even obtain authorization for them to take time off from their regular assignments to work with your team.

Schedule individual one-on-one meetings between each of your user representatives and an interviewer from your project team. The interviewer should ask the user to describe the task in as much detail as possible and with as many variations as come to mind. Next, the interviewer should write the text narrative of the use case; even if the members of your project team prefer working from diagrams, you should always create the text version because most users have more difficulty understanding diagrams. Show the text draft to the interviewee and make revisions until the interviewee declares that you've got it right. Then submit the draft for a second opinion to at least one more user who performs the same task. When your users agree on a version, give it to your product manager for a last review. After your product manager approves it, you can consider it authoritative enough for your developers to begin translating it into code.

Once the code is written, the use case still has value to the project. Your testers will adapt it for their test cases, and your documentation writers and trainers will incorporate it into their educational material.

Usability Reviews

Whenever you design a screen, map a navigation path, establish a workflow, create an administrative rule, or configure a report, you should conduct a usability review before you assume that your version is final.

A usability review is a show-and-tell meeting at which your project team presents something to your users and invites them to critique it. The method of selecting the participants and arranging the meetings is the same as for the development of use cases. Usability reviews, though, don't have to be one-on-one encounters: the process works just as well with a single individual as with a group of as many as five or six.

At the usability review you unveil your UI component(s), explain the features and functions, and ask questions:

- Is the purpose of this component clear to you?
- Can you envision when and how you would use it?
- Does it have all the data elements it needs? Are the program rules determining the display of data correct?
- Are there any data elements that should be eliminated?
- Is the layout clear? Could it be organized or formatted better?
- Does it have all the control elements it needs?
- Are the controls easy to identify? Is their function immediately evident?
- Does the navigation path leading to this component accurately model your behavior?
- Can you guess where you would go after leaving this component?
- Are the program rules determining the behavior of this component correct?

No matter how well you believe you have done your homework and have put together a design everyone will love, your usability reviewers will find plenty to criticize in your first draft—of anything. Novice project managers usually emerge from such meetings in a state of high dudgeon, cursing the benighted users under their breath. Veteran project managers arm themselves with an implacable smile and take it in stride. When the users talk, you and your team members should listen. Make notes. Nod. Ask questions. Under no circumstances should you ever argue with them or criticize their comments. Thank them for their advice, and then go back to the drawing board and create another draft. Repeat this process until you give them what they want.

In the early stages of development, the best tools for preparing a presentation for a usability review are a pencil and paper, and the best medium for distribution is a copy machine. You want your users to treat your material as a rough draft, so it should look like one. In all probability, you will have an eager beaver on your project team who will want to create a stunning four-color screen mockup or functional prototype, but be firm. Users are much more reluctant to criticize such impressive models. They overestimate the amount of work necessary to prepare them, and they are afraid that they're wasting project resources if they insist on a revision. They also are unconsciously influenced by the authority of the professional look and feel: they devalue their own perceptions or fail to consider alternative approaches. People will spot bad ideas much more quickly if you don't dress them up. Template 4.1 is a good example of an usability review form that you can adapt for your project.

Be prepared for different groups of users to give you conflicting advice. For example, let's say you have a screen that shows information about a customer. The telephone order entry clerks might want to see marketing details about the customer's personal preferences, while the billing clerks might want to see financial details about the customer's invoice payment history. Each group might feel the other's data just clutters up the screen and makes it harder to read. In these situations, most of the time it is possi-

Usability Review Form

USER NAME: _____

COMPONENT: _____

- Is the purpose of this component clear to you?

  _____

  _____

  _____

- Can you envision when and how you would use it?

  _____

  _____

  _____

- Does it have all the data elements it needs? Are the program rules that determine the display of data correct?

  _____

  _____

  _____

- Are there data elements that should be eliminated? If so, which ones?

  _____

  _____

  _____

- Is the layout clear? Could it be organized or formatted better?

  _____

  _____

  _____

- Does it have all the control elements it needs? If not, what is missing?

  _____

  _____

  _____

- Are the controls easy to identify? Is their function immediately evident?

  _____

  _____

  _____

Template 4.1   Usability Review Form

Usability Review Form (*continued*)

- Does the navigation path leading to this component accurately model your behavior? If not, what would you change?

  _____

  _____

  _____

- Can you guess where you would go after leaving this component?

  _____

  _____

  _____

- Are the program rules that determine the behavior of this component correct?

  _____

  _____

  _____

Template 4.1   *(Continued)*

ble to reach a compromise eventually. Keep redesigning the product and scheduling usability reviews until you invent a solution everyone can live with. If you encounter certain users whom nothing you submit will satisfy, bring the problem to the attention of the product manager and your client. These users' objections may indicate a critical flaw in the design specifications or project requirements.

Workflow Analysis

Replacing an old computer system or building a completely new product is like remodeling your house or moving into a new one. The process forces you to sort through your stuff and throw things away. It encourages you to think about your habits and needs and perhaps rearrange your life a bit.

So it is with your users. They probably haven't spent much time recently evaluating their processes or considering whether they work as efficiently as they could. Now here comes your team, asking a lot of questions and forcing them to pause and take stock. The result may very well be a committee charged with analyzing and improving their workflow and inventing a new model you can then encode into your product.

Reengineering your users' processes is not the responsibility of your project team. If your research into their procedures indicates that anarchy prevails, it is your responsibility to suggest to your client that an analysis of the situation would be a good idea. You can point out that it will be much more expensive to build and test a workflow with 15 alternate paths than with 5.

If your client organizes such a committee, the role of your project team is to stand by and wait until your user community decides what it wants to do. In the meantime, work on other functions of the product. Send a representative from the project team to attend the committee meetings and report back on the progress of their discussions. This delegate can offer advice, if asked, but by no means should he or she attempt to take charge.

An important exception to this principle arises when you perceive that a minor change in user behavior could have a huge impact on your product. For example:

- Consolidating several variants of a form into one standard document
- Forwarding draft documents for approval to a single administrator instead of many
- Establishing consistent rules for data validation, approvals, deadlines, routing, and formats, for example, across multiple independent user groups that have always done things their own way

Modifications such as these can be a simple matter for your users but can dramatically reduce the complexity of your development effort. Nonetheless, changes that seem logical and trivial to your project team often entail many other issues for your users and therefore can be frustratingly difficult to implement. Make the most persuasive case you can, then let them decide. If any pressure is exerted, it should come from the client and the product manager, not from your team.

Ultimately, the users will have to live in the house you build for them. If they insist on putting the Jacuzzi in the attic, even if you think they are crazy, your job is to make sure the floor is thick enough to support the weight and the water pressure is strong enough when they turn on the tap. On the other hand, it may never have occurred to them until you mentioned it that the basement might be a better place.

Testing

When users participate in the product design, they are, in effect, telling you what they want you to do. When they participate in the testing, they are confirming whether you've actually done it. Whereas design sessions can often have a fun, playful atmosphere, end-user testing is inevitably a more serious, tedious, and sometimes contentious activity—and therefore both your users and your project team may prefer to avoid it. Testing performed by your users, however, will give you information you can't obtain from anyone else. It will also give everyone more confidence in the product. Early in development, ask your product manager to notify your users that you'd like their help with the data verification tests, the beta test, and the user acceptance test.

Data Verification Tests

During your research and requirements gathering, your users explain to you in theoretical terms how your programs should manipulate the data they input. They might say something like, "If the Contact Code is A, the system should print the Red Report. If it's B, print the Blue Report. If it's X, send an alert to the department manager that displays a skull-and-crossbones on her screen."

You get to work and faithfully write your code to make all this happen. Yet when you give the program to your users, suddenly you get an apologetic call: "We're sorry, we forgot to tell you about Contact Code Z. There's only a few of them, but they're really important. For a Code Z you should print the Green Report, and could you maybe add an audio file that plays Beethoven's *Ode to Joy*?"

There's no way your developers are going to be able to find out on their own about all the Code Z's in your users' lives. The solution to this problem is to ask your users to provide you with a set of test data that includes a few normal, ordinary examples and a lot of examples that represent extreme, unusual circumstances. These might include the following:

- The record with the largest number of entries
- The record with the longest or most active transaction history
- The record with the most complex or most varied types of data

Once you explain this concept to your users, they tend to catch on fast and are delighted to provide you with the most bizarre examples they have encountered. The number of examples you will need depends on the functionality of your product, but it is generally based on the outputs at the end of the workflow: the invoices, the confirmation lists, the summary screens, and the reports. Your developers should be able to identify the best places in the system for data verification to be performed.

The users who have the expertise to furnish this kind of test data are often not the ones who volunteer to be usability consultants, beta testers, or point people. Typically, they are the more reclusive, overworked, detail-oriented members of the user community. But your product manager should know who they are. Ask your product manager to contact them and schedule a meeting; you should attend along with your development manager and QA manager.

At the meeting, summarize your goals and then let the users and the members of your project team work out the details. Collectively, you should agree on the format for a spreadsheet where you will store the test data submitted by all the participants. Each record in the set of test data should be numbered. It should identify the data elements to be verified and explain why the examples were selected. You should then agree on and record the actions to be taken to produce the desired result. Start with the input of each data element, and follow it through every decision point in the process until you reach the output where the data will be verified. Number each action or decision and indicate the expected result.

Based on the notes you take at the meeting, your QA manager and testers should be able to document the test cases and test data so that anyone on your project team or in your user community could execute the tests and validate the data. Before you begin to depend on them, though, you should e-mail the documents to the users who attended the meeting and ask them to confirm that you transcribed everything correctly.

As you build the product, your developers and testers will employ the test cases and test data over and over again to check their work. Most of the time there's no need to involve the data experts again. If your users reengineer their processes or if you alter the product design, you should consult with your data experts to help you update the test cases and test data sets. After any major changes in the product, give them a version running in the test environment and let them experiment with it. Finally, make sure that your data experts participate in the beta test and user acceptance test.

Beta Test

Most computer users are familiar with the concept of a beta test: after a product has passed the ("alpha") tests run by the project team, it is given to a select group of end

Figure 4.2   Give the users what they want, but give them your advice, too.

users who then find as many problems as they can. Many developers have been approached at some point during their career by a large software company promising them a free copy of a product in exchange for participation in a beta test, and as a result they have the impression that only large organizations can afford beta tests. This preconception is simply not true. Any software product will improve its accuracy and reliability with a beta test, and any organization can arrange one. All it takes is including the beta test in your project plan and persuading your users to cooperate.

Even if you've been meeting regularly with your users throughout the development process, when the time for beta testing arrives, the relationship inevitably changes. Once users get their hands on the almost-final product, issues that in earlier phases might have seemed abstract and theoretical suddenly become very concrete. The tone of communication often changes, taking on a new edge of urgency. A beta test can be a helpful episode of collaboration and fine-tuning, or it can be a donnybrook of mutual recrimination, or it can be a chunk of time when nothing much happens at all. As usual, what makes the difference is clear expectations and advance planning.

Early in development, before you have completed unit testing of the various modules and components, you, your project manager, and your client should agree on the scope and purpose of beta testing. The amount and complexity of testing your users plan to do—and will be given time to do by their managers—will strongly influence your development team's plans for integration testing and system testing. If your users are simply going to start up the application and spend a couple of hours randomly checking for glaring errors, then your own testing efforts will be far more rigorous and take longer than if your users execute an end-to-end test plan that activates every step of the workflow and includes error conditions.

Of course, the ideal approach would be to have both comprehensive integration and system testing and a thorough end-to-end beta test, but many projects start to run out of time and money as the deadline approaches and managers are forced to make a choice. In addition, certain circumstances may prevent your testers from duplicating your users' environment to an extent necessary for reliable system and integration testing. For example, if your users are located in many different countries and input data using localized settings and configurations, you may not be able to afford to build a test environment that replicates all these conditions. As a result, your beta test would play a much more critical role.

The spectrum of the possible coverage a beta test provides is quite broad, but generally beta tests can be divided into three types:

Comprehensive. A test plan incorporating documented test cases and test data to verify the end-to-end data flow for all routine processes.

Basic. A test plan describing recommended test cases and test data to verify the end-to-end data flow for the most important routine processes and a list summarizing other functions to be verified.

Checklist. A test plan outlining the functions to be verified without any end-to-end throughput of data.

Your Quality Assurance manager should be able to give you a preliminary estimate of how much time and effort it will take to develop, execute, and analyze the results from each of these three types.

Once you have established the scope and purpose, you, your project manager, and your client can negotiate a schedule. As you envision your beta testers' activities, make sure you add in enough time to do the following:

- Deliver and install the beta version
- Troubleshoot installation problems
- Attend training, read the user documentation, and/or independently figure out how to use the product
- Review the test plan and design test cases
- Become familiar with the problem reporting procedures

Ask your client to be realistic about how many hours the beta testers will actually be able to devote to your project every week. Find out how much advance notice is desirable for the beta testers to rearrange their own priorities and for technical support staff to make themselves available.

A beta test with a smaller number of carefully chosen participants is usually much more effective than one that is open to all volunteers because communication with a smaller group is more manageable and less time-consuming. The people you want most are likely to be the hardest to recruit—either because they're so good at what they do that everyone wants their help or because their senior position makes their time too valuable. It's often worthwhile to campaign for their participation, using whatever methods of persuasion and political leverage are available to you, even if they can help only for a limited time and on certain specific tasks.

Your volunteers will probably come from two categories: younger new recruits who are technologically sophisticated and eager to make a name for themselves in the organization and older veteran staff members who are worried that your product will not work properly and will make their jobs harder. Each type of tester can provide valuable criticism and insight. It is important for you to arrange a wider representation from your user community. Every step in the workflow, every job category, every security type, every hardware platform, and every foreign office with localized configurations should be included.

To accomplish this, you will have to ask your client and project manager to recommend specific people. The first users on the list should be your data verification experts, but there will be other types of users who can make an important contribution. You will need to explain to the beta testers' managers exactly what you want the testers to do, how long it should take, and why it is important for the success of your project. There will be meetings and phone calls, and you will repeat your speech enough times to learn it by heart. You may be obliged to offer some kind of reward or recognition so that the beta testers and their managers feel the sacrifices they are making of their other projects or of their free time are worthwhile.

In a beta test utopia, you could create your test plan and then schedule the time and find the people you needed to execute it. In the real world, the opposite tends to be true: you will be able to test for only as long as the schedule permits and only with the people you have available. To obtain the most value from your beta test, you should adapt the test plan so that it can easily be accomplished by the testers you have within the alloted time. They key concept here is *easily*. Professional testers almost always overestimate what average users can accomplish. It is far more helpful to have simpler tasks that beta testers can complete than more complex tasks that they abandon halfway because they've run out of time.

If possible, the test plan should meet the following criteria:

- Simulate the hardware configuration and operations procedures of the production environment.
- Begin with a backed-up copy of a baseline database that can be restored if the test needs to be rerun.
- Create an end-to-end data flow.
- Execute every step of the process for your users' ordinary tasks.
- Include both newly input data and records migrated from legacy systems.
- Allocate a significant amount of time for the beta testers to experiment with the system and invent their own test cases.

When you set up the beta test, you will need to customize your tools and prepare supporting documents. First consider how you want the beta testers to communicate with your project team. You could give them full access to your change management database, but then they would be able to see the change history of the entire project and all the defects discovered by your testers. You would have to train them to use the system properly, and there might be licensing issues. Therefore, it is generally preferable to create a special input form and a view of the database that shows only those items contributed by the members of the beta test group.

Distribute a detailed outline of the full beta test plan to all the beta testers, along with a spreadsheet listing test data, a file containing test cases, a form for recording tests executed and the results, an input form for submitting change requests, and a form documenting new test cases and test data invented by the beta testers.

After the communication tools and procedures have been developed, the documentation has been sent out, and the beta version has been deployed and successfully installed on the participants' machines, you should schedule an orientation session. If you don't, your beta testers will probably ignore all the instructions and carefully crafted test data you have given them and do whatever they please whenever they get around to it. Your project manager should give a demo of the product and then show how you would like the beta tester to execute the test plan, record the results, and submit a change request. The orientation should be as face-to-face and hands-on as possible—ideally with the product manager standing beside the beta tester's desk or at the front of a classroom. When this is not possible because the beta testers are at remote locations, the product manager should arrange a teleconference or a meeting. Beta testers should be able to see the product projected on a screen and hear the product manager's voice explaining how it works while the product manager inputs data and navigates through the functions. At the very least, the product manager can send out a presentation or a document containing screen images, plan a conference call with all the beta testers at their computers, and ask them to follow along together one step at a time.

You should expect your beta test to uncover problems. That's what it's for. Even if some of the problems seem serious, and even if your release date seems to be approaching faster and faster all the time, tell everyone that you're delighted the problems were found before the rollout.

Evaluate the results of the beta test in a meeting with your client, your product manager, your development manager, and your QA manager. Prioritize the changes and estimate the time and effort required to implement them. Your project plan should provide for another phase of coding; if the changes necessary are really major, you should revise the plan and add another round of integration and system testing.

Your product manager should respond to every change request submitted by the beta testers. Inform them of the action you're planning to take:

- Rejected (with thanks and an explanation)
- Deferred until a later release
- Approved for this version

When they see the list of approved items, they'll know what to look for when they participate in the user acceptance test.

User Acceptance Test

Whenever a product gets delayed, it's tempting to drop the user acceptance test (UAT) from the plan. After all, the product has been through several rounds of testing already. Often a project manager figures that any remaining problems would be too insignificant to bother with.

It's true that if you've done a good job in your testing so far, the likelihood that a showstopper bug suddenly appears during a user acceptance test is small. But this does not diminish the value of the user acceptance test. The purpose of a UAT is less to verify the product's data and functionality than to obtain a consensus that it's ready to be released.

No software product is ever completely finished from every user's point of view. There will always be features that you didn't have time to implement, special circumstances that require workarounds, improvements that could be made in the look and feel. But at some point you have to stop, declare that you're as ready as you're ever going to be, and launch.

Without a user acceptance test, you run the risk of being criticized later for releasing the product prematurely.

A user acceptance test consists of two essential sections: the test plan document and the signatures (manual or electronic) of the people who approve the release. Within this framework, everything else is negotiable between your project team and your users. As you work out the details, you will want to consider these points:

- How long should the tests last?
- Who ought to approve the release?
- Who should participate in the testing?
- What should the test plan include? Should it incorporate structured test cases and test data, or should it be based on exploratory testing?
- What are the pass/fail criteria?

The user acceptance tests should last as long as it takes for the participants to feel confident about making a decision to approve or reject the product. Depending on the product, the user community, and the organization, this could take hours, days, weeks, or months. Let the users tell you what they think they need.

Obtaining unanimous consent to approve the release is not always possible. You can reduce the political infighting that such decisions sometimes provoke by creating a hierarchy of approvals and encouraging dissenters to record their objections. You might stipulate in advance that the deployment will occur if 75 percent of the managers in the user community vote yes. Of course, ultimately your client casts the final and pivotal vote—but he or she will be less anxious about it if the decision is a representative rather than an autocratic one.

Ideally the participants in the user acceptance test should include some if not all of your usability consultants, your data verification experts, and your beta testers who have in-depth knowledge of the workflow and processes. The method of recruitment should be the same as for the beta test; very little training in either the product itself or in the test procedures should be needed because the participants should already know what they're doing. When briefing your testers on change management issues, instruct them to submit change requests as they have in the past, but advise them that anything less urgent than a catastrophic failure will probably be treated as an enhancement and scheduled for the next version.

The contents of the UAT plan are largely determined by the duration of the tests and the nature of the product. Tests that are scheduled for one Friday afternoon are inevitably more cursory and exploratory than tests that can be set up, executed, and interpreted over a six-week period. If your product is replacing an older application, it may be sufficient for you to run the two systems in tandem for a while, let your users perform their regular jobs, and compare the results. If your product automates manual processes, you should provide your testers with some guidance in the form of documented test cases and test data.

Formulating the pass/fail criteria is typically the most difficult activity of the user acceptance tests. When you first ask your client to define the pass/fail criteria, chances are you'll get a response like "The product has to work." If you press for a more specific answer, your client will probably say, "It has to work *perfectly.*"

Yes, but . . . everyone knows perfection does not exist here on Earth, and you must persuade your client to acknowledge this fact. Quote statistics, quote the Bible—whatever it takes, move the discussion into the realm of measurable behavior. Explain that the criteria should be based on percentages and categories, such as the following:

- In version 1.0, 80 percent of the data output by your product's reports will match the data from the old application. This should improve to 95 percent in version 1.1.
- Fifty percent of your Web pages will load in three seconds, 25 percent will load in five seconds, and 25 percent will take eight seconds or more.
- With 1000 users logged in to your database, 80 percent of your queries will return data within 10 seconds.

You get the idea. If you need suggestions on criteria to measure, your product manager and your usability consultants should be able to give you some hints. They can also remind your client that managers who demand perfection sooner or later cause 100 percent of their staff to quit.

If your users have never been involved in testing a software product before, you can expect that at first they will be puzzled and perhaps even annoyed by your requests. The people who volunteered during your interviews may wonder what they've gotten themselves into, and the people who are selected by your client or product manager may grumble. Yet over the course of the project they will figure out why they have been brought in to help, and they will develop greater respect for your project team. By the time the product is launched, they will feel more of a personal stake in its success.

Process Adjustment

Keeping up with your users' activities during the course of the project may remind you of trying to bundle toddlers into snowsuits: it would all be so much easier if they could . . . just . . . hold . . . still!

But they don't. While you and your team are busy building the product, the users are going about their usual business, doing whatever it is they do, responding to problems and opportunities, having new ideas, dismantling old structures and processes, constantly changing. And you need to find a way to stay informed. Perhaps they are contemplating some major initiative that will depend on the information in your database—one that would be much more effective if you added a few fields to a table before the product was launched. Or perhaps they are negotiating with another organization or department to undertake a joint venture, assuming that your system will be compatible with the other entity's systems, and in reality it's not. Perhaps they are being reorganized, and the new decision makers don't thoroughly understand the purpose of your product. Under any of these circumstances, your knowledge of the issues and the players, and your presence at planning meetings, can have a major effect not only on the success of your project, but also on your long-term relationship with your client.

Even if your organization is the sort of place where the same things have been done in the same way since the invention of the typewriter and the same people have been holding the same positions for so long that everyone has forgotten about their predecessors, your team's relationship with your users will change as you collaborate. Whether it's a usability review, a status report, a risk analysis, or any other forum or document through which the two groups communicate, you will learn what works best by trial and error during each phase of development. Experienced project managers turn this into a conscious, rational process by focusing everyone's attention on the forms and methods of interaction as well as the content. The goal is a continuous adaptation so that each participant always has access to the appropriate people and the relevant information. Among the questions you might ask are these:

- Did everyone receive this document/meeting invitation/status report who should have? Should anyone be added to or removed from the distribution list?
- Was everyone consulted about this decision whose experience or perspective should influence the outcome?
- Are any steps missing from this process? Are there any steps that merely create bureaucracy and can be eliminated?
- Are the tools and procedures for sharing information among the users and the project team adequate? How could they be improved?

The amount of time you and other members of your team can expect to spend with your users will depend on a number of factors. If your project is only one of many systems they commission, then you'll probably be treated like all the other development managers they deal with—at least until you've demonstrated to them how interested you are in their activities. For your part, you don't want to waste your team's time sitting through endless internal discussions about matters of no concern to your project.

Ideally, you as project manager should attempt to get invited to as many management-level user meetings as it takes for them to think of you as a regular guest and for you to find out about their long-range plans. You should also be empowered to call meetings that your users feel obliged to attend so that they can consult with your project team and be kept informed about your progress.

Because the advisory role is time-consuming for your users, gauge you participants' attitudes carefully. If they start to act like you are imposing on them, scale back your plans. Prioritize the product features for which you need usability information and testing before you proceed further on the project. This is particularly important when the users whom you must consult are senior managers. If possible, try to set up the meetings with those users first because they are the participants who are most likely to cancel and reschedule.

In all your relations with your user community—during user interface design, testing, or process adjustment—the key to success is your client. With your client's support, you will obtain your users' cooperation. People will show up for your meetings, invite you to their meetings, perform the tasks you request, send you the information you need. Without your client's support, none of this will happen. Therefore, above all else, be sure to pay attention to and nurture your relationship with your client. As we will see, communication with management is an essential part of a project manager's job.

Communicate with Management

Like your users, senior managers probably aren't very interested in your daily travails. Basically they're aware that you've got an assignment, and they expect you to let them know when you're done so they can give you another one. In the meantime, the less you bother them, the better.

Even Michelangelo probably needed to get together with Pope Julian now and then when he and his staff were painting the Sistine Chapel. You may have to apply for an audience, but you should maintain regular contact with the senior management of your user community and your IT department. In many organizations, senior managers' meetings are regular events, and you'll just need to remind your client and your boss to invite you periodically. If your work environment is more informal and unstructured, you will have to take the initiative in maintaining communication with senior management about important issues affecting your project. Among the matters you will want to discuss with them are scope creep, organizational change, outsourcing, the resolution of conflicts, and progress reports.

Scope Creep

Scope creep is what happens when your users want to keep adding features to the product long after they've approved the project proposal.

Requests for design changes are an inevitable consequence of users' involvement in the user interface design and their testing efforts. You may be on the third round of system testing with all code frozen except for critical bug fixes—but from your users' point of view the release date is still several weeks away. You've still got plenty of time before release, so what's the big deal?

How you respond to their pleas for just one more input screen or admin function or hardware platform, and how they react to your estimates of risk and explanations of the software development process, will reflect the relationship you have been building with them from the beginning of the project. Of course, you will have to listen to them—but they will need to listen to you, too. And that's where senior management comes in. If you want to maintain control of the project, it is essential that the senior managers of your user community—particularly your sponsor(s) and your client—understand and endorse two key development concepts:

Feature freeze. The point at which you stop adding functions to the product without adjusting the project plan.

Code freeze. The point at which you stop making changes to the product except for major bug fixes without adjusting the project plan.

Scope creep puts project managers in a very difficult position. On the one hand, you want to build a solid, usable product. On the other hand, you need to be responsive to your users. Some very demanding clients simply won't listen to your discourses on risk and methodology; their attitude is, "I don't care what it takes . . . just do it or I'll find someone else who can." If you are unfortunate enough to find yourself with a client like this, try comparing your team with independent consulting firms. You might even do some research and provide evidence in the form of competitive bids on your project proposal from actual consultants. Attend a meeting of your user community's senior managers and diplomatically call your client's bluff. Remind your users' senior managers that consultants wouldn't work for a fixed price regardless of how many changes the client made in the requirements. And consider other ways in which you and your team can market your efforts and make your users feel that you care about providing good service.

Organizational Change

At some organizations, if you take a leave of absence for six months you won't recognize the place when you get back. People quit or get fired, departments are reorganized, divisions combine or split. The work may stay the same, but the players change constantly.

Change comes from outside as well. Businesses are acquired and divested and merged for the sake of stockholders' profits. Government agencies are created and dissolved and reconfigured by legislation. Nonprofit groups expand and contract in response to funding.

After every change, the organizational chart is redrawn. Standards and processes are revised. New formal communication patterns are established, and informal ones evolve on their own. The collective vision of the organization's function and purpose may alter. At times it may seem as though the changes in your organization have nothing to do with your project—and perhaps they don't. But before you assume you're not going to be affected, ask yourself three questions:

- Will the organization's activities in the marketplace or the community be any different?
- Will any new technology be introduced into the organization?
- Will any new people have an influence on the budget for my client or IT?

If the answer to any of these questions is yes, you should make every effort to inform the new players about your project and to find out about their long-term strategy and priorities. How you accomplish this will depend on the culture of your organization. If you work in a structured, hierarchical environment, ask your client to arrange for you to be invited to the appropriate meetings and have your project put on the agenda. In a more casual environment, it's probably acceptable for you to walk right up to the new senior VP, say hello, and start a conversation. No matter how you accomplish it, make sure that your project is noticed and understood and that you stay alert to the forces shaping its future.

Outsourcing

Whether you plan to include consultants on your project team from the very beginning or you decide to bring them in at a later phase, the senior management of your user community and your IT department should be told who they are, what they're doing, and why they're necessary.

Some IT departments maintain lists of approved consultants or consulting firms, so check into this before you make any commitments. Even if there is no official list, you may be able to negotiate a better rate by involving your IT management or your purchasing department in the discussions—many consultants will lower their prices if they foresee the possibility of repeat business or additional assignments from other project teams. If you do have complete freedom to choose whomever you want, obtain thorough documentation about the consultant's qualifications and experience with the specific tasks he or she is being hired to perform, and make it available to anyone who asks. It should go without saying (but it bears repeating nonetheless) that as a project manager, you should never sign a contract with any consultant who is in a position to provide personal favors or services to you or any member of your family. If the best person for the job just happens to be your bridge partner or the spouse of the admissions director of the school to which your child is applying, you should acknowledge this fact in a written memo to your management before the deal is done.

The scope of the consultant's assignment should also be carefully outlined in advance. The more specific you can be, the greater your chances are of avoiding both disputes over the bill and conflicts between the outsiders and your internal staff. If the consultant will be working on a self-contained project, such as a user manual or a stress test, the written agreement should include these points:

- A description of the final product the consultant will deliver
- Your acceptance criteria
- The project plan
- A list of dependencies on other project variables that could legitimately cause the consultant to change the product or fall behind schedule
- A list of the required documentation

If the consultant will be working alongside other members of your team in a joint effort to build or test your product, you should formalize the consultant's supporting role. No consultant ever feels the same degree of ownership or accountability for a project as a staff member does. Assign a staff member to supervise and take responsibility for the work of every consultant. Let your management know that after the consultant leaves there will still be someone on your team who will follow up on and resolve any problems related to the work the consultant has done.

You should also be prepared to explain to management why you want to hire a consultant for the task rather than assigning the work to one of your own staff members or temporarily borrowing a resource from another project team. In fact, you should think long and hard about this. Unless you work for an organization where IT subcontracting is the standard *modus operandi*, in the long run your goal should be to augment the technical expertise and promote the career development not only of your own project team but of the IT group as a whole. Therefore your consultant should perform one of the following functions:

- Boring, repetitive work that involves old technology so that your staff can focus on creative new challenges in a state-of-the-art development environment
- Exciting, innovative work with cutting-edge technology so that they can teach your staff how it's done
- The same work as your staff because there's too much of it for them to be able to complete the project on schedule

If both management and your team clearly understand into which category the consultant falls, he or she or they will be treated as a valuable asset to the project.

Conflicts

Differences of opinion among the members of your team are routine, and it is the project manager's job either to resolve them by executive fiat or to make sure the disputants work things out among themselves. Management will not want to hear about these incidents.

Conflicts between your project team and your client or between your project team and other project teams are another matter entirely. These differences of opinion are also routine, but they need to be handled with special care. For example:

Process. Conflicts between your project team and your client might occur over issues of workflow or cooperation. In the beginning everyone might agree on how developers should communicate with users about questions regarding details of implementation. Yet in spite of their original commitment, the users might not devote enough time to thinking about and answering the developers' questions, or they might be collectively unable to reach a decision. Your project team might also be in for trouble if your client doesn't understand or accept the concept of a code freeze and insists on making changes to the product right up to the release date.

Configuration. Another project team in your organization might decide to take advantage of a new architecture or tool or program feature that wasn't available when you designed your own product. You don't want to stand in anyone's way, but you might realize that the other project will introduce a change in your users' desktop environment. It might be only a newer version of a shared system file or a later release of a shrink-wrapped office application, but you might discover that your product could be affected in unpredictable ways. Testing and possibly revising your product to operate in the new environment would affect your schedule. You might try to persuade your project manager colleague to postpone implementing the change until after your own product's next release—but to no avail.

Data ownership. Your product's developers might create a new database to store most of the information they will need, but then realize that several pieces of important data are already being maintained in another database for a different product. You might obtain permission from the other project manager to link your product to that database, but the story often doesn't end there. If your product updates the information, you might later determine that the two products have different interpretations of end-user roles or processes. Even if the information is a read-only input to your product, changes to the other product might make its database temporarily unusable until you revise your queries, stored procedures, or field lengths. As with changes to the technology environment, you might find your product's rollout schedule is at the mercy of another project manager.

In any of these situations, or others of a similar nature, your best approach is to acknowledge and document the problem as soon as you conclude that negotiations are no longer making any progress. When you report the problem, you should be as neutral as possible in your tone and avoid accusations. The issue should be stated in terms of risk to the project, for example, "If we cannot confirm the business rules for the Member Discount field, we estimate that 30 percent of the invoices may be calculated incorrectly," or "If FileZap 6.2 is deployed before our release, the additional coding and testing will take 250 work hours and delay our release by 9 work days." Be frank and realistic and forceful, but try at the same time to step back from the emotional confrontation and envision how your project fits in with your user community's other priorities and the IT department's objectives. In most organizations there are myriad competing interests, and you should be prepared to act like a good sport if the umpire's decision is not in your favor.

It is often helpful to use the influence of one management group to resolve issues with another. Senior IT management can sometimes intervene effectively to focus your client's attention on working more closely with your developers or to restrain your client's demands for last-minute design changes. Your client's senior management can sometimes lobby the IT powers to have your project's requirements and schedule take precedence over others. For the sake of your reputation, such maneuvers are best done openly, with witnesses, rather than in secret.

Status Updates

Your senior management may be inquisitive, pestering you for news all the time, or aloof, keeping their distance until you call for help. You can minimize the annoyance of the former type and protect against a surprise "But you never told us!" inquisition from the latter by providing regular, written status reports. Even if they're never asked for, even if you suspect nobody really reads them, their existence will be noticed and your project will benefit by your considering it periodically from management's point of view.

Your client and your IT department have different perspectives, and you should adapt your presentation to your audience. You have only one project plan, but you should be able to derive from it two distinct types of status report. For your client, you should explain your progress in terms of functionality:

- Features you've implemented
- Features you're still working on
- Problems your testers have encountered
- Open issues awaiting resolution from your usability consultants
- Evolution of your user documentation and training materials

For your IT managers the content should instead focus on the stages of the development cycle. It should cover the following:

- Development of detailed design specifications
- Building of program modules
- Creation of system and test documentation
- Open technical issues awaiting resolution
- Statistics describing the product's behavior during unit, system, and performance testing
- Arrangements for deployment

Putting together two separate status documents for every reporting period is actually less of a burden than it sounds. You will soon discover that you are, in fact, looking at the product through these two different lenses all the time, switching back and forth constantly, depending on whom you're talking to. Once you've created the templates and used them a couple of times you'll find it a very useful exercise to strengthen your project planning, and senior management will give you high marks for communication and accountability.

Plan Education and Support

Often it's not until the product is almost ready to be released that the project manager begins to envision it actually being used.

At first the image is a pleasant one: busy, contented folks interacting with the product the way they're supposed to. But then the project manager suddenly has an anxiety attack, and the picture changes. One of the users is puzzled about the meaning of a field name. Another user tries to enter data that the system considers invalid. A third clicks on a link and gets an error message, and so on, until the entire user population is transformed into a mob of scowling, muttering malcontents. Simultaneously they all reach for their phones and fire off flaming e-mails. The product manager receives all the messages but can resolve only about a third of the complaints. In horror, the project manager hits the Do Not Disturb button on the phone as dozens of voice messages accumulate in the queue and shuts down e-mail as the list of items in the in box scrolls down off the screen . . .

To avoid this nightmare, you should acknowledge at the outset that in the matter of education and support the issues are complex, the necessary skills are specialized, and the work should begin at the same time as the construction of the product. From a distance, documentation and training and troubleshooting are nearly indistinguishable—they seem like three different names for a single activity that one might call "Helping the User." In reality, each of the three functions has a unique set of goals and methods and serves a particular purpose.

User Documentation

User documentation explains how to perform specific tasks. Typically the user consults the documentation either when he wants to figure out how to do something new or when she is unpleasantly surprised by something the system has done. Thus the user's state of mind when reading the document is goal-oriented and probably impatient. He or she is like a driver who wants directions on how to get from point A to point B and is not interested in a description of the scenery along the way or details about how the road is constructed.

In all likelihood your product will have several types of users, and you should already know who they are based on your earlier research. They may have different levels of literacy and language skills, different senses of humor, different degrees of computer expertise. If your product will be installed and/or supported by technicians other than the members of your development team, this subset of users will require altogether different information than, say, the data entry clerks. As you design your documentation, you should create an outline listing all your user types, the average reading level and computer skills for each group, and the tasks you expect each group to perform. Template 4.2 is a good example. You should also make a list of any use cases you've developed that would be helpful in organizing and prioritizing the product's functions.

Next consider the format of the documentation. Based on your understanding of your user community, are users more likely to look up the information they need in a book or to search for it electronically? Most technology professionals assume that by now any human being who prefers reading words on paper can easily print out a few pages of a PDF file, but many people still feel that they're not getting a "real" computer system unless it comes with a loose-leaf binder they can keep on their desks. Even the savviest hypertext jumpers often resort to printed "cheat sheets" they can thumbtack to the bulletin board next to their workstation.

Electronic documentation can be presented to the user in several ways. The simplest is the online manual in PDF format, which is organized and laid out just like a printed book. You can search for any word in the PDF file and print as many pages as you want. Hyperlinks can be added to the file for ease of navigation. The file can be stored on the user's hard disk or on a CD-ROM, or it can be maintained as a Web site with different pages for each chapter.

Then there's the Help file. Anyone who has ever used a computer for more than a half hour knows where to find it: it's the last item on the right of a Windows main menu (and somewhere equally prominent on the Web site's home page). The information contained in a Help file is usually broken up into smaller chunks. It focuses on the users' interaction with the program functions rather than the accomplishment of a complex task—for example, how to sort a list rather than how to produce a monthly report. Although it is possible to set up a Help file so that you can search for any word in it, the database necessary for this operation can become very large and the retrieval process can often be quite slow. The printed output from a Help file is also generally less attractive than from a PDF file. Assembling a helpful Help file requires a great deal of indexing, but the process of labeling the chunks of information enables the designer to include synonyms or text strings by which a typical user might search. Most Help files are installed on the user's hard disk along with the program files; they can also be configured as a Web site linked to the pages of the product's site.

Context-sensitive Help is another form of electronic documentation now included with most mass-market applications. In format it ranges from Microsoft's infamous Mister Paperclip, who interrupts what users are doing to offer his assistance, to function keys that display the Help file entry for the active dialog box or field, to mouse-over text that identifies the object on which the user is about to click. In proportion to the amount of coding required to deliver it, the amount of information furnished by context-sensitive Help is relatively limited. Its most worthwhile application is probably mouse-over text answering the user's question, "What on earth does this icon stand for?"

Developers are very rarely able to write good user documentation. Their services are valuable in creating the electronic delivery medium, but the content should not be their responsibility. Because they are so familiar with the structure of the system, they have great difficulty adopting the user's perspective. If you do not have a technical writer on your team, consider hiring one as a consultant. Your next best choice would be drafting the product manager or establishing a task force of end users. No matter who writes the text or develops the electronic package, you should submit drafts to your product manager, your client, and your usability reviewers for their comments. The usability of the documentation is nearly as important as the usability of the product itself (at least if you want to avoid the overflowing phone message queue and e-mail in box). The first

Documentation User Type List

PROJECT:	VERSION:
DOC ID:	DATE CREATED:
DOC TYPE:	CREATED BY:
DESCRIPTION:	FILE NAME:

User Type	Literacy/language	Technology Skills	Tasks

Template 4.2   Documentation User Type List

draft of the documentation should be ready at the same time as the first prototype, and it should grow and change along with the product.

Training

Training materials differ from user documentation in scope, content, and context. They focus on larger questions of how the new product will affect the users' thought processes, physical habits, social interactions, and daily routines. In addition to concise explanations about how to perform specific tasks, training materials provide conceptual models of how the system works and sample exercises enabling users to try out new activities in a safe environment. Their structure and tone are based on several assumptions: that the user has set aside time for training, is ready and willing to learn, has enough patience for a trial-and error approach, and will give the process his or her undivided attention. Documentation designers often come from a publishing background and know a great deal about how to edit and lay out information on a two-dimensional page or screen so that it can be easily understood; training developers are frequently former educators with expertise on how people learn.

Most software products are complex enough that training every user to perform every possible function would be either impossible or an outlandish waste of resources. The first step in developing training materials is to consult your outline that describes all your user types and decide what goals the members of each group will try to accomplish with the help of your product on a regular basis: hourly, daily, weekly, monthly, quarterly, and annually.

The next phase should appeal to anyone who has ever daydreamed of being a novelist, playwright, or screenwriter. Basically you invent a bunch of fictional characters to act out your users' roles. Depending on what your product does, you also make up fictional customers, suppliers, products, schools, classes, government agencies, and countries. When you are done you should have an entire alternate universe modeling the data your system tracks.

Then you write the scripts. For each goal of each user group you portray, step by step, how the fictional characters interact with your product to get the job done. Your use cases should provide you with many essential scenarios. Your sample data should consist of ordinary cases—typical, normal examples, not exceptions to the rules. The script should be descriptive enough that you could round up a group of random people on the street, hand them copies, assign them roles, and they would all know what to do. As a rough estimate, the fictional activities should represent about 75 percent of the product's functionality.

Once you've determined the content of the training materials, you can evaluate the alternate methods of presenting it:

Demo. The simplest choice is a demo, with the trainer projecting the product on a screen and executing the scripts while the audience watches. This is, of course, better than nothing. When a product is being launched in many locations and it is not feasible for trainers to visit each site personally, a teleconference demo is often the best solution. Passive members of an audience, though, do not retain as much information as do active participants in a hands-on exercise. If due to resource limitations a demo or series of demos is all you can arrange for your product, you should at least hand out printed copies of the scripts to your audience so that they can refresh their memories when they try to use the product themselves.

Classroom training. A structured class gives your users a more thorough understanding of the product and more confidence in their ability to perform their assigned tasks with it. The trainer still projects the product on a screen and executes the scripts, but the students also execute them at their workstations simultaneously. One student per workstation is ideal; two are feasible if they take turns controlling the keyboard and mouse; if there are any more than two, you might as well have a demo instead. With any class, the trainer should write down the students' questions and comments and give them to the project manager for review. Recurring questions often identify elements of the product that may need to be changed in the next release.

Tutorials. A tutorial provides the user with scripts and step-by-step instructions on how to execute them. A tutorial can be a simple checklist document, or it can be a fully interactive program with prompts and error checking and triumphant music when the correct answer is typed in. Unlike a live demo or a class, a tutorial can be executed at the user's convenience. It can be interrupted and restarted. It can be available to teach the moment the user needs to know something. On the other hand, the tutorial is usually run in private and you often have no way of knowing whether the user has actually done it. If the user has any questions or problems, there is typically no one around to ask.

Developers generally are better at performing demos and doing classroom training than at creating user documentation. They know the product inside out, and their pride in their work kindles users' enthusiasm. The main drawback to asking developers to act as trainers is that they tend to forget about the carefully crafted scripts that portray the activities of fictional users and instead wander off on technical tangents until the audience's eyes glaze over. No matter who gives your demos or teaches your classes—a professional trainer, your product manager, your developers—rehearsals are the key to success. The project manager, product manager, and several end users who represent different user types should evaluate both the trainers' performance and the content of the training materials far enough in advance of the product rollout so that improvements can still be made.

A tutorial program is a development project in itself, and you should consider the costs and dependencies carefully before you make any rash promises to your end users. Any type of tutorial needs to be reviewed for usability, but this task is not as straightforward as with a demo or class. The private nature of a tutorial makes many usability problems more difficult to identify: unless you have a controlled laboratory where you can observe or videotape the person going through the steps of the tutorial, you'll have to trust the user's memory and self-recording skills. One low-tech, high-value strategy for creating a tutorial is simply to recycle and reformat any scripts you prepare for demos and classes.

Any type of learning requires a protected space. Classrooms and workshops enable students to make mistakes and figure out how to do things the right way without fearing the consequences. The same principle holds true for your system and your users: before you begin to offer training, you should establish a separate database on your development or test server to store the fictional information created by your scripts. Any training data stored on your users' computers should reside in its own clearly labeled files and directories. Once you have built this training environment, it should be monitored and maintained as part of your development infrastructure.

Troubleshooting

No matter how well you train your users so that they know what to expect, no matter how thoroughly you document your product's features, at some point something just won't work. Training is like preventive medicine, and documentation should be part anatomy textbook and part first-aid manual. Support is equivalent to a personal consultation with a doctor.

The calls for help that you and your product manager receive from your users will often turn out to be about problems that have nothing to do with your product. When something bad happens with their computer, most users have no idea what's wrong, and their impulse is to blame the last application they saw on the screen. For example, you might get a call from a user who claimed that clicking on the Submit button on your Update Personal Data page crashed his machine. Unable to reproduce the problem, you go to his desk and discover that at the same time he clicked the Submit button his network connection suddenly failed.

Over the years many users have become much more computer-savvy and will report problems with enough supporting information for a technician to make a quick diagnosis. Even if your user community is a graduate department of computer science and they e-mail you machine language output along with their problem reports, there will be times when your product is merely revealing an error in the data or a failure somewhere else in the IT infrastructure.

Under these circumstances, the appropriate response to your user's complaint is not "Sorry . . . it's not my problem." Although you may lack the authority or influence to resolve the situation, you should be able to let the user know the following:

- What you believe is the real nature of the problem
- Who is responsible for fixing it—the individual, the department, and department manager
- How you are letting the responsible individual know that the problem exists
- What you and the user can do to follow up

To accomplish this, you and the product manager and anyone else on your team who will help support the users should make sure you know the people and processes involved. Your technology environment survey should have documented this information. Your project procedures guide should provide it for reference and for training new team members. However it works in your environment, you should always transmit your problem reports to other IT groups in writing and keep a record of the user who reported the issue, the recipient to whom you sent the report, and the dates.

If your organization has a Help Desk to which users are supposed to report all hardware and software problems, you should ensure that the Help Desk staff is adequately trained and has appropriate technical documentation—not only at the product launch, but throughout the life of the product as changes and enhancements are introduced. The Help Desk manager should agree to let you inspect the call logs or database records or perform any other type of audit you feel would be necessary to convince you that the Help Desk staff is maintaining its commitment to your project.

In the end, what matters most to your project is the relationship between your team and your user community. When your users report a problem with your products—to you, to your product manager, to anyone on your staff, or to a Help Desk—they should feel confident that they will be taken care of. If the problem is a usability issue, the product manager should call the person on the phone or show up at his or her desk and explain how the product works. If the problem turns out to be a defect or an enhancement request, the product manager should enter it into your change management database and send the user an e-mail or phone message acknowledgment. If the problem has nothing to do with your product, you should notify the appropriate contact and send the user an e-mail or phone message explaining what was done. You and your client should agree on a reasonable time frame for these responses. Finally, you should appoint a member of your project team as support coordinator to monitor compliance with these procedures, serve as your liaison with the Help Desk, and check up on whether your users generally are receiving the information and consideration they need to do their jobs well.

The quality of a project's education and support is hard to quantify. The number of pages written, the number of users trained, or the number of troubleshooting issues resolved unfortunately doesn't indicate the effectiveness of the effort. The best measurement you'll have of success or failure in this area is your users' subjective feelings about you and your team. Education and support form the human face of your product. Make it an attentive and caring one.

Milestone Marker

Real-world entrepreneurs are like bloodhounds, always tracking the scent of their customers' whims. It's an instinct, and some people are naturally endowed with it. But even if you're not, you can train yourself to practice certain behaviors that achieve the same result. During the development of your product, if you follow the guidelines suggested here to collaborate with your users, keep in touch with management, and create a strategy for education and support, you can be confident that you'll stay on track and find your way through the forest.

Meanwhile, your project team is hard at work building the product. There are features to be coded and components to be assembled and tests to be run. Each team member presumably knows how to do his or her particular job—yet somehow all the parts need to get assembled and all the functions need to mesh. In the next chapter, we'll explore how you can lead your team out of its natural state of development anarchy and bestow upon the project the blessings of good government.

Governor and Legislator

In the realm of technology, the leadership functions of a software project manager vary depending on the type of authority you are exercising. To your project team, you are like the governor of a territory. You oversee the condition of your domain and the welfare of your people; you make sure that your government has good laws and that the citizens follow them; you resolve disputes among your agencies. To other software project managers and IT colleagues, you are more like a legislator in a parliament. On behalf of your team, you stand up for their interests and lobby for their fair share of resources and influence. Fortunately, you don't have to solicit campaign contributions or run for reelection.

During the development phase, your administration should focus on several key policy initiatives. The top priorities of your domestic agenda should be thorough product testing, efficient organization of your project resources, and comprehensive change management. You should establish strategic alliances with your IT colleagues on plans for deployment. You may not be able to promise everyone a tax cut, but as a Technology Partner you can earn high approval ratings by adhering to your principles for the sake of your product.

Create Appropriate Test Plans

Novice software project managers generally lack a strong background in testing. There are a number of reasons for this, not least of which is that by temperament the average tester shuns the limelight and therefore is rarely promoted to a leadership position outside the QA group. Anyone who is promoted to the position of project manager certainly should realize, based on his or her own experience, that software testing is an art and a science unto itself. It requires a different mentality, a different array of skills, a different knowledge base, and a different set of tools than software development.

As project manager, you are ultimately responsible for your team's product testing efforts. Your testers and your quality assurance manager can create test plans, test cases, and test data; they can also offer valuable advice. It is up to you, though, to set the priorities, decide on the strategy, and allocate the resources. Before you can do this effectively, you'll have to become familiar with basic testing concepts. You should evaluate the criteria influencing the design of your test plans and understand the ways you can adapt your test plans to suit various strategies and priorities. It also helps if you're aware of certain factors affecting the success of your testers and test plans in improving the overall quality of your product.

Basic Testing Concepts

Like most technology professionals, software testers speak in their own jargon. Mostly what they talk about are the components of tests, the phases of testing, the varieties of tests, the methods of testing, and the types of test data. To the uninitiated these things all sound pretty much the same, but as you will see, they're not.

Test Components

Organizations and tool vendors have different names for the components of the testing process. No matter where you work or what tool you use, you will accomplish your testing by means of the following:

Test data. Reusable sample data. The four principal types are these:
- Valid data—Examples that produce correct answers
- Invalid data—Examples that are not allowed or that produce wrong answers
- Boundary data—Examples from the outer limits of allowable functionality, defined parameters, or system tolerance
- Environment data—Examples that verify how the product performs in its environment

Test cases. A list of actions performed by the user and the expected results. Cases can be documented at different levels of resolution ranging from keystroke by keystroke (high resolution) to function by function (low resolution). Some common synonyms for test cases are test procedures, test scripts, and test scenarios.

Test log. A detailed list of test cases executed, including cases that were planned to be executed but could not be for various reasons.

Test results. A summary list describing the test cases executed, the pass/fail status of each test, and any new problems discovered or questions raised.

Test statistics. A summary list for a specified build or version indicating the number of program changes tested, the number of changes that passed, the number that failed, the number of new problems discovered, the number of test cases created, revised, and executed, and any other quantitative data the QA manager or project manager wants to analyze.

Test plan. A report specifying who will test what, and when, where, and how. It lists the changes to be verified, the test cases, and test data. It summarizes the design and strategy of the tests, describes the test environment, and establishes the pass/fail criteria.

These documents give the project manager enough information about the testing process to determine which functions of the product have been verified and how much effort doing so required.

Test Phases

When a change is made in a program, the revised code should pass through three phases of testing before it is approved for release:

Unit test. The function is tested separately, disconnected from other functions. To accomplish this, it is sometimes necessary to create special programs that input data into the function being tested and intercept the output before it can be transmitted to any other function. Often developers create their own unit tests to verify code they have written, although testers can provide guidance on selecting effective test data.

Integration test. The function is incorporated into the workflow of the product. Data is passed through the system end to end from initial inputs to final outputs. State transitions between functions and components are verified.

System test. The product is loaded into the environment (or a facsimile thereof) where it will be used and tested. The product's behavior on all approved platforms and under all approved configurations is verified. Inputs from other systems and outputs to other products are connected, and their viability is confirmed.

No matter what methodology you are following, for best results these three phases should occur in sequence. If you skip a step, identifying the cause of any problems you discover later on will take longer and be harder.

Test Types

Depending on the circumstances, testing has different goals and different methods. Among the types of test plans you might create for your project are these:

Smoke test. Test cases to verify that a new build is robust enough to be subjected to system testing. This plan should take no more than an hour to execute manually. If it produces three fatal errors—either program crashes or data inaccuracies—then the build should be sent back to the developers for further unit testing.

Regression test. Test cases to verify that changes made to specific functions do not affect other functions of the product. This plan is long and comprehensive, and it includes both valid and invalid data. It may also include performance and load tests.

Beta test. Test cases your users execute to confirm the usability, functionality, and accuracy of the product.

User acceptance test. Test cases your users execute to determine whether the product is ready for release.

Performance test. Test cases to verify the product's behavior in a particular environment with a specified number of users.

Load test. Test cases to verify the product's behavior with increasing numbers of users and increasing transaction volumes.

Stress test. Test cases to determine the product's behavior when the maximum number of users or maximum transaction volume is exceeded.

Environment test. Test cases to verify your product's functionality when something changes in your technology infrastructure.

Many of your test cases will be reused again and again in these different types of tests; some will be used rarely or even only once.

Test Methods

When planning a test, you'll have to consider the best approach to take. Some of the alternatives available to you are the following:

Positive/constructive. The tester does what the user is supposed to do.

Negative/destructive. The tester tries to break the rules and cause the product to fail.

Structured. The tester follows a test plan and performs actions according to the instructions in a test case using previously selected data.

Exploratory. The tester improvises.

Manual. The tester interacts with the product directly.

Automated. The tester develops a program that executes the test.

Functional. The tester verifies the accuracy of the data and the workflow of the product (in contrast to the processing speed or response time).

Performance. The tester verifies the product's processing speed and response time under normal, load, and/or stress conditions.

Black box. The tester has no knowledge of the product's internal design and verifies its behavior from a user's point of view.

White box/glass box. The tester refers to the system documentation and verifies the product's behavior based on its architecture, design, and code.

Each of these approaches is useful and provides a different kind of information. Your testing should incorporate as many of them as your resources permit.

Test Plan Criteria

Because there is no type of test that can verify every possible function, state transition, data element, workflow pattern, user action, or hardware configuration for a product, when you design your test plans you will need to prioritize risks and decide on an acceptable level of coverage in each area.

So far, QA experts have not yet invented a formula to determine what methods you should employ for testing or how much testing is enough. Experienced project managers discover that every project has its own complex equation balancing various critical factors.

Scope of the Project

In layman's terms, the scope of a project can be defined as the product's size multiplied by its complexity. You can use a variety of measurements to describe a project's scope:

- Number of lines of code
- Number of objects
- Number of input and output fields
- Number of screens or reports or Web pages
- Number of program functions

For testing purposes it is often most helpful to know how many different paths data can take through the system and how many branches are made on each path. Your test cases will be a lot quicker to design and execute if the system performs 1 calculation on your users' input than if the data has to pass through 15 distinct conditional steps in the workflow before it arrives at its final output destination. To familiarize yourself with this type of analysis, and to equip yourself with useful information in case you have to defend your budget and/or schedule before senior management, compare your product with others that seem to have similar scope. Try to select products for which you can obtain internal numbers (such as objects, lines of code, program functions, and workflow decision points). Of course, your product is not built yet—but you can ask your developers for their estimates on these metrics. This process will not only help you discern the difference between clutter and volume or between awkwardness and complexity; it will also give you more insight into your developers' decisions about the structure and design of your product.

Deadlines

Some project deadlines are real, and some are artificial. If your organization has an old mainframe that it has decided to stop leasing as of a certain date, then the replacement system you are building has to be up and running before the old machine leaves the premises. If you are trying to launch a new product or service before your competitor does, you may have more flexibility. If you are creating or upgrading an internal application, your deadlines will be ruled more by the whims of senior management than by external necessity.

Early in the project, look ahead past your initial release. Try to find out how often your users will expect to receive new features and bug fixes. Perhaps they will be satisfied with a release every six months or every quarter, or perhaps they may be operating on "Internet time" and will demand a release every week or two. These scheduling parameters should help determine how you allocate your testing resources and select your testing methods.

A fixed deadline should alert you to place a greater emphasis on testing earlier in the project: make sure the unit testing is very thorough, so that as the weeks go by and the pieces of the product start to come together there are fewer errors in the individual components. Even before there is a single completed screen or module of code to test, you can put your testers to work learning about your users' requirements, exploring the tasks the users will perform with the product, and writing the first draft of the user acceptance test plan. If your product will be on a short release cycle, you should begin preparations early in the project to develop an automated regression test so that each new release can be verified quickly.

System Documentation

For any test, there are right answers and wrong answers. A tester needs to know what the right answers are before he or she can certify whether the program being tested has passed or failed. If you plan to have your end users do all your testing, then you may be able to rely on their knowledge (as long as everyone agrees about what the program should be doing). Otherwise, you'll need some form of system documentation. Among the types of documents your project team will find useful are the following:

System architecture schema. A diagram of the hardware infrastructure and major software components, showing the linkages and processes connecting them.

Data dictionary. A list of the fields in the databases, describing their table, type, length, source, and other characteristics.

Procedure inventory. A list of the programs stored with the database, describing their input and output parameters and processing fields.

Object/script inventory. A list of program objects, COM objects, Java script, and other components which manipulate the data between its entry via the user interface and its storage in the database.

Data model. A diagram of the databases, showing relationships between the fields and the tables.

Data flow schema. A diagram of the path data elements follow through the database tables and user interface components.

Design specifications. A document describing the functions of the system and the technology environment.

User interface components inventory. A list of the system's windows, screens, forms, dialog boxes, Web pages, and reports, indicating user type access, security restrictions, and program rules.

User interface elements inventory. A list of the data elements, control elements, and other objects contained in each user interface component, indicating user type access, security restrictions, and program rules.

Data element specifications. A list of characteristics for a data element, including storage location, default status, pick list selections, validation criteria, and program rules.

Control element specifications. A list of characteristics for a control element, including activation criteria, accessibility via keyboard or mouse, tab order, behavior during creation, display, update and deletion of data, and program rules.

Data itinerary. A list describing the progress of a data element through the system, including inputs, storage locations, processing procedures, outputs, and program rules.

Program rules list. A list of the logical rules affecting the processing of data elements and the behavior of program controls.

Message list. A list of all the messages the system displays to the user, describing the circumstances that trigger them.

User type list. A list of the categories of users the system employs to determine the security restrictions and program rules.

Templates for many of these documents are available on the companion Web site (www.wiley.com/ensworth).

Organizations vary in their assumptions about who should prepare the system documentation. Sometimes developers diligently record everything while they are designing the system to ensure that they fulfill all the users' requirements. Sometimes testers receive a totally undocumented product and are then forced to interview developers and users to piece together how the system works. The latter approach can be more time-consuming, but it can serve as a worthwhile check of the developers' work and improve the testers' knowledge of the product.

Test Documentation

The purpose of test documentation is to show how much of the product has been inspected and to prove what happened when the tester performed the inspection. As with system documentation, if your end users are your testers you may find they have a very casual attitude about keeping written logs and using checklists. You'll give them a version to test, and after a while they'll tell you, "It's fine—it works okay except for those three bug reports we sent you." Have they verified all the features? Have they input invalid data and observed the error handling? You don't know. They don't remember very clearly. You won't know until after the product has been released and someone calls you to complain.

Before you develop your test plans, evaluate how much test documentation your project will require. At a minimum, you'll want a checklist to give to any end users who do testing for you. You'll want to prevent the project from being seriously delayed if a tester quits. If you're expecting to create automated tests, you'll want an easy-to-read description of the automated scripts.

Unless you personally have a background in software quality assurance, your estimate of how long it should take to create and maintain test documentation will probably be way off. Consult with your QA manager and explain your goals in detail before you start typing numbers into your project plan. Make sure you have the resources to do a decent job; test documentation is one of those easily overlooked tasks that can invisibly consume many project hours.

Test Plan Methodologies

After you've taken all these criteria into consideration, you'll have a better sense of the proportion of the testing effort to development work and the type of testing resources you may require for your product. Next you can begin to evaluate the various testing methods and decide which ones will best suit the project and the team.

Positive versus Negative

Novice project managers and inexperienced testers often make the mistake of thinking that once they've verified what the users are supposed to do, the test is done. Sooner or later, when a user makes a mistake or a connection fails and the product crashes, they realize that they've been overly optimistic.

The amount of negative testing you'll need to do will depend on how fault tolerant your product needs to be. The higher your users' standards of reliability, the more your testers should abuse your developers' work. (Emphasize the *work*, not the developers themselves.) For a relatively low-risk internal product, the proportion of negative test cases should start at 25 percent. For products available to the public, allocate 50 percent. Products responsible for health, safety, or large financial transactions can devote 75 percent or more of their QA resources to negative testing.

Testers like to create negative cases. By and large, testers are a methodical, orderly group, but during negative testing they can give free rein to their defiant, mischievous, disruptive impulses. This energy, however, needs to be channeled toward achieving the most productive goals. You and your QA manager should confer and agree on what parts of your product must be made fail-safe, such as the following:

- Fields where data must be valid
- Processes that must complete to avoid deadlocks on the server
- Links between subsystems that must inform the user and cache input data if the connection is lost

You may or may not want your testers to go as far as some of their colleagues in California, who periodically knock over their server racks to verify their products' behavior during an earthquake.

Structured versus Exploratory

The structured approach to testing is based on the idea that you should analyze your requirements and your code and create your test plans and test cases before you start testing. First you run the cases for the unit tests, and only when the number of new problems reported and open problems pending falls below a certain level do you deem the product ready to advance to integration testing. Then you run the cases for the integration test, and you keep on fixing things and creating new builds until the defect rate drops to within your target range. Then you move on to the system test, the beta test, the user acceptance test, and so forth. At each stage the documentation is audited to verify that the tests focus on the program behavior under review and provide enough coverage for valid data, invalid data, and boundary data.

Structured testing is essential for the reliability of your product. It is measurable, repeatable, and verifiable. The planning and documentation require a substantial investment during the early stages of the project. The maintenance of the documentation becomes an ongoing responsibility. Although a well-documented structured test can be executed by a junior tester with little knowledge of your product or your user community, such tests and testers sometimes miss or fail to investigate problems not explicitly mentioned in the test cases.

Exploratory testing is just what it sounds like. You get a bunch of people together—developers, testers, end users, telephone support operators, summer interns, your kids—and tell them to play with the program. You give them no requirements document, no design specifications, no user manual, and no road maps of any kind. You do make it clear that you want them to break it, and you encourage them to submit problem reports about anything they find that looks wrong or that they don't like. You set a time limit. You might offer prizes for the most defects submitted, the most obscure defect, the most catastrophic defect, or the most annoying defect. You leave the unit testing and integration testing to the developers because these phases require more disciplined procedures and better documentation, and you deploy your exploratory testing team intensively during the system test and user acceptance test.

The exploratory method has several advantages. It requires no advance planning and no voluminous documentation. An expert tester can often roam freely through a new product and, by applying certain rule-breaking diagnostic techniques, discover many major problems in short order. The converse, though, is also true: an inexperienced tester can roam through the same product aimlessly and discover nothing much. With exploratory testing it is hard to measure coverage, nearly impossible to repeat the tests unless you install a record-and-playback tool to log the tester's actions, and sometimes problematic to verify results. Nonetheless, exploratory testing is a good technique when you want to get acquainted with the product or to investigate program behavior that seems vaguely peculiar.

Most successful projects employ both methods in varying proportions. Organizations with a strong engineering culture favor structured testing from the outset and include exploratory testing primarily to address concerns about a product's usability. Organizations with a more entrepreneurial culture prefer exploratory testing and may acknowledge the need for structured testing only if persistent data errors or infrastructure failures create a liability for their product's end users.

Team dynamics also play an important role. The more people you have on your staff who hold engineering degrees, the more comfortable your group will be with the process of structured testing. On the other hand, if your developers majored in business or graphic design, they're probably going to think structured testing misses the forest for the trees and trust exploratory testing to uncover the problems that really matter.

Your role as a manger in this area is to counteract the prevailing tendency and provide balance. If everyone is gung ho for structured testing, make sure you schedule time in the project plan for exploratory testing as early as possible in the system test phase. You can present this as a kind of blind audit to verify that the test plans and cases and data accurately reflect how the product is going to be used and misused. If exploratory testing is going to dominate your QA effort, be aware that you will receive a large number of problem reports that will be of no use to you whatsoever. To ensure the ongoing cooperation of your testers, each report will have to be reviewed, evaluated, and responded to politely. It is also very important to ensure that each tester keeps a log of the actions he or she has performed so that you can compile reports on how much of the product has actually been tested.

Manual versus Automated

Manual testing occurs when a human being sits in front of a computer, executes a test, and documents a result. The test can be positive or negative, structured or exploratory, black box or glass box. It's manual as in "by hand," as opposed to "by machine."

Human testers are, of course, slower than computers. They can be more inconsistent in their methods of execution and their powers of observation. Yet they are still undeniably smarter, more curious, and more intuitive. A person performing a manual test will notice problems outside the scope of a test case and follow hunches to locate additional errors.

Automated testing occurs when a human being records a script of a computer executing a test correctly and then plays back that script on a different machine or after changes have been made to the program. The script compares the actual results with the expected results, decides whether the program passed or failed, and documents the outcome in a file. The script can be run from remote locations at any time, can be installed on multiple machines simultaneously, and can sometimes be configured to use input from a table to test different user logins or queries.

In theory, automated testing always sounds like a great idea because it's faster, more efficient, and more available than humans. The reality, of course, is more complicated. For one thing, automated tests suffer from the same lack of intelligence as spell checkers: sometimes what looks correct really isn't. Conversely, when an automated test encounters a variance between expected results and actual results, it often is not smart enough to figure out that the program is fine but the system date changed or the currency exchange rate fluctuated. If there really is a problem, it can't stop what it's doing and poke around and gather enough information to explain the context and help the developers recreate the condition.

Automated test tools perform their verifications in two ways: by comparing either the bitmaps on the screen or the properties and content of the objects that create the screen images. This means that many automated tests remain valid only so long as the user interface does not change. With the former type of tool, if a developer changes the color of a button or reorders the list of the links on a page, the test will fail. With the latter, the test designer could instruct the test to ignore such cosmetic changes, but if the developer adds or deletes a field the test will still fail.

Finally, automated test tools require care and feeding. The test scripts become a product in themselves; they need to be designed, coded, tested, archived, and updated. Testers must be trained to create, execute, and interpret automated tests in a consistent manner. Simple, inexpensive record-and-playback tools that capture bitmaps are relatively easy to set up and use right out of the box, but they have the least intelligence and flexibility. They can drive your testers crazy by indicating that a test has failed when it turns out that the only variation between expected results and actual results was the cursor blinking at the wrong time. The smarter and more configurable a tool is, the more expensive and more difficult to learn it will be. Organizations that invest heavily in automated testing often find themselves in permanent relationships with consultants from the tool vendor.

Nevertheless, automated testing can be very helpful if you understand what you're getting into and carefully manage the resources. It does a much better job than human beings at verifying program behavior after the environment changes. It can save you many headaches when you are trying to debug a problem in a foreign office where communication with local users is hampered by time differences or language barriers. It can dramatically increase the speed and reliability of your regression testing when you make a few changes to your product and want to verify that everything else still works. It is indispensable for performance testing.

If you decide to employ automated testing, here are a few guidelines to keep in mind:

- Allocate enough time and resources in your project plan for building and maintaining the automated test cases.
- Insist that every test case to be automated must first be documented as a manual test case so that everyone can read it even if they aren't familiar with the automated tool's programming language.
- Wait to record the test scripts until your user interface is stable.
- Automate only the test cases that you will use over and over again.
- Don't ever rely exclusively on automated tests to verify the functionality of a new version of your product.
- Prepare a detailed explanation of the value of automated testing to your project for senior management because the costs can be large and the benefits difficult to understand.

One final word of advice: keep an eye on your testers, and watch out for signs of automation mania. Once testers start coding automated scripts, particularly with one of the more powerful tools, they tend to get caught up in the creative process of building more and more elaborate test procedures. They begin debating the finer points of function libraries, and they work obsessively on optimizing their scripts until their eyes glaze over and they forget all about the actual product they're testing. When this happens, drag them away from their tool and send them off to do usability testing with the product manager until they snap out of it.

Functional versus Performance

Functional testing verifies that a product operates correctly. Performance testing verifies that a product operates both correctly and reliably for a certain number of users. All software products should receive thorough functional testing. The extent of the performance testing a product requires depends on the size of the user community, the network and telecommunications infrastructure, and the system architecture.

Nowadays many people associate performance testing with notorious Internet e-commerce disasters. Such failures result when a new Web site becomes so popular all of a sudden that the application, the network, and the servers are paralyzed by the unexpected traffic, like an expressway interchange during an emergency evacuation. Yet no matter what platform your product runs on, how large your user community is, or how fast you expect it to grow, performance is still an issue. Without testing, most of the time you just can't predict the performance of your product after it leaves the development and test environments and is deployed among actual users. Among the unknown factors are these:

Query size. What will happen when someone creates a query that returns a data set so large it exceeds the memory capacity on the user's computer? Will the system freeze, or will the program display a helpful message suggesting that the user modify the query?

Query volume. What will happen when a lot of users send queries at the same time? Will everyone's system slow down? Will some queries be rejected? Can you gather statistics on the behavior of the database?

Server contention. What will happen if your product shares a server with other products? Will your application cause the others to slow down, or vice versa?

Replication and load balancing. Will the data your users input be replicated to every database where it needs to go? Will your users' logons and queries be distributed evenly among the servers?

Network traffic. What will happen if your users fill up the bandwidth on your LAN or WAN? Will your product be unusable in certain locations because the line speeds are too slow?

To answer these questions you need two things: an automated testing tool and a performance testing tool. The automated testing tool records the test cases and test data that simulate user behavior. The performance testing tool loads the automated tests onto different machines, manages the timing of the tests, monitors the various components of your infrastructure, and reports the results.

Expertise in performance testing is highly specialized knowledge. It requires a greater familiarity with software development concepts, coding practices, and programming languages than any other type of testing. To succeed in this effort, you should designate the tester with the strongest engineering background as coordinator of performance testing for your project. Treat the construction of a performance testing infrastructure and the development of automated performance tests as projects in themselves, and monitor them diligently to verify that you are building realistic models and writing effective test cases. When you run the tests, hang up the graphs and charts as hallway decorations.

Black Box versus Glass Box

Black box testing is by far the most common method of verifying the functionality of software products developed for an organization's internal procedures. Testers who adopt the users' perspective are more capable of designing not only integration and system tests, but also beta tests and user acceptance tests. Black box test cases can be created based on existing use cases and training materials, and they are easier for a product manager to understand and prioritize.

Developers invent many glass box test cases during their unit testing. The glass box method is very helpful in providing criteria for negative tests because the tester needs to know about field types, size limits, processing rules, and error conditions. Glass box test cases are important for verifying state transitions and interactions among the components of the system architecture, and they trace decision paths through the code with mathematical certainty.

Your assessment of which method better suits your project will probably be influenced most strongly by the skills of the testers on your team. Testers who have worked as developers will be most adept at glass box testing; testers who have been documentation writers or business analysts will naturally gravitate toward black box testing. Both methods can provide adequate coverage, and it's a good idea to include a combination of both—but play your strong suit, and let each tester analyze the product and create test cases using the method he or she prefers. Your QA manager should be able to evaluate the results and identify areas where coverage is lacking or the alternate method would be more effective.

Test Plan Priorities

So far in devising your test plans you've considered a number of general criteria that affect what you should include, and you've evaluated several methods appropriate for your project. Whether your testers are end users, consultants, or QA professionals on your organization's staff, the next issue is always the same: Where do you start? Given that you can't test everything about your product and the environment where it will be used, how do you decide what is most important?

Risk Assessment

A risk assessment analyzes the functions of your product in terms of the potential consequences if they fail. It ranks the consequences by severity, probability, and recoverability.

This is an opportunity for you and your team to get together and pretend, collectively, that you're writing a screenplay for a horror movie. Most QA professionals have a dark, paranoid element to their imagination, so they'll be delighted to participate in this exercise. Ask yourselves: what is the absolute worst thing that could occur if our product fails to operate or operates incorrectly? If you can't come up with anything truly grisly, there's always the possibility of people losing their jobs or going bankrupt. Once you get started, you'll probably have no trouble envisioning a number of disastrous scenarios. Reproducing the program behavior that creates these conditions will give you your first set of test cases. These cases should form the core of your regression test and should be run on every new version before you release it.

Legal Considerations

After your team has exhausted its own imagination, go visit some lawyers. They may not completely understand what your product does or the risks inherent in your technology, but they will open your eyes to a whole new dimension of trouble. You will probably be amazed to learn the number of reasons why your organization could be fined, sued, or prosecuted—all because of some inadvertent error or omission by your innocent, well-meaning product. Ask the lawyers to prepare a document for you that describes the issues they identify, and use it to design your next set of test cases.

User Nightmares

Every single person who will use your product has a private vision of the ways in which it could make life worse instead of better. These nightmares will be based on the details of each individual's tasks and activities, and nobody on your team will be able to guess what they are. Maybe if a document is routed incorrectly in the workflow a billing clerk will get hundreds of phone calls from infuriated customers. Maybe if a form is missing a crucial field, a sales person will have to track down the information, and a backlog of incomplete forms on a Friday will force her to cancel her weekend plans. For a completely new product, many of these issues won't surface until after it has been released. But some can be predicted, especially if your product will replace an existing system.

With patience, you can encourage users to articulate their fears. Your product manger can interview them personally and ask each user, "What is the worst thing that could happen to you if this product malfunctions?" You might also schedule an informal meeting and let your testers free-associate for a while to get everyone in the mood. If you choose to call a meeting, try to have a tape recorder running: some of your best test cases may be based on discussions where everyone is talking fast and interrupting each other with escalating tales of doom.

Success Factors

Even when you as project manager have a clear idea of your goals and methods and priorities, the effectiveness of your test plans can be helped or hindered by other factors. Some are within your control, and some are not. Nevertheless, you can often influence what you cannot control.

QA Manager Expertise

An experienced QA manager can save you months of project time. A QA manager is not a tester: a manager evaluates what needs to be tested, supervises the test environment, selects the appropriate testing tools, forecasts the schedule and resources necessary for each phase of testing, and reviews the test plans and test cases for optimal design and coverage. The role of a QA manager on any project is to lobby for best practices—in other words, to annoy the project manager with demands that cannot possibly be met without missing the deadline. Of course, as project manager you are free to reject or ignore the QA manager's recommendations and to accept the responsibility for the consequences. If your QA manager does not occasionally make you seethe with exasperation, you should reevaluate both the person's qualifications and your ability to empower people who disagree with you.

Management Support

Testing is a bottomless pit. You can test your product from now until the sun goes supernova without finding all the latent problems. Testing is also expensive, consuming money and time without much noticeable change in the product. Unless your organization is run by engineers, you will have to fight hard to obtain testing resources for your project from senior management.

Professional QA managers and consultants have two reliable methods for stating the issues in terms that senior management can understand. One is a simple graph showing how much more it costs to resolve a problem when it is discovered after the product has been released than earlier in the development cycle. You may be able to assemble this information based on your own organization's measurements and statistics. If you can't, a textbook example should still get your senior management's attention.

The other method is to present test cases as potential risks. For example: "If we don't test 5,000 simultaneous login attempts, we won't know if our site can withstand Marketing's projected traffic." Or: "If we don't test invoice adjustments for invoices with more than 100 products, we won't know if our biggest customers' orders can be processed correctly." The idea is to give senior management a sense of the damage to their wallets and their reputations if things go wrong.

Frequency of New Versions

When developers create a new feature or fix a problem, they are naturally eager to find out whether it works. Their instinct is to immediately move the program into the test environment and ask for testers' reactions. On poorly managed projects, this can result in many new versions being created every day.

In the early stages of development, this might not cause serious problems. After a while, however, small changes to any program can have many unforeseen consequences. The only way to find out about those consequences is to run the system through a complete regression test. Regression tests demand a relatively large amount of resources to set up, execute, and document. Frequent regression tests will exhaust your testers and ruin their morale.

The proliferation of versions also creates administrative difficulties for your change management system. It becomes extremely confusing to document whether item #362 had a fix submitted in build 6.1e or in build 6.1f three hours later, and was it the fix that failed, or is it a new error? Before long everyone is scratching their heads, wondering what has been tested and what hasn't.

A better approach is to bundle changes and create new versions less often. Ask your developers to do their own unit testing and to provide testers with documentation of the test cases and test data they employed. For each new version, compile a list of the new features and fixes submitted and decide how much regression testing is necessary. While the testers are verifying the items on the list, performing the regression test, and updating the change management database with the results, the developers should refrain from creating any more new builds or moving any new versions into the test environment.

At first, this process will seem much slower, but over the life of the project you will save a great deal of time and reduce the stress on your entire team.

Developer's View   **Tester's View**

Figure 5.1   Different views.

Developers' Support

Developers and testers are natural adversaries. Most novice developers feel personally attacked when testers zealously find defects in their work. Many testers feel that developers are ivory-tower idealists who would rather write elegant code than create a product that actually satisfies the users' needs. Over the course of a project a lot of antagonism can build up between the two—but it doesn't have to be that way.

A project manager can do a great deal to reduce the tension and turn the relationship into a collaboration. First and foremost is to focus on the product instead of the personalities. When discussing errors, insist that your team refer to "the code" in the abstract, not modules written by a particular developer. The same rule applies to test cases and test results. For example: "We discovered a GPF in the query by product line, but the test case didn't catch it because it used only valid data." This helps create the impression that everyone is working together toward a common goal.

Another message you should convey to the developers is that testers make them look good. Very early in their careers, testers learn to accept the notion that nobody outside the development group ever notices or appreciates them. Like editors, they labor in obscurity to perfect someone else's creation. Most talented writers, though, understand how important an editor's contributions can be. In publishing, there are basically three levels of editing: proofreading, which catches spelling and grammar mistakes;

copy editing, which focuses on the clarity and accuracy of ideas being communicated; and developmental editing, which examines the design and scope of the project in relation to the audience and the market. Similarly, software developers should welcome criticism from testers on everything from cosmetic details to the fulfillment of user requirements.

Using a standard form for your test plan can help ensure that you've taken all these issues and factors into consideration. Template 5.1 is a suggested format for the test plan, and it includes each of the listed spreadsheets within the document. Each individual spreadsheet is available on the Web site for download.

Test Plan

PRODUCT: _____ VERSION: _____

I. PROJECT OVERVIEW

A. INTRODUCTION

B. TESTING REQUIREMENTS

  1. New features

  2. Fixes

  3. Regression tests

C. REFERENCES

II. TEST STRATEGY

A. TEST ENVIRONMENT

  Test server(s):

  Test database(s):

  Operating system:

  Database version:

  Test machines:

  Test Ids:

  Other:

B. TEST LOG

C. REPORTING AND TRACKING

D. PASS/FAIL CRITERIA

Template 5.1   Test Plan

III. TEST CASES

A. CHANGES

Test ID	Test Name	Description

B. REGRESSION TESTS

Test ID	Test Name	Description

IV. TEST DATA

For Test Case:
Test Data ID:
File Name:

Case	Type	Field 1	Field 2	Field 3	Field 4	Field 5
1	Valid					
2	Invalid					
3	Boundary					
4	Environment					

For Test Case:
Test Data ID:
File Name:

Case	Type	Field 1	Field 2	Field 3	Field 4	Field 5
1	Valid					
2	Invalid					
3	Boundary					
4	Environment					

Template 5.1 (*Continued*)

V. TEST RESULTS

A. TEST LOG

The execution of the test procedures revealed the following:

Build A

Test ID	Test Name	Pass/Fail	Description/Reason

Build B

Test ID	Test Name	Pass/Fail	Description/Reason

Build C

Test ID	Test Name	Pass/Fail	Description/Reason

B. CHANGE MANAGEMENT

The following items in the change management database were resolved:

_____

_____

_____

The following items were added to the change management database:

_____

_____

Template 5.1   (*Continued*)

There are many more ways to test a program than to develop it. A program expects the user to follow a particular path, but people wander. They take unexpected detours. They get lost and go blundering into areas where they don't belong. Furthermore, they don't always use a tool in the way the designer expected. If you give people a wrench, sometimes, if they're desperate, they may try to hammer nails with it. The scientific part of testing is designing experiments to prove whether a product does what it's supposed to do. The artistic part involves imagining what weird user behavior or unforeseen environmental glitches could cause the product to fail.

As project manager, when it comes to testing your greatest challenge is to understand what your testers are doing and how much confidence their efforts can give you in the quality and robustness of the product.

Organize the Workshop

If you've been a developer yourself, it may be hard to resist the temptation to grab some design specifications, join the programmers, and start coding. If you were promoted to project manager from some other job in the organization, you may find yourself hovering nervously at the edge of the team's work area, wondering what's going on in there. Neither behavior is appropriate for the project manager role.

Developers and testers will not welcome you as a peer, nor will they appreciate your spying on or pestering them. Yet they will understand the need for you to supervise their practices and enforce project procedures. You will be able to stay both involved with and informed about your team's efforts if you focus on organizing the project resources. For example, you'll want to make sure that everyone can find the information they need about the current status of the product. You'd like everyone to be confident that they can do their work without accidentally undoing someone else's work. And you don't want anyone to lose any sleep worrying that the separate pieces won't fit together when you try to assemble them because you've built them out of the wrong materials. You can accomplish all of these goals by monitoring documentation, version control, and configuration management.

Documentation Library

By the time the first line of code gets written, your project already has amassed a large number of important documents. As you proceed with development and testing— and after you release your first version, when you move on to maintenance and enhancements—the documentation will continue to grow. To facilitate communication among your team members, and between your team and your IT department colleagues, it's important to create a single location where everyone can find the information they need: your project's research library.

Many organizations require that project documentation be stored along with source code in the version control database. A version control system is designed as a secure archive, however, not as a public reading room. Access to materials within a version control database is usually restricted by team membership and job function, and the user interface rarely permits interproject searches or casual browsing. Over the life of the project the version control database will accumulate many revisions of the same document. Most of the time, your team members and your colleagues are interested in only the current versions.

Although you will be obliged to file two copies of every document—one in the version control database and one in the documentation library—the benefits are worth the minor additional effort. Nevertheless, you'll need to consider several significant issues before you can expect to depend on your documentation library as a valuable resource.

Format

Once upon a time, all project documentation was maintained on paper in three-ring binders. When changes became necessary, each document was retyped, and copies were made using mimeograph stencils or carbon paper. Version control consisted of taking out the old pages, storing them in a manila file folder, and putting the new pages in the binder. Because copies were so slow and expensive to create, the documentation library was an actual room where people had to come to do their research.

If anyone misplaced the three-hole punch device, the project could be delayed for weeks.

Before you dismiss paper-based documentation as a relic of a bygone era, remember that on occasion you'll need to bring the documents to a meeting and show them to people. No matter what other, more high-tech formats you may employ, having one official project binder is still a useful practice.

For an electronic documentation library, the simplest approach is to create a documentation directory on a shared file server. Establish four subdirectories:

- Project Documentation (user profile, project profile, site survey, etc.)
- System Documentation (data model, design specifications, message list, etc.)
- Test Documentation (test plan, test case, test log, etc.)
- User Documentation (help files, user manual, training materials, etc.)

Within each subdirectory, make a separate folder for each type of document. To keep track of the documentation for different versions of your product, you can either recreate the entire directory structure or append new folders under each document type. This arrangement does not enable you to view detailed information about a document or to search by keywords or criteria, but it is easy and cheap to set up and requires little maintenance.

Your research into your organization's technology environment should have shown you whether your IT department maintains a central documentation library database. If it does, all you'll need to do is contact the administrator, make arrangements for your project to be added, and train your team to use the system. If it doesn't, your next step would be to find out how other projects in your organization are managing their documentation: you might be able to install the same tool and benefit from their experience. Then there is always the possibility that no other project manager has paid much attention to this issue, and you're on your own to come up with a solution.

If you find yourself in the position of designing a brand-new documentation library database, don't get carried away and squander your resources on the task. A simple relational database with a few linked tables will suffice. Among the important fields of information you should include on the input form are these:

- Document category
- Document type
- Version
- Author
- Creation date
- Last revision date
- Document/test ID
- Document/test name
- Description
- Comments

Provide some basic queries that select and sort the documents by type, version, author, and creation date. Build views and reports based on these queries, and make them accessible to everyone on your project team. Find a shared server with space available for the many large files you will be attaching. Once the database is installed and your team has begun using it, and once word gets around, put a welcome mat outside your door and get ready to receive visits from other project managers.

Maintenance

Every documentation library requires maintenance, even if it's only a matter of putting new pages into your three-ring binder.

For your documentation library to be useful to your project, it must be kept up to date and organized consistently. This should be an ongoing commitment over the life of your project. Maintenance is not simply a matter of adding new team members to the Authors table or arranging for a corrupt file to be restored from a backup: it also implies an obligation to monitor the integrity of the data. Just as a book librarian might occasionally stroll through the stacks and notice an overdue return or a misshelved volume, your electronic documentation librarian should audit the contents of the database for missing files, miscategorized items, and other anomalies.

To accomplish these goals, you should designate one of your team members as documentation coordinator. The coordinator should supervise and maintain the documentation library and should be held accountable for the quality, accessibility, and usability of the documentation therein. You should make it clear to the entire project team that the coordinator is empowered to uphold standards, enforce deadlines, request revisions, and notify you of any chronic compliance problems on matters such as these:

- Submitting required documents
- Following standard formats for documentation
- Updating documents to reflect changes
- Filling out database input forms completely and correctly

Besides giving the documentation coordinator a state-of-the-art three-hole punch device, you should also arrange for any necessary training. If your project will be using a central database managed by the IT department, your coordinator will need to be taught its procedures for updates and modifications. If you are building your own database, it may be advisable to enroll your coordinator in a course on the software's advanced functions so that he or she can serve as a competent system administrator.

Procedures

How much documentation you should create for your project, and the level of detail it should contain, will depend largely on the character of your organization. If your staff doesn't have much turnover and people tend to stay in the same jobs for several years, then your documentation can be more cursory than if you need to train a new team member every couple of months—or if you have a lot of consultants. If your product is used under conditions that entail serious potential risks to life and property, you will undoubtedly be expected to compile a great deal more documentation than if the worst problem your product could cause would be a billing error or a missed appointment. Certain organizations have no choice about the kind of documentation they produce: they are required by law or regulation to demonstrate exactly what was done, when, where, by whom, how, and what the consequences were—for every build of every version.

Whatever standards you establish, your documentation library will enable you to determine whether you are meeting them. Team members who became accustomed on other projects to storing their documentation in the form of attachments to e-mail messages might at first grumble at this degree of scrutiny. When approached by your documentation coordinator for revisions in the format of their test cases, they might initially complain about being micro-managed. Technology professionals are just as sensitive and as stubborn as any other user community about being told they have to change their behavior and all do something in a different, standardized way.

As project manager, it's up to you to educate and persuade your team. At a staff meeting, describe the documentation standards you want to introduce. Explain why these standards are necessary and appropriate for your project. Point out that the documentation library will help everyone communicate and collaborate more effectively. If your library is a database, give a demo and show how it works. Summarize the role of the documentation coordinator, then turn the meeting over to your coordinator and let him or her present the documentation templates and the procedures for using them. Emphasize that the documentation library is a tool and that it will be modified and adapted in response to suggestions from the team.

Once you're sure everyone understands your expectations, form a pool and take bets on how many gigabytes each participant thinks the files in your documentation library will occupy on the day of your rollout.

Version Control

A version control database archives source code, database tables and procedures, documentation, and any other materials you choose to include. When you retrieve a file, you check it out of the database, and nobody else can edit it until you check it back in. If you make changes to the file, both the old copy and the new copy are saved when you check it in, but the system assigns the new copy a different version label.

You can't run any kind of professional software development effort without a version control system. Your organization probably already has one; as project manager, your mission is to make sure that everyone on your team has access to it, knows how and when to use it, and uses it correctly. If your organization is very new, or new to the software development process, and you discover that it lacks a version control system, the single most worthwhile improvement you can make is to install one.

Sounds relatively simple, right? In theory, it is—and it requires not much more behavior modification than learning to make regular backups. In practice, however, people encounter a number of issues and difficulties that discourage them from using version control:

Definitions. What is a version? Is it the product you release into the production environment? Is it the collection of files, procedures, configuration settings, and database tables you promote from the development environment to the test environment, which for compiled programs is usually called a "build"? Is it the new copy of any file modified by anyone involved in the project? Early in the project, your team members should collectively decide on names for each of these entities. Post the glossary in the documentation library so that everyone uses the same terminology.

Labeling. A version of your product may have multiple components: files installed on the user's computer, templates, frames, database procedures, data tables, daemons, middle-tier applications, and object layers, for example. What happens when you modify one of the components but not the others? A common solution is to divide the version label into several ID codes, with one for each component. As with the definitions, your labeling conventions should be agreed on by your team and posted in the documentation library.

Maintenance. Version control is in itself a system. To be implemented properly it requires its own database and front-end application, its own administrator, its own documentation, training, and change control process. Many off-the-shelf version control products now available have clear, intuitive user interfaces and can be mastered by the members of a project team in a few hours. Setting up the database and maintaining the user accounts and permissions is a sizable job. If your organization already has a version control system and you're merely plugging your project into it, then you don't need to worry much about this. If you're the one introducing version control into the organization, be sure to do some research before you incorporate the task into your project's schedule. Ask your developers for advice in choosing a product and estimating the implementation effort.

Development environment. The platform on which you are developing and the language with which you are coding will influence your choice of a version control product. Some products work well with C++, Visual Basic, or JavaScript, but not with UNIX. Some products can handle front-end code and documents smoothly but are more cumbersome for database procedures. Lotus Notes databases have their own idiosyncrasies and sometimes need to have their own tool. Often when version control is sporadic or incomplete, it's because the product has multiple components written in different languages or running on different platforms, and the version control system does not treat all the components equally.

Performance. A poorly implemented or carelessly administered version control system can be frustratingly slow. It can behave differently to users who dial in from remote locations. Because it is not a production system, it can be neglected by the operations and security staff—with disastrous consequences if the server crashes and there is no current database backup or nobody on duty who knows how to bring the machine up again. If you experience performance issues with a version control system administered by your IT department, and if the administrators can't fix the problem, bring the situation to the attention of IT senior management—and emphasize the risk to your project. If you're frustrated by a system you purchased and installed yourself, contact the vendor for technical support and research the problem among any user groups you can locate. Be candid with your client about the negative impact of these technical difficulties.

Procedures. The system is only as reliable and helpful as the human beings using it. Version control is designed to prevent more than one person from making changes to a file at the same time. On a development team, this can cause problems if one of the members is a file hog. There is nothing more aggravating to a developer than having an inspiration about how to fix a nasty bug, getting all set to modify the code, logging into the version control system to retrieve the file, only to discover that another developer checked it out a few days ago and subsequently went on vacation, leaving the file locked and inaccessible. Such absent-minded lapses can be the bane of global development projects, causing lots of short-term delays that add up to a cumulative nightmare—as weary developers in the United States who are eager to go home leave the office at night without checking in their work, just as their colleagues in Asia arrive in the morning and want to begin to update the same files (or vice versa). To avoid this problem, ask your team members to discuss and agree on appropriate rules for file sharing. Post the rules in the documentation library, and enforce them consistently. Penalties for inconsiderate and costly behavior can range from public humiliation by being listed on a project bulletin board's Hall of Shame to official job probation.

Now that you've read about all these challenges and obstacles, you're probably wondering if a version control system could really be worth the trouble. It is. The investments you make to select the right product, set up the database, configure the application to work properly in your environment, and train your staff both to use the tool and to understand the cooperative nature of the process will be repaid the very first time something bad happens to a new release and you have to roll back quickly to an earlier version. No matter how well you plan, how attentively you manage, or how thoroughly you test, that day will eventually come—and, wisely, you will be prepared for it.

As the Internet makes an organization's internal data processing operations more and more visible to the outside world, the role of version control becomes more important. No matter what kind of business or activity an organization engages in, the software it creates becomes part of its capital assets. When accountants audit an organization, they now look more closely at the condition of the software and the tools and practices employed to build and maintain it. If you need to explain to senior management why you're asking for resources for version control, remind them that part of your job is to strengthen and protect the organization's productive assets.

Training your team to use version control consistently and properly should begin during the initial project phases with the product definition document. As soon as the developers start writing code and the testers start creating test cases, their understanding of and compliance with the version control system should be a major factor in your evaluation of their performance. Let them know this in no uncertain terms.

Designate a member of your project team to serve as version control coordinator. The coordinator should audit the database once a month and notify you of any problems arising from the issues discussed previously. Good version control habits instilled early are more likely to last beyond the first release into the maintenance phase and to be communicated to new members of the team. Within the IT department, your emphasis on version control will enhance your professional reputation.

Configuration Management

How often have you heard the plaintive cry, "But it works on *my* machine!"

Let's assume you've gone to the trouble of finding out the hardware and software configurations on which your product will be expected to operate. You've narrowed the list to an agreed-on number of supported machines and versions. You've made it clear to senior management that the specifications are final and, no, you will not adapt your Web site to run on wireless devices unless they extend the project deadline and give you additional resources. You've built your development and test environments. You've hired your staff, created your team, and are ready to go.

It would be nice if your team could now focus their undivided attention on building the product. But to make sure that the product you build actually works when you deploy it, you'll have to keep a sharp lookout for unexpected changes in your technology environment. If any changes occur, you will need to test your product and possibly modify it to keep it compatible.

There are two types of changes you should be concerned about: your team's deviation from the desktop standard and your organization's modification of the production environment. The former is accidental, the latter deliberate.

Development Desktop

Your organization probably has a standard image for the desktop and laptop computers it distributes to its employees. Somewhere in your IT department, there exists a master machine from which the registry settings, directory structure, common files, and office applications are copied. Every member of your team should have started out on the project with a machine bearing this standard image. If your organization does not follow this practice, you'll have to figure out the most common configuration among your users and adopt it as the standard image for your team.

Users often wreak havoc on their machines by installing games and personal finance programs; with developers and testers, it's tools. Every developer and tester has his or her favorite utility that does something he or she can't imagine getting along without. Because the average end user has no need to track memory leaks or search for unexecutable modules of code, these tools are rarely included on the list of programs in the standard supported configurations. Every one of the tools installs files and creates registry entries on the machine that have the potential to create conflicts with other machines.

The potential for chaos increases exponentially with the size of your team and the number of locations where they work.

Although you can't expect to maintain control over every registry setting on your developers' and testers' hard drives (nor would you want to), you can reduce the likelihood of unpleasant surprises. Start by asking each team member to document what already exists on his or her machine. Get a list of the tools and a description of what they're used for—you might discover one that would be helpful to others. Even if the programs were installed by an IT technician who downloaded the standard image from a secure server, document the settings for all commercial applications. People tend to make changes in their Web browser configuration or word processing document templates without thinking about the consequences, and then they forget that they've done anything. If your team members work in different countries, or if your product is going to be installed in more than one country, make sure everyone starts out using the same international settings for language, keyboard, date/time, currency, and so on. For the record, get printouts of every machine's registry and store them in a binder.

Collecting this information is a chore, but it serves two purposes. First, it will make debugging much easier if you encounter some weird intermittent error that cannot be traced to the application code—and you won't be scrambling to pull it together in the midst of a deadline crisis. Second, it will force your team to think about their environment and become aware of the effect any changes they make might have on the project.

Once you've assembled the data, you'll need to review it periodically to ensure that it's still current. You might make a speech at a staff meeting to the effect that the machines belong to the organization and are not to be tampered with in any way. Depending on the culture of your organization, you may or may not want to enforce this. If creativity and independent thinking are important to your project, your developers will demand more privacy and flexibility, but it doesn't hurt to go on the record clearly stating an official policy.

Production Environment

In addition to the changes introduced by your developers individually, you'll also have to take into account the changes in the production environment imposed by the organization collectively. These include front-end, network, and back-end enhancements. Your mission, as soon as you accept the role of project manager, is to stay informed about every change in your organization's technology infrastructure. Whenever a change occurs, you should decide whether it affects your project. If it might affect your project, you should determine the risk it creates.

For example, a new ODBC driver distributed by another project might interfere with your product's ability to communicate with a database. A new .DLL file might change the way your program objects appear on the screen. A change in the Web browser settings might affect the speed of your connections or the display of your .PDF files. An upgrade in the database software might cause your queries to return different results. A reorganization of the databases on the servers or the installation of a new server might alter IP addresses and interfere with your connections. Adapting your product in response to any of these modifications might involve a five-minute change to one line of code, or it might take two weeks to reengineer a different approach.

For monitoring changes in the production environment, it helps if your organization has a Change Control Board. If it does, find out when they meet and send a representative from your project team. Make sure they put you on their e-mail distribution lists. If there is no Change Control Board, you'll have to do the research and establish the relationships on your own. Consult your technology environment profile, and find out who is responsible for each piece of the infrastructure. Introduce yourself to every manager and database administrator, and describe your project to them. Ask them to keep in touch with you and notify you several weeks in advance if they are planning to make any changes. After you have gotten to know them, suggest that you create an electronic bulletin board or discussion database where everyone can post information about infrastructure changes.

Inevitably, you will occasionally need to test your product in a new environment. This will consume resources and disrupt your schedule, so if you find it happens often you should incorporate the activity into your project plan. At some organizations where the data architecture is very complex and there are many independent software development teams, changes in the production environment are so frequent that every project budgets a certain percentage of resources to this type of testing. You can minimize the impact on your project by adopting a consistent approach and measuring the effort it takes. Here are some suggestions from the QA front lines:

Plan. Create an environment test plan. Each plan will be slightly different depending on the specific changes being tested, but the core test cases will remain the same. They should include your product's most basic functionality: startup; login; creating, displaying, editing, and deleting records; and printing. If you have an automated tool for functionality testing, you should automate the environment test as soon as your product's design is stable enough. To this template you can then add manual test cases designed for each change in the environment.

Environment. Test the changes in a separate test environment. Although this may sound redundant and obvious, in reality it can become quite complex. To begin with, you don't want to test the changes in your development environment because it may be difficult to undo the changes, and if you encounter a major incompatibility you may want to go back to the Change Control Board and ask that they reconsider their plans. In addition, your project's test environment is not normally configured to match the production environment because your product is most likely planning to introduce some changes of its own. Therefore you need a special test environment that duplicates the new production environment where you can run the current version of your product to verify how it behaves.

Version. Test your current production version (when you have one), and then test your most recent build in development. If you know there are going to be several environment changes within a few months, try to group changes and test them as a version.

Metrics. Keep track of the amount of time it takes your team to create and customize the test plan, load the changes into the test environment, execute the tests, document the results, modify the product, and retest the changes. Use these metrics to estimate the effect on your project plan of future environment changes. For example, if you know from experience that for the last database software upgrade it took you 250 hours to test and modify your product, the next time the IT department announces a similar upgrade you will be able to inform your client how long the project will be delayed.

After a change in the production environment has been deployed, make sure your developers and testers receive it. Some organizations isolate development groups in their own domains on IP subnets on the theory that developers and testers require more control over their machines than end users do. Such a policy could cause your development and test environments to become out of sync with your production environment and lead to version control problems.

All this data gathering and monitoring and communicating with other groups within the IT department require ongoing effort, organization, and coordination. You will be better informed and better prepared to cope with environment changes if you appoint a member of your project team to serve as configuration coordinator. This coordinator maintains the binder with the records of the other team members' desktop files and periodically checks people's machines to make sure the information is kept current. He or she attends the Change Control Board meetings, stays in touch with IT department colleagues who routinely make changes in the production environment, and collaborates with your QA manager to ensure that the environment test plan and the test environment are continuously updated and available when necessary. Because version control and configuration management are closely linked, the coordination role for both functions is often combined.

Organizing your workshop naturally takes effort away from other, more measurably productive tasks. When you ask your team members to stop building and testing and instead pay attention to the documentation library requirements, the version control standards, or the configuration management procedures, the less experienced among them may smirk at you like teenagers who've been told to clean up their rooms. As project manager, you need to consider the timing and nit-pickiness of your organizational efforts. Professional chefs understand that the kitchen is going to be a mess during the dinner rush; surgeons don't stop to sterilize their instruments and put them away until after an operation is done; sailboat captains order the crew to secure the cleats and coil the lines only when the boat has completed a tack. So pace yourself, and schedule your audits and enforcement drives at appropriate intervals. But do it consistently, or else the project will begin to suffer from the effects of disorganization. In a messy kitchen the cooks can't find the spices; surgeons who use unsterilized scalpels can infect patients; crew members whose feet get tangled in uncoiled lines can be dragged overboard. Based on what your product does for your organization, you can probably imagine some comparably unpleasant potential incidents caused by your workshop's disarray.

Track Program Changes

At the beginning of development, the participants in a software project share a vision of the final product. The project proposal has been agreed on. The requirements have been documented. Everyone forges ahead confidently and enthusiastically. But as soon as you present the first UI sketches or demo the first prototype, changes are suggested. No matter how good your developers' work may be, someone will always want to improve on it. One day scientists will probably discover the location of the criticism gene in our human DNA.

Everybody enjoys making comments and offering advice. Users and testers are, of course, entitled to do this. They will send you e-mails, leave you voice messages, write you notes on paper, and sit down next to you in the cafeteria to give you the benefit of their wisdom. The trouble is, they will also do this to your product manager and your developers. Furthermore, they expect all of you to listen to them, to remember what they say, and to do what they ask.

You could ignore them and do it your own way (many developers favor this approach). Or you could keep track of their requests and establish a process for change management.

The Change Management Process

Change requests come from two sources: your users and your development team.

Your users will all have complaints and suggestions. From the lowest to the highest, they will regard your software product as an intimate friend or foe in their daily affairs. It will be their servant, and in their eyes your job is to get the servant to wait on them properly. They will all want the product to do different things. Some of their ideas will be silly, and some will be visionary. But every single one of your users will expect their comments to be given a fair hearing—and will treat their servant with more respect if they understand how changes are evaluated and implemented.

Your testers and developers will regard the product not as a servant but as a machine, and occasionally as a work of art. They too will all have different visions of how it should behave, based on both the users' specifications and their own imaginations. They too will all want to be heard—even the most junior testers and documentation writers. For the team to function effectively, every member must understand the steps by which a program change evolves from a spoken or written thought to a tangible result.

In many ways, the software development process is like an assembly line. You could picture each modification to the code as a manufactured unit progressing from raw materials (the change request) to finished product (the new version containing the change). The workflow of the change management process—the amount of time the unit spends at each stage of the assembly line and the person who works on it there—will vary according to the scope and design of the product. The overall pattern, however, remains consistent.

The following numbered list describes the sequence of a typical change management workflow. Template 5.2 is a change management form that records all the information you need to keep track of the process. The text in bold on the list corresponds to fields on the form. If you read through the list and refer to the form while you're reading, you should be able to visualize the phases, the actors, and the tasks.

1. Status: *New*
   Actor(s): Any user or member of the project team
   Tasks: All change requests should be recorded in writing and stored in the same place. If it isn't written down, it doesn't exist. The initial request should be forwarded to the product manager. It should provide the following:
   Submitter. The name of the person who submitted the item.
   Date and time of submission.
   Originator. The name of the person who reported the problem or suggested the modification.
   Priority of the item.

Change Request

PRODUCT: _____ CHANGE ID: _____

GENERAL INFORMATION

Priority:	Severity:	Category:	Type:
Urgent	Fatal	System crash	Requirement
High	Serious	Application error	Design Change
Medium	Moderate	Data error	Enhancement
Low	Inconvenient	Usability issue	Defect

Summary:	**Current status:**
	New
	Evaluation
	Verification
	Research
	Submitted for development
Date submitted:	Accepted for development
Submitted by:	Development in progress
Contact type: Phone / E-mail / Meeting / Fax / Database entry	Submitted for testing
	Accepted for testing
Reported By:	Testing in progress
Name:	Change verified
Title:	Change failed
Department:	Approved for release
Location:	**Resolution type:**
Phone:	Problem fixed
Fax:	Change implemented
E-mail:	Not reproducible
Environment:	User error
Version found:	Works as designed
URL:	Training issue
Browser version:	Design issue
Configuration:	Resource issue
Database:	Environment issue
Server:	Data issue
Hardware:	Duplicate

Description (with steps to reproduce):

Response date:	**Response type:**
Response by:	Answer question
Comments:	Investigate problem
	Submit for development

Template 5.2 Change Management Form

PRODUCT: _____   CHANGE ID: _____

DEVELOPMENT INFORMATION

Developer assigned: **Date:**

Developer comments:

Estimated scope:	**Estimated complexity:**	**Estimated hours to complete:**
Minor (< 24 hours)	Easy	
Routine (24–80 hours)	Medium	
Project (> 80 hours)	Hard	

Client approvals: **Date:**

Projects impacted:

Databases impacted:

Servers impacted:

IT manager approvals: **Date:**

Analysis:
   Start date: End date: Peer review date:
   Document IDs:

Design:
   Start date: End date: Peer review date:
   Document IDs:

Coding:
   Start date: End date: Peer review date:
   Document IDs:

Unit Test:
   Start date: End date: Peer review date:
   Document IDs:

Version fixed: **Target release:**

Actual scope:	**Actual complexity:**	**Actual hours to complete:**
Minor (< 24 hours)	Easy	
Routine (24–80 hours)	Medium	
Project (> 80 hours)	Hard	

Template 5.2   (*Continued*)

PRODUCT: _____ CHANGE ID: _____

QA Information

Tester assigned:		Date:

Tester comments:

Test plan:	Estimated complexity:	Test method:
None	Easy	Manual
Unit test (Developer Only)	Medium	Automated
Usability review	Hard	Both
Integration test	**Estimated hours to**	**Test case status:**
System test	**complete:**	No test case
Beta test		Existing test case
UAT test		New test case

User documentation: Y N	Technical documentation: Y N

Usability review:
  Start date: End date: Peer review date:
  Document IDs:

Test case design:
  Start date: End date: Peer review date:
  Document IDs:

Integration testing:
  Start date: End date: Peer review date:
  Document IDs:

System testing:
  Start date: End date: Peer review date:
  Document IDs:

Beta testing:
  Start date: End date: Peer review date:
  Document IDs:

UAT testing:
  Start date: End date: Peer review date:
  Document IDs:

Actual scope:	Actual complexity:	Actual hours to complete:
Minor (< 24 hours)	Easy	
Routine (24–80 hours)	Medium	
Project (> 80 hours)	Hard	

Resolved by:	Date:

Resolution comments:

Template 5.2   *(Continued)*

PRODUCT: _____ CHANGE ID: _____

CHANGE LOG

Status:	Change effective:	Changed by:
New	Date:	Name:
Evaluation	Date:	Name:
Verification	Date:	Name:
Research	Date:	Name:
Submitted for development	Date:	Name:
Accepted for development	Date:	Name:
Development in progress	Date:	Name:
Submitted for testing	Date:	Name:
Accepted for testing	Date:	Name:
Testing in progress	Date:	Name:
Change verified	Date:	Name:
Change failed	Date:	Name:
Approved for release	Date:	Name:
Resolved	Date:	Name:

Code changes:

UI changes:

Database changes:

Server changes:

Configuration changes:

Workflow changes:

Operations changes:

Documentation changes:

Template 5.2 *(Continued)*

Product. The name of the product if the database is used by more than one project.

Summary. A brief statement of the request.

Description. A more detailed account, including the steps to reproduce the situation.

Resolution: The change request may be closed during this phase for the following reason(s):

Withdrawn. The submitter may withdraw it.

2. Status: *Evaluation*

Actor(s): Product manager

Tasks: Every day, or at intervals agreed on by the project manager, the product manager, and the client, the product manager should review the new change requests. If the change request was submitted by a developer or tester, the product manager should forward it directly (and, if possible, automatically) to the project manager.

Resolution: The change request may be closed during this phase for the following reason(s):

Training issue. If the issue is a lack of understanding, the product manager should respond to the submitter and the originator and explain how to use the product to achieve the desired results. The product manager should then record the response and close the item.

3. Status: *Verification*

Actor(s): Product manager

Tasks: If the issue is a legitimate problem or suggestion for a design change or enhancement, the product manager should first attempt to reproduce the situation.

Resolution: The change request may be closed during this phase for the following reason(s):

Not reproducible. If the situation cannot be reproduced, the product manager should close the item.

4. Status: *Research*

Actor(s): Product manager

Tasks: Once the situation has been reproduced, the product manager should record the following:

Information about the environment. For example, the version or build in use at the time, the server and database, the hardware configuration, the Web browser, the URL, the user interface component, the specific data involved in the situation, or the user's login and security level.

Contact type. For example, a phone call, an e-mail message, or a direct entry into the database.

The product manager should then forward the item to the project manager. Periodically, on a regular schedule, the change requests should be reviewed. For urgent operational problems like a server crash or a major processing failure, the review should occur immediately—and immediate action should be taken by whoever is on hand and qualified to fix the problem.

Resolution: The change request may be closed during this phase for the following reason(s):

Problem fixed. The person who fixes the problem should record any modifications made to the product, the infrastructure, the operating procedures, or the documentation. If the problem was reported by someone outside the project team, the product manager should respond to the submitter and the originator and confirm that the problem has been fixed. The product manager should then record the response and close the item.

5. Status: *Submitted for Development*
Actor(s): Product manager, project manager, development manager, QA manager
Tasks: For routine change requests, the review schedule should be agreed on by the product manager and project manager. At the beginning of a project, the review meetings tend to be widely spaced, usually biweekly. As the deadline approaches they happen more frequently—but don't let anyone drag you into more than one meeting a day. The review team should consist of the product manager, the project manager, the development manager, and the QA manager. Each new item should be discussed and evaluated, and the project manager should record additional information about the request. The **priority** should be updated based on the users' needs, as well as the **type** of request, the **severity** of the issue, the **category** of the issue, the program **function** affected, the **estimated development effort**, and the **estimated testing effort**. The participants should determine whether the requested change would affect any other **projects** and whether it would be advisable to obtain **approvals** from the client or other IT department project or service managers. Following the review, an item could be classified in several ways. If it is accepted for development, it should be forwarded to the development manager. Otherwise, it will be sent back to the submitter for more information, postponed, or closed.
Resolution: The change request may be closed during this phase for the following reason(s):

User error. The situation might have been caused by a user's error. The project manager should close the item.

Works as designed. Some items might have been submitted because the developer or tester didn't understand what the product was supposed to do. The project manager should close the item.

Design issue. Some suggested enhancements might not serve the product's purpose or might require an altogether different architecture. The project manager should close the item.

Resource issue. Some changes might be too costly or difficult to implement. The project manager should close the item.

Environment issue. Some items might be impossible to reproduce because they were caused by problems in the technology infrastructure that have subsequently been resolved. The project manager should close the item.

Data issue. Some items might have been submitted because of errors in the data that your product is not responsible for fixing. The project manager should close the item.

Duplicate. Many items may be submitted that describe the same issue from different points of view. The project manager should close the item.

6. Status: *Accepted for Development*
   Actor(s):   Development manager
   Tasks: The development manager should assign the item to a specific **developer**. The developer thereby assumes responsibility for coordinating all interdependent changes to the product, creating or updating the code, and revising the system documentation. The developer should also track the item through all phases of development.

7. Status: *Development in Progress*
   Actor(s):   Developer
   Tasks: The developer should determine the **scope** and **complexity** of the task and indicate which **databases** and **servers** will be affected; forecast the **estimated work effort** required to implement the change; record the **modifications** made to the code, the database, the user interface, the workflow, the infrastructure, the operating procedures, and the system and test documentation; and note the **dates** when the item began and ended the phases of **design, analysis, coding** and **unit testing**. After the item has successfully completed the unit tests, the developer should calculate the **actual work effort** during each development phase and forward the item to the project manager. Periodically, on a regular basis, the changes submitted for verification should be reviewed.

8. Status: *Submitted for Testing*
   Actor(s):   Project manager, development manager, QA manager
   Tasks: The project manager, development manager, and QA manager should schedule a review meeting to decide which changes will be incorporated into a particular build or version of the product for testing. Once the project manager has compiled the list for the build or version, the items included should be forwarded to the QA manager.

9. Status: *Accepted for Testing*
   Actor(s):   QA manager
   Tasks: The QA manager should evaluate the amount of testing required for verifying the change and decide on a **test plan**, determine whether manual or automated testing would be the most effective **test method**, identify whether the item should be discussed in the **user documentation** or **technical documentation**, and assign the item to be tested to a specific **tester**. The tester thereby assumes responsibility for creating or updating all test cases and test data, executing manual and automated tests, and recording and analyzing the results. The tester also should track the item through all phases of testing.

10. Status: *Testing in Progress*
  Actor(s):   Tester
    Tasks: The tester should determine the **complexity** of the testing task and the availability of any **test cases** to verify the change. The tester should forecast the **estimated work effort** to verify the change and update the documentation, record the **modifications** made to the test environment and the test documentation, and note the **dates** when the item began and ended the phases of **usability review, integration testing, system testing, beta testing,** and **user acceptance testing.** Following the integration test, the tester should indicate whether the item has passed or failed and forward the item to the QA manager. It should be understood, however, that sometimes an item verified during an integration test may be recategorized as a failure during later testing phases. After the item has successfully completed the user acceptance testing, the tester should calculate the **actual work effort** during each test phase.

11. Status: *Change Failed*
  Actor(s):   QA manager
    Tasks: After all the changes in a particular build or version have been tested—or as many as possible within the limits of the schedule and the technology environment—the QA manager should compile the test statistics showing which items passed, which items failed, and which items could not be tested for various reasons. An item that fails the integration test should be sent back to the development manager for review. In most cases, the item will be returned to the developer originally assigned.

12. Status: *Change Verified*
  Actor(s):   QA manager
    Tasks: When an item has been verified, the QA manager should record the **version** or build where it was **fixed** and the **target release.** The QA manager should then forward the item to the project manager.

13. Status: *Approved for Release*
  Actor(s):   Project manager
    Tasks: Prior to a release of the product, the project manager should review all verified items and compile a list of change requests incorporated into the new version. The announcement of the new version should mention all important changes, with special emphasis on items submitted by users. Each verified item should be forwarded to the product manager for a final approval.

 Resolution: The change request may be closed during this phase for the following reason(s):

       Change Implemented. If the change request was submitted by someone outside the project team, the product manager should respond to the submitter and the originator and confirm that the change has been implemented. The project manager should then record the response and close the item.

14. Status: *All*
    Actor(s):   All
    Tasks: Whenever an item is closed for any reason, the person who closes it should record the **date and time of the resolution**, the **name of the person** who resolved the issue, the **resolution type**, and any appropriate **comments**. The project manager and product manager should be notified. If the change request was submitted by someone outside the project team, the product manager should respond to the submitter and the originator and explain the outcome. Whenever any member of the project team responds to a change request submitted by someone outside the project team, the team member should record the **date and time of the response**, the **name of the person** responding, the **response type**, and any appropriate **comments**. Whenever an item moves from one status to another, the **date and time** should be recorded. It's helpful if you also record the old and new status and the name of the old and new assignee.

It should be possible at any stage for any team member to include comments and attach supporting documents such as screen images, report files, test logs, test data, or output from debugging programs. The change requests should be accessible to everyone on your team, and everyone should understand the entire process, to the point that they can recite it from beginning to end. Your QA manager should act as coordinator of your change management process, auditing the data and notifying you of any compliance issues or discrepancies between your project's workflow and the model on which the system is based.

Now that you understand the principles of a well-engineered change management process, you're ready to evaluate what kind of tool would be most suitable for applying those principles to your own project.

Change Management Tools

The ideal change management tool would be fully integrated into other software development support systems. It would be linked to the software modeling tool, so that problems and design changes could reference the original design specifications. It would be linked to the documentation database, so that the system documentation and test documentation could be easily modified. It would be linked to the automated test tool, so that test results could be appended to change requests. It would be linked to the version control database, so that alterations to specific files or sections of code could be noted. It would be linked to the product itself, so that users could input change requests directly to the database. It would provide a discussion view, so that users could debate the merits of an enhancement request or developers could collectively investigate a problem without affecting the workflow. It would do all these things, yet the rules encoded in the system would be flexible enough to make any of the links or steps optional if, for example, you wanted to input a problem report that was not related to a design specification or not associated with an automated test. On the back end, it would employ any of the standard, industrial-strength relational databases. The data in the tables could be modified via SQL statements through an ODBC connection from an external application without disrupting the indexes or triggers. Finally, a novice user could install the tool out of the box in less than two days and could customize and administer it without outside training.

Alas, such a tool does not yet exist. There are products that provide subsets of change management functionality packaged together—such as linkages between design specifications and change requests or between change requests and automated test cases. Some integrated systems offer a broad spectrum of features, but their workflow is inflexible, their data is inaccessible via ODBC, and their maintenance requires a specially trained, dedicated resource. So far, a user-friendly, flexible, end-to-end change management system remains the Holy Grail of software tool developers.

The good news is that you really don't need any tools for change management. The key to efficient and effective change management is a well-defined process. If you capture the data you need on your change request form, you could print out the form on a piece of paper and then store the paper in a different file folder at each step in the workflow. As long as everyone on your team understood when the paper should be moved, where it should go, and what data should be filled in at each step, you'd have a change management system. You could even gather statistics from it.

Moving up the technology ladder from a paper-based system, you could store the change request as a word processing document and move it into different folders on a shared server. You could create a spreadsheet to store most of the data elements in the change request form, although spreadsheets are not good at recording or searching for the information in long text fields. You could build a database using one of the popular office applications.

If your organization already has a centralized change management system run by a QA administrator, your task will be relatively simple. You'll need to provide the administrator with a list of your project team members and their roles. You might be asked to specify the major functions of your product so that change requests can be categorized and to explain the method you will use for labeling builds and versions. You'll schedule training for your staff and arrange for their logons to be added to the system, and you'll be ready to go.

Before you provide information to the administrator you should talk to other project managers and ask them about their experiences with the system. Make sure the tool can model your project's workflow. The QA literature abounds with stories of organizations that wanted to implement process improvements but were prevented from doing so because their change management systems couldn't be adapted without losing years of critical data. But this is certainly not always the case. The database template can often be modified without too much fuss and bother if you provide detailed specifications of what your project needs. Just be aware that the change management system is a software product in itself, which means that the enhancements you request will have to be analyzed, designed, coded, tested, and deployed, and this process can delay your project. Weigh your options carefully, and find out if other project managers have created viable workarounds.

As you will soon realize once you begin to delve into the issues yourself, the subject of change management tools is complex. Your QA manager should be able to advise you on the advantages and drawbacks of the various approaches described here; there are also articles devoted to the topic in QA journals and relevant chapters in books on software testing.

Change Management Issues

As you design, configure, and/or implement your change management system, you will find yourself considering (and reconsidering) a number of strategic issues.

Participation

Depending on the size and the temperament of your user community, you may or may not want your users to be able to input items directly into your database. The most effective way to do this is to create an automatic electronic feed from your product directly into the database—for example, a "Contact Developers" entry on the main menu or a "Comments" link on the home page. If you would like your users to be able to view the items they have submitted or to access the database independently, you will need to provide them with the database software itself. This probably means that someone will have to add the cost of copies of the software or licenses to their budget.

Filtering

If your users do have access to the database, it is inevitable that they will add a great many items that require no attention whatsoever from your developers. Especially in the first weeks after a new version has been released, the database will become cluttered with urgent problem reports that are, in fact, the result of the product behaving exactly the way it should and the user being confused by a new or revised feature. Although such reports are valuable when determining whether your training and documentation are adequate, you don't want your developers wasting their time sifting through them. The product manager can perform a valuable service by responding to these items and closing them out. This must be done tactfully, because users can become unhappy if they see a lot of their items rejected or deferred. The product manager should also be the designated data entry person for user complaints and suggestions that the users themselves do not input directly.

Privacy of Test Results

Your testers are going to find flaws and errors in your product—that's what they're paid to do. Many of them will be trivial. Many of them will be documented in highly technical language that users cannot understand. Some managers, in an idealistic spirit of openness, have allowed end users to view every item in the database. They have regretted this decision. To a typical client, a long list of change requests means not that your testers are doing a thorough job, but that your product is a mess. If your users have access to your database, do not let them see the items posted by your testers. The QA section should be private and restricted to members of your development team.

Discussions

When a user submits a suggestion to the database, it is only one person's opinion. Other users may not agree with the idea, or they may have alternative solutions to propose. Your database should provide a means for people to engage in a public discussion, either with each entry visible as an e-mail thread or with the author and subject lines displayed in a summary format. This feature is also very helpful for the members of your development team when they need to collaborate on locating the cause of an error or implementing a fix simultaneously across several modules of code. The same guidelines for filtering and privacy apply to discussions: you don't want your developers to be distracted by users' ruminations on their workflow, and you don't want your users to be horrified by arguments between front-end and back-end programmers over whose fault it was that a query failed. You, as project manager, and the product manager should monitor these discussions and read through them periodically to make sure contributors are being civil and constructive. Communication difficulties and negative vibes that may not be noticeable during meetings or while the project leader is around can often be spotted in the tone of a discussion, enabling you to intervene early while there is still a good chance for harmony to be restored.

Administration

Your product manager may not mind sifting through change requests input by users and responding to and resolving items that need no attention from developers. After all, the product manager's job is to represent the users. In contrast, he or she may not feel the same way about items submitted by testers—and there are going to be a lot more of those. It is important to clarify at the outset who is responsible for resolving, closing, and removing from the active queues all items in the database that have been through the entire change management process and have no further interest except as archived statistics. This is a big job, and a tedious one, but it is essential if the database is to remain a useful tool.

Ownership

Developers sometimes feel that the purpose of the database is for them to store all the notes they need about interdependencies within the code, the users' reasons for wanting a feature to work a certain way, and the different approaches they've taken to solving the problem and why they failed. Testers may regard the database as a convenient place to record ideas for test cases or offer hints to the documentation writers and technical support staff. Users take a more forensic view of the database, searching through it for clues about what the development team is actually doing all day long and why a change that seems so simple to them requires the budget of a Hollywood thriller and a cast of thousands to implement. This can result in a multidirectional tug-of-war over the system design and the type of information it contains. All of these various uses are possible and feasible under the right circumstances. The project manager, though, should be the only person who can authorize a change to the system or its usage. You should make it clear to your staff and your users that you own the database. In an environment where an organization-wide change management system is controlled by a central QA administrator, you are that administrator's designated representative for your project.

Secrecy

On rare occasions, a tester may encounter a problem so horrible that nobody wants to mention it for fear of provoking senior management's wrath. This is more likely to occur with a product that is already in production; it also takes a very close-knit development team to try to pull it off. For example, let's say a tester decides to try a new sequence of steps on a Web site and suddenly discovers that he can display a table containing customers' names, e-mail addresses, credit card numbers, and recent purchases. Shocked, he rushes over to the developer and shows her what he's found. Together they reproduce the problem, and they realize that anyone on the Internet could do it, too. The sequence of steps is fairly obscure, so by their estimate the risk to the organization is low. They consider what to do next. They know that if they report the problem in the database all hell will break loose. The developer might get in trouble for having such a huge security breach in the code. The tester might get in trouble for not finding the defect sooner. The project manager might get in trouble because project managers are supposed to make sure that things like this don't happen. The crisis will provoke many meetings and follow-up reviews, which delay the project. After agonizing over the situation for a while, the tester promises not to record the problem in the database and the developer promises to fix it in the next release.

This scenario illustrates a failure of leadership on the part of the project manager. To prevent it from happening on your project, you should make it clear to your team that you want all issues recorded in the database. You should let them know that you value open communication, honesty, and rapid response. You should assure them that if an event like this were to occur on your project, you personally would take the heat from senior management, attend all the unpleasant meetings alone as much as possible, and do your best to shield them from any negative repercussions.

Performance Evaluations

Professional athletes expect that statistics about performance will be published in the daily newspapers, but not software developers. It often happens that a new tester who does not yet fully understand the product, or a zealous tester who is overflowing with enthusiastic ideas about how to improve the product, will flood the database with defect reports and enhancement requests. When the developers look at their work queues, they see dozens of items assigned to them, most of which turn out to be not a problem, impossible to implement, or of such low priority that they can be deferred for several geological epochs of Internet time. The developers may corner the innocent tester by the coffee machine when no one is watching and strongly hint that such items should not be input into the change management system because they make the developers look bad.

It is tempting for a project manager to use the statistics in the problem tracking database as a measurement of developers' and testers' job performance. After all, it's easy to run queries that show who has the most items on his or her work queue, who has the oldest outstanding items, who submits fixes fastest, whose fixes fail most often, and who certifies that fixes are acceptable only to have the items rejected or reopened by end users. The data is all there for the crunching. But the reality is always more subtle than the numbers. If you get to know your team well, you'll know how they work without running any queries. Certain developers on a team assume the role of deep-thinking gurus: they're the ones who tackle the hardest problems that take the longest to resolve. If you look at their statistics, they're not very productive—but everyone knows the project would collapse without them. The same holds true for testers. Many fixes can be verified in 10 seconds, but others may require hours of preparation. The most analytical and creative testers, the ones you can trust to reproduce problems that occur only under complex, interdependent conditions, will have the worst verification rates. Often testers have no way of knowing in advance whether an item is significant or trivial; if a tester has trouble figuring out the product's design specifications or persistently focuses on only cosmetic issues, it is up to the project manager—not the developers—to take appropriate action.

You should avoid creating and distributing reports with the data sorted by team members' names. By focusing on individual performance, you introduce a team-disrupting element of competition into the process and invite people to abuse the system in various unsavory ways: bombarding an unpopular member with trivial bug reports, filing false reports so that defects can be quickly "fixed," or submitting fixes too quickly without adequate analysis or testing.

It is much more helpful in the long run to present statistics from the change management system sorted by program function, or by current status, or by average workload. This reinforces your staff's sense that you regard them as a team, and it nearly always provides enough information about the state of the project for your end users or senior management.

Change Management Politics

How an organization communicates internally about the work to be done and measures its own progress essentially defines its culture. In an environment where senior management maintains tight central control and uniformity among different teams, you are likely to find a very formal software change management system in use across development projects and throughout the organization. In contrast, a more decentralized senior management structure may condone a more ad hoc approach to change management, allowing different software development teams to select whatever tools they believe best suit their projects. The former type tends to pay much greater attention to the actual productivity of the software development teams, as measured in features implemented and bugs fixed, and to the overall quality of the software products, as measured in defects reported over the course of the development cycle. The latter type often focuses instead on less quantitative indicators, such as the popularity of the software development teams among the user communities and the perceived value of the software product as a tool to accomplish certain organizational goals.

Because of these cultural variables, change management isn't only an engineering process—it's very much a political process. Many conflicts over power and control and resources present themselves disguised as gaps and bottlenecks in change management procedures. Under these circumstances, fixing a problem with a procedure requires that you step back and deal with the larger forces as well.

Regardless of your organization's culture, or the political machinations within your IT department, or the tools you have at your disposal, you can do a good job of tracking product changes. The effort you invest in your change management system will be repaid exponentially.

It will help you monitor the relative workloads of the members of your team. It will alert you if any steps in the development or testing process are being skipped. It will enable you to evaluate the progress you are making in relation to your project plan. It will provide you with insight into risky or troublesome functions of your product.

Most importantly, it will demonstrate to your users that you care about their responses and pay attention to their needs.

Rehearse Your Deployment

Once your product is ready to be released, the programs will have to travel. Unless your software runs on a mainframe with dumb terminals or is a background process linking data from several systems, you will be transferring files to your users' computers. These files could range from huge directories requiring lots of memory, to shared resources such as .DLL files or ODBC drivers, to cookies, to registry entries. In addition, no matter what type of product you have created, you will need to move files from the QA environment to the production environment.

Many new project managers do a very thorough job of planning, scheduling, and budgeting their projects right up to the very end. Then they assume that when everyone has signed off on the product and it is ready to go, it will just somehow get launched. It's not that they believe in cybermagic; they simply have not scoped out the details. Often they are surprised by the complexity of the issues they are forced to deal with at the last minute.

Choreography of a Product Launch

Depending on the architecture of your system, the order of the steps, the intricacies of each phase, and the timing of the processes may vary. But the basic choreography is essentially the same.

1. **Identify your users.** For an internal system you should be able to find out exactly who your users are: name, title, department, location, phone number, e-mail address, and hardware configuration. If your product grants access to different functions or data depending on the user's logon type or permissions, your list should also include this information.

2. **Build the production version.** The production version comprises the programs, templates, settings, and data you plan to copy to the users' computers. It also includes the database tables, procedures, and the settings on the servers.

3. **Develop the setup script.** This is the installation program that checks the available space on the user's computer, proposes a directory location, copies the production version files to the specified directory, and offers configuration options. For a Web site, it might also create a registered user whose identity and profile are recognized during future visits. To facilitate testing, the code pointing to the servers should be easy to find and edit so that you can run the installation in the development, test, or production environment. The script should also include an uninstall/unregister option that removes all traces of the product's existence from a user's computer.

4. **Create the delivery package.** There are a variety of ways to deliver the production version and the setup script to your users. You can personally walk around to all your users' desks carrying a disk and load the software on their machines

one at a time. You can cut CDs and send them via interoffice mail to your remote branch offices. You can create a new directory on a shared server and leave all your users a voice mail message asking them to map to the drive and double-click on `setup.exe`. You can send out an object package as an e-mail attachment. You can include a link to a Web site in an e-mail message. You can use an automated software management system to locate your users by logon ID, machine name, IP address, or other criteria and install your product either with their permission or silently and invisibly without their knowledge. Whichever method you prefer, make sure your network can handle the traffic you anticipate. It is also a good idea to have a second method available as a backup. Chances are, you will always have a few users who are out of the office on the rollout date, or whose machines are powered off, or who simply cannot follow your instructions, or whom the automated software management system cannot locate.

5. **Set the version counter.** Whenever you release a new version, you will want to be certain that all of your users install it. You can do this by creating a version field in the database and a version setting in the user's registry. For the software to work, the setting and the field must match. The setup script for the new version should write the version setting to the registry. At the same time you announce your rollout, you should create the entry in the database field.

6. **Migrate to the production servers.** Transfer your databases and stored procedures and settings to the designated servers. Turn on replication.

7. **Release the desktop production version.** Deliver the setup script and program files to the users' computers.

8. **Confirm installations.** If you use an automated software management system, you should be able to obtain a report listing successful installations, failed installations, and pending installations. (These reports should be viewed with a critical eye: some systems count aborted installations as successes.) Or you could ask all users to log on within a certain period after installation and then you could analyze the database logs. You could send an e-mail message to everyone on your user list and request a confirmation. Whatever method you employ, you should make an effort to find out how well your deployment succeeded. If a lot of users do not receive the delivery package, then you have problems with your distribution method and/or tools. If all of your users receive the delivery package and run the installation but for a lot of them the script fails, then you need to make some quick changes in your setup programs. If all of your users receive the delivery package but many of them ignore it, you should call an emergency meeting with your client and product manager and investigate who is responsible for the communication failure. If all of your users receive the delivery package, run the installation successfully, and happily begin using your product, you should offer a sacrifice to the technology gods in thanks for the miracle.

As with the choreography of an actual dance, it's important for everyone to keep their eyes open and perform their steps on cue—or else the audience may witness a large, ugly, embarrassing pileup of bodies on stage.

Advance Preparations

Even if you understand all the steps in the deployment process—even if you have lived through several product launches already—there are good reasons for beginning your preparations well in advance of the rollout date. With so many activities to coordinate, scheduling can become difficult. It is not going to be feasible to migrate your databases to the production servers the same week the operations staff is planning a major hardware upgrade. Nor do you want to discover suddenly that the three days remaining for a developer to create the setup script are the same three days that she told you a long time ago she was going to be absent for her brother's wedding. And then there's the inevitable loss of focus as your team sprints for the finish line: exhausted people are more likely to overlook critical details and make dumb mistakes under deadline pressure.

Around the time of your first system test, you should begin by reviewing your environment. Many organizations provide standard tools and well-defined procedures for software distribution, and all the project manager needs to worry about is making sure that his or her team follows the established guidelines. In other organizations, central control is less strict, and project managers are given more choice at different stages of deployment. Find out what activities are governed by policy and what others leave you free to improvise. For the steps where you are on your own, consult with your team about the tools they have used and the procedures they have followed on previous projects. Other project managers may be willing to offer advice. Be sure to include your product manager, so that you obtain an accurate assessment of your users' capabilities and preferences.

Once you have decided how you are going to handle the deployment of your product, tell your team about your plans. Prepare a summary of the activities during each step, and assign roles to the appropriate members. At a staff meeting, review the procedures in sequence. If some of the tasks are supposed to be handled by people outside your group, invite them to the meeting, too. Verbally rehearse the entire process. After everyone understands what is expected of him or her, ask all the participants for an estimate of how long their tasks will take.

You can save time and reduce errors by automating as many steps of the process as possible. Compiling the production version, creating the installation script, setting up databases and administrative utilities on production servers—these activities can be labor-intensive, and they demand unflagging attention. Even if you can depend on your own team members to be careful, you might not have a choice in the matter. Some organizations may insist that all production versions be compiled and built by a central operations group; they may also keep all their servers at a remote, low-rent, disaster-proof site far away. To the operations technicians at such a site, your excellent product will be indistinguishable from the hack job running on the node next door. Whatever parts of the deployment you can automate are functions you will not have to trust to the kindness and diligence of strangers. If you cannot automate the actual tasks, you might create an automated test that certifies that the tasks have been performed correctly and completely.

Installation Test

Novice project managers tend to regard the product launch as an afterthought. To use an old-fashioned metaphor, it seems like addressing an envelope after a letter has been drafted, typed, and signed. It should now be evident that the construction of your product, the creation of the delivery vehicle, and the configuration of the supporting environment are parallel and interdependent endeavors.

Ideally, the first version of the installation program and the entire suite of files and settings it copies to the users' computers should be available at the time of the first integration test. If it is not, different testers are likely to end up testing different versions. It also becomes more difficult to determine whether a problem is caused by a program error or a missing file or conflicting settings in the users' options or permissions. The idea of a integration test is to pass data through the application from the first user inputs and automated feeds to the last display outputs and printed reports. The state of the user's machine as determined by the setup script is an essential but frequently overlooked input variable.

The same holds true for the database and server environment. Rehearsing the deployment of the production version as part of the integration test avoids confusion and delays and radical changes later. For example, you might discover that your data does not replicate the way you expected. Or an update to a single field causes the entire record to be refreshed and retransmitted, and the traffic quickly exceeds your network's bandwidth. Or a null value in a field in one database is interpreted as a zero when it is imported into a different database, with disastrous consequences for your calculations. Or a process becomes deadlocked when it requests data at 2 a.m. from a server that is taken offline every night for routine maintenance . . . and so on. The sooner your testers can discover these problems, the longer your developers will have to come up with solutions.

Milestone Marker

Throughout the development phase, in your role as Technology Partner you'll be asking your project team to do lots of things that aren't directly related to building the product. Whether it's reviewing test plans, organizing project resources, participating in change management, or planning the deployment—none of these activities will actually cause anything to happen in your product's user interface or send a single byte of data through your product's workflow. Therefore in the beginning some of your team members may be inclined to ignore your requests, claiming that in their opinion such matters aren't important. If this happens to you, you should suddenly morph before their eyes from governor/legislator into absolute monarch and let the recalcitrant foot-draggers know that, in your opinion, such matters are very important indeed.

The relationship between you and your staff will undergo many similar challenges. The development phase of your project is volatile; everyone improvises a great deal and figures out the solutions to unexpected problems on the fly. The role of Team Captain is much easier at the start, when the gung-ho players are all fired up and listening impatiently to the national anthem, than later on when they're tired and wishing the game was over already. In the next chapter, we'll consider how you can help maintain their energy, their teamwork, and their positive attitude even if your project goes into extra innings.

CHAPTER 6

Artisans in Their Workshop

Outstanding development teams don't just happen by chance. Nor is it a matter of fate or luck providing you with a lineup of star talent. Throughout the ages, quality engineering work has been done in all kinds of environments—from medieval tapestry guilds to modern aerospace assembly lines. The key to success has always been and will always be the same. You can remember it as the four Cs: a collective commitment to craftsmanship and cooperation.

As project manager, you are not part of the team. You are the boss, and no amount of informality or schmoozing with the staff is going to change that. In your Team Captain role, your job is to establish an environment where creativity, perfectionism, hard work, and open communication can occur. You can also praise and reward individual team members' behavior that promotes the four Cs and criticize and punish behavior that thwarts them. Your skill in managing the workshop will be judged by your ability to convey high expectations, promote a constant exchange of information, and keep the peace.

Maintain Standards

We hear a lot about standards these days. Parents want schools to impose standards for student performance. Consumers want the government to create standards for genetically modified foods. But what exactly is a standard, and what purpose does it serve in software development?

Defining Standards

A standard is a statement of shared expectations within a community. Parents expect that by fourth grade, children should have memorized the multiplication tables. Americans expect that the water coming out of their taps should be safe to drink. In the 1950s, moviegoers expected that actors in love scenes would keep their clothes on.

A standard is different from a rule or a custom. Rules are mandatory. They are enforced by laws and regulations, and if you break one you are subjected to public disgrace, loss of status, a fine, and/or a jail sentence. Customs, on the other hand, are optional. In your community it may be the custom to serve salad before the entree, but if you decide to serve it afterward you probably won't suffer any negative consequences beyond a few people making remarks behind your back about how weird you are.

Within an organization, the rules are obvious—they're what you have to do to get things done and stay out of trouble. You have to turn in your time sheets on Friday afternoon. You have to attend the strategic planning meeting. You have to notify your staff in advance when you shut down the telephone system for routine maintenance. The fact that you've been asked to manage anything proves that you already know the rules.

Customs are more ambiguous and sometimes harder to notice. If you've been promoted within a group where you've been working for a while, chances are its customs have already become part of your daily routine to the point where you don't think about them anymore. If you've been asked to lead a different team, however, you'll have to start watching and listening carefully. Consider people's behavior and their routines. Do team members eat lunch together or socialize out of the office? Do they expect to be fed pizza in the conference room? Do they listen to music on their headphones and exchange CDs? Do they play with toys at their desks or shoot sponge darts at each other? Are they taking courses in the evening and helping each other with their homework? Do they shout back and forth through the partitions of their cubicles a lot? Do they trade stock tips? These sorts of activities are all examples of customs in a typical American office.

Workplace standards are often neither completely optional nor strictly mandatory, yet if you violate them members of the organization feel that it's bad both for you as an individual and for the group as a whole. People who uphold standards are regarded as admirable and trustworthy, while those who ignore them are viewed with suspicion.

When you become a project manager, one of the first things you have to do as a leader is size up the organization and the team and figure out which of their practices are rules, which are customs, and which are standards. This usually takes a couple of months, and it's an exploratory process. Other project managers are the best sources of information; try to find a veteran who is willing to act as your mentor until you have developed a discerning eye.

The rules are the easy part: you simply enforce them. You present them to your team and indicate that you expect obedience. You may not agree with all the rules—and before long you may start lobbying your peers and senior management to change them—but as project manager it is your responsibility to carry out the policies set by authorities higher than you.

Customs are more idiosyncratic and more variable, and therefore they are much more dictatorial to impose on others. Naturally, you have your own ideas about how your team should behave. Before you start issuing edicts, spend a while reflecting on what they're accustomed to and why. Of course, it is possible that you were brought in as a manager in the first place because what they were accustomed to wasn't so good for the organization. If that's the case, try to determine which behaviors were counter-productive and which were basically harmless. Introduce changes slowly and diplo-matically, and give people a reasonable amount of time to adjust to your priorities. Adopt some of their customs: order the pizza for the conference room, put some toys on your desk, bring in CDs and share them. Be sensitive to gestures of rebellion or resentment. If the discontent over any of your new policies is widespread, you should talk to a friend outside the organization whose opinion you trust and ask his or her advice about whether your ideas are in the project's best interest or if you're just acting like a control freak. In general, you should give your staff as much personal freedom as you can without jeopardizing the project or incurring the wrath of senior management.

When it comes to standards, you have greater authority and accountability. As proj-ect manager, it is your right and your duty to establish standards. Your standards com-municate how you expect certain jobs to be done. The clearer your standards are, the more effectively your team will collaborate with each other and the more focused they will be as individuals.

Modifying Standards

Because standards are statements of *shared* expectations, it would be futile to attempt to implement them by fiat. Worse than futile—such authoritarian methods inevitably lead to resentment, cynicism, foot-dragging, lame excuses, and other forms of passive-aggressive nastiness among the team members. If you want your staff to comply with your standards willingly, include everyone in formulating and updating them. It is good practice for a manager not only to articulate but also to defend his or her expec-tations: you may find you are being unrealistic, and your team members may propose a better way to accomplish your goals.

The procedures guide you created at the beginning of the project to train your team members should contain your first attempt at establishing standards. During the devel-opment phase, you may find that your initial expectations were either too stringent or too lax. Deadline pressure may force you to adopt a more cursory approach, or com-munication problems within your team may force you to expand the details. If, as time goes by, you discover that your standards are burdensome or inadequate, go ahead and modify them. Discuss the matter at a staff meeting, obtain a consensus, and revise the procedures guide.

A standard increases uniformity and decreases ambiguity by answering a frequently asked question. Among the questions that are likely to recur during the development phase are these:

Workflow. If there are gateways between steps in your development process, how detailed should the entrance and exit criteria be? Who should certify that the cri-teria have been met, and how long should the evaluation take?

Design specifications. How much detail must each specification contain? Can you work from a simple statement such as "For subscribers with premium service, deduct 5 percent from their shipping and handling fee," or do you need supporting business analysis documents and formal approval by your client?

Code commentary. How often should the comments be updated? How extensive should the comments be? If more than one developer works on a section of code, whose job is it to write the comments? How extensive must the changes to code be before comments are required?

System documentation. What system documentation is essential for your project? What tools may be used to prepare it? How neat does it have to be? Who will see it besides your developers and testers?

Test documentation. Do you expect your testers to create test plans and test cases before they begin testing, or will it be acceptable if they compile the documentation afterward as a record of what they have done? Should your test cases describe every keystroke and mouse click, or can they summarize a function, such as "Enter a new product"?

User documentation. How closely should the writers collaborate with the developers, testers, and usability consultants? When should the writers submit their draft material for review?

Version control. What comments should developers include when checking in a version? How long can a shared file remain checked out by one person? What constitutes a version, and who decides when to create a new one?

Configuration management. What types of programs may your team members load onto their computers without notifying the configuration coordinator and obtaining permission? How often should they expect to have their machines audited, and how much privacy will they have?

Change requests. When your testers and/or users submit a problem report, an enhancement request, or a design change, do they have to fill out every field on the input form? Should your product manager be allowed to veto change requests before the developers see them? If a request is rejected, how much explanation should be provided?

Procedures guide. How often should the guide be updated? How much detail should it provide? Should there be a change log?

Status reports. How often do you want your team members to give you individual status reports? How detailed should they be? Will they be organized by tasks accomplished within a certain time period, by milestones on the project plan, or by open and closed issues? Should you have status reports for group functions (development, testing, documentation) instead of or in addition to the individual status reports? What arrangements will you make for people to bring to your attention problems that they are reluctant to describe in writing or speak about openly at a staff meeting?

Time management. Does your organization require staff members and consultants to fill out time sheets? If so, how detailed must they be? If not, how will you keep track of your team's work? What type of personal activities and communications are permitted during work hours?

Metrics. In addition to the number of hours your team members work and the time they spend accomplishing particular tasks, what other statistics will you gather to measure how your project is progressing?

The process of evaluating standards can degenerate into unproductive, irrelevant collective introspection—or bickering. Remember what it was like when you were eight years old, and you and your friends would meet in the park, and one of you had a ball, and you decided to make up a game, and then you spent most of the afternoon arguing about the rules instead of playing? To avoid such exercises in futility, focus on aspects of your project where the lack of a uniform approach is causing confusion or risk. Start with the critical areas, and expand your coverage as needed.

Upholding Standards

In principle, everyone thinks standards are a great idea. Code with comments is incontrovertibly better than code without comments. A product that has system documentation is obviously better than one that forces people to guess how it works. But deadlines have a way of creeping up, and then suddenly you start to hear, "I'm sorry, I would have done it that way, but I just didn't have time."

Establishing standards is of absolutely no use unless your entire team is ready, willing, and able to uphold them. Actually, it's worse than useless—if you go to the trouble to discuss, draft, document, and train, and then just look the other way while everybody does their own thing, you've wasted a lot of your team's time and sabotaged your own credibility as a manager.

The creation of coordinator roles helps instill a collective sense of responsibility for upholding standards. When you assign different team members to coordinate such tasks as project documentation, version control, configuration management, the procedures guide, the change management process, and user support, the auditing function is distributed throughout the group, and no single person acquires the role of über-enforcer. If your project continues for more than six months, you should consider rotating the roles: this practice prevents one individual from being lenient with friends and draconian with others in any specific area for very long.

Even auditors need to be audited sometimes. Your QA manager should plan a quarterly review of all the standards you and your team have set for your project. The review should monitor the levels of compliance, assess the thoroughness of the inspection procedures, and provide you with a report on the current state of affairs. If you discover any problems, ask your QA manager to follow up and try to resolve them with the team members involved. Occasionally you might need to intervene and back up your QA manager, but whenever possible it's preferable to reserve your authority for urgent matters.

Share Information

Everyone has too many meetings. This seems especially true the closer you get to an important deadline, when all you really want to do is tell other people to leave you alone so that you can finish your work. Recurring staff meetings are the worst: every week the same faces around the table, the same items on the agenda.

As a project manager, though, you know that you're supposed to call meetings. You know there's no better way to get members of your team to communicate with each other across social ties and job functions. The challenge is to make meetings effective and enlightening. You can avoid group gripe sessions and boastful individual presentations if you set a clearly defined purpose and an established structure for your meetings.

A couple of days before each regular meeting, send out a reminder and ask everyone on your team if they have any items they would like to add to the agenda. Before the meeting, type up the agenda and rank the items submitted (including your own) by order of importance. Be sure to include old business—items discussed at previous meetings but left unresolved.

At each meeting, distribute the agenda and ask if there are any last-minute additions. Then follow the list until you run out of time. As meeting leader, it is up to you to keep an eye on the clock and focus the discussion. Assign someone to take minutes, and rotate the job periodically. After the meeting the person who took the minutes should type them up and distribute them within two or three days.

Your team will hold meetings throughout the life of the project. Before you begin coding, the main topics at the meetings are getting to know the users and the technology environment, creating the project proposal, and figuring out how to work together. At the time of deployment, the meetings deal primarily with scheduling and logistics. After the rollout, the emphasis of the meetings shifts to maintenance issues and plans for future versions.

During development, the range of issues about which your team members need to share information is much broader than during other phases. Although you won't cover every subject at every meeting, over time you should expect to include the following topics on your agenda.

Requirements Review

The change management process requires communication among your entire team. Change requests that have been approved by the product manager, project manager, development manager, and quality assurance manager should be presented to the group at your regular team meeting.

The developers and testers should evaluate each item and analyze the nature of the changes, the effect on various objects, architectural tiers, modules of code, and the amount of effort required for implementation. Sometimes the analysis will not be possible without referring to the code or the system documentation. When this happens, any team member should be permitted to defer discussion on the item until the next meeting. As the project progresses, and as the system becomes larger and more complex, you will no doubt begin the meeting with old business, usually with a follow-up discussion of deferred change requests.

Your team's evaluation of changes in the product's requirements will affect both your project plan and your schedule of versions. By listening as your developers and testers brainstorm about the details of program changes, you will have an early warning of issues that could overwhelm your resources and derail your schedule. You will also be able to group changes intelligently so that all items that affect a particular function can be coded and tested as an integrated unit.

Developers can become very impatient with the review process. As soon as they hear about a problem, they like to find out what's wrong. Once they have the code in front of them, it's hard to resist the temptation to start experimenting with it. Without totally dampening their instinct to tinker, you should make it clear that their work needs to be planned, organized, and scheduled. They should not work on any change requests that haven't been reviewed and approved. If they can't resist, they should do this work on their own time—and their version of the code should be stored on only their own machine, away from the team development builds in the project's version control system.

Progress Review

"So, how's it going?"

The tone of the question makes all the difference. It can be hopeful, encouraging, anxious, or aggressive. How you choose to answer will, of course, depend on who's doing the asking.

Among your team members, candor is essential. Unless you are gifted with precognition, not a single one of your original estimates is going to hit the mark precisely. Every task will require more (or, rarely, less) effort than you predicted. For your team members there should be no shame attached to this. If they are working conscientiously they should not have to worry about getting in trouble when they take longer than expected to finish a task. Rather than reassuring you that everything is hunky-dory, you need them to be honest about variances from the schedule and budget and to recalculate their forecasts to the best of their ability.

These assessments should occur on a regular basis throughout the life of the project. In the beginning of the development phase, it is easy to postpone them because the product still seems rather intangible. If you're preparing adequate system and test documentation, though, you should have enough material to scrutinize. Close to the release deadline it is tempting to avoid progress reviews because everyone on the team feels pressured. Nevertheless, no matter how loud the groans are, you should put this topic on the meeting agenda. During the home stretch wishful thinking often clouds people's judgment, and you'll probably be surprised by the number of outstanding unresolved issues. Keep track of the causes of each delay in the change management database. After a while, if you discern patterns of problems, you may be able to alleviate the situation with more training, better tools, or upgraded hardware. As a rule, you should plan to review your progress every two weeks and after each major build. A complete revision of the project plan should occur every quarter.

Sooner or later in your career as a project manager, you'll find yourself leading a team that is working as hard as they can and yet seems to be falling farther and farther behind each day. For every problem they resolve, three new ones appear. For every task they complete, a newly discovered dependency forces them to go back and redo something else. You miss deadline after deadline, and still there is no end in sight.

Faced with such discouraging (and occasionally career-threatening) circumstances, novice project managers tend to make certain predictable mistakes:

Cannon fodder. The first desperate measure usually involves recruiting more developers and testers. This tactic probably dates back to low-tech military strategy for ground combat, when it was possible to overwhelm an enemy by sheer numbers. Unfortunately, it does not work for software projects. The investment of time and effort it takes to train the new people, establish new lines of communication, install new equipment, obtain new security IDs, divide the work to be done, perform additional integration and regression testing, and settle territorial disputes is seldom recouped by any added productivity. Thirty years ago, Frederick Brooks recognized this truth in *The Mythical Man Month* when he stated: "Adding manpower to a late software project makes it later." Times haven't changed much (except now he'd say "personpower"). If under deadline pressure you are forced to expand your team—including hiring temporary ad hoc consultants for specified functions such as load testing—you should remember to adjust the schedules of your existing staff members to reflect the time they will spend helping the newcomers get up to speed.

Body snatching. The next thing project managers usually try (or the first, if they don't have the resources to enlarge the development team) is to move people around. They might reassign the challenging work to the most talented and productive developers within the team and marginalize the others with trivial tasks. They might try to trade their back-bench developers for recognized stars from other projects. While it certainly makes sense to ensure that your team members' assignments are consonant with their abilities and to recruit the best staff available, these tactics can have subtle but damaging and long-lasting repercussions for your product. You might not have to cope with obtaining new equipment or office space or security IDs or with training anyone about the way things are done at your organization, but you will face very disruptive interpersonal dynamics.

Developers normally take great pride in the code they create and have a strong sense of personal authorship. If someone on your team isn't performing up to par, it is far better to find that person a mentor who can coach him or her than to reassign the person's tasks to someone else. The humiliation and resentment and trauma caused by shifting responsibilities in the midst of a project will lead to further delays as the members of your formerly cooperative team take out their anger on each other. No one will feel quite as personally committed as before. Everyone will have to figure out the new lines of communication. The developers with new assignments will take a look at the code they've inherited and propose different ideas about how things should have been done in the first place—often at staff meetings with the original creators present, listening in silent fury. If the new person on the team is a star traded in from another project, you can expect to witness major ego battles over product design and development standards. Try as hard as you can to keep your team and their assignments stable during the course of the project, at least until the group has completed one major release together. If you need to have the developers on your team help each other more, or if you need to bring in an expert from another project, make sure everyone understands that the person who is receiving the assistance is still in charge of and responsible for the task originally assigned.

Death march. A third common error committed by panicked project managers is mandatory overtime. They look at everything that needs to be done before a deadline and decree that the entire team must put in as many hours as it takes to get the job done. Exactly how many hours that entails varies according to the culture of the organization: a "death march" schedule at an investment bank would probably involve cots in the conference room, while at a nonprofit foundation it might result in some canceled dinner plans. In any event, no matter where you work, this measure is effective only for a week or two at most. After that, your staff may appear to be laboring effectively in their places, but they will be sleep-deprived and dull-witted, and their minds will actually be elsewhere. Their ability to cooperate and communicate will be hampered by their lack of patience, and their error rates will be high.

In the end, as a manager whose project is running seriously behind schedule you have two choices: you can cut back on what you promised to deliver, or you can extend the deadline. Learning how to present these options to your client cheerfully, firmly, and diplomatically is a difficult but crucial skill for any project manager.

Your behavior during progress reviews will have a strong influence on the morale of your team. When a project is behind schedule, everyone understandably gets discouraged, and a mood of doom and gloom begins to infect the meetings. The harder people are working, and the closer the deadline looms, the easier it is for this presentation to turn into mass hysteria—the kind of "uh-oh, we're dead" mentality that causes your staff members to run out of the conference room and call their headhunters.

You can put the brakes on this downward spiral by acting confident and optimistic at all times. No matter how scared or depressed you might feel, don't let your team know it. Practice two expressions in the mirror at home: a frown of thoughtful concern and a wry, world-weary smile. Assume these masks in public whenever anyone tells you bad news, and reassure everyone that things are going to turn out fine in the end. Find a confidant outside the organization. Remember Franklin Delano Roosevelt's pronouncement during the Great Depression that "we have nothing to fear but fear itself"? If you don't seem worried, your team won't waste as much energy on anxiety attacks and will remain more focused and productive.

Code Review

At a code review, a developer submits samples of his or her work for others to evaluate. There are two types of code reviews: a peer review and a project team review.

A peer review occurs when the developer presents the code to other developers and solicits their criticism. Some organizations establish a formal review process and require that all code be inspected by peers at the end of the analysis, design, construction, and unit testing phases prior to implementation. To ensure fairness and objectivity, there are usually rules that govern rotation of developers among review boards, time commitments, conflict resolution, and the length and complexity of the material under review. With this type of peer review it is generally regarded as a bad idea for the project manager to be included in the review sessions. The goal is to encourage a free exchange of questions, suggestions, and criticism, unimpeded by the judgmental presence of the person who writes everyone's performance evaluations.

A project team review occurs at a regular staff meeting. Its purpose is to help others understand the design of the system, the flow of the data, and the configuration of the environment. Your developers ought to be able to do the following:

- Clearly explain the functions of the different layers of architecture
- Diagram the layout of the tables and show the relationships between key fields
- Map the path through the system of the most important data elements
- Describe the actions of daemons and stored procedures
- Talk about the functionality of the Web server and indicate why they chose particular settings

No doubt your documentation writers can produce a perfectly good user manual without knowing much about connection pooling, and your testers will notice that a button doesn't work whether or not they're aware of database triggers. But they look at the product from different points of view than your developers. They ask the kind of basic, uninformed questions that compel developers to step back from the code and contemplate a bigger picture. And if a developer on your team can't explain what he or she is doing in plain, nontechnical language, you as a project manager should be concerned that he or she does not understand it well enough in the first place.

There are important areas in which your other team members' work can be influenced by the information your developers provide. Testers who understand the system architecture and the configuration settings are in a much better position to create test cases that verify the behavior of the product when various components fail. If they know about the structure of the tables and the behavior of daemons and stored procedures, they can invent more effective test data to violate the rules and baffle the logic. When documentation writers and trainers are aware of a system's limitations they can create procedures to bridge any gaps between what the product does and what particular users might need. Conversely, if they know your product provides features and opportunities that your users don't already have, they can focus on showing the users in detail how to adapt their routines and take advantage of every new bell and whistle.

Test Review

Testers also benefit from peer reviews and project team reviews.

A peer review makes it necessary for a tester to document his or her test plans, test cases, and test data in such a manner that they can be understood and evaluated by someone else. It ensures that every tester follows the correct format and procedures, and it promotes an exchange of ideas among your testers on test types, methods, and tools.

A project team review enables your testers to present their test plans, test cases, and test data to the rest of the group. This process helps your testing efforts maintain appropriate priorities and match the correct methods with the functions and data to be verified. It is easy for testers to become obsessed with a small subset of the product's functions or sidetracked into tinkering with the test tools. Any good test plan should include the user interface, the data, security and permissions, performance, and the system environment, but the challenge is to figure out how thorough you ought to be in each area given the limits of your time and resources. By periodically explaining their test plan to the rest of the team, your testers will be obliged to reflect on their strategy. By submitting their test cases and test data for review, they will learn how to adjust their coverage to address the actual risks more realistically.

Furthermore, if your project employs any kind of automated testing, then your testers are also writing code. Most test tools have their own programming languages that are extensions of Visual Basic or JavaScript, and the more advice your testers receive from your developers about programming techniques in general, the better they are able to implement the tool's advanced features. There are also particular ways in which a program can be made more testable based on the tool's requirements and limitations: the properties assigned to objects and controls can determine whether the tool can automatically recognize and verify them or if it needs manually input instructions. Often developers don't have a choice about the kind of objects and controls they use, but in situations where it doesn't really matter an understanding of testers' needs can do a great deal to improve the effectiveness of test cases and speed up the test development process.

User Documentation and Training Review

Your regular team meetings should also occasionally include a review of user documentation and training materials because the requirements for these components evolve as the product is being built. As developers make decisions about system architecture and workflow, their model of user behavior changes. The longer a project goes on, the more developers become absorbed in the intricacies of their program logic, and the more inclined they are to assume they understand how users will respond to what appears on the screen. Testers who focus on whether actual results match expected results also can easily lose sight of the users' perspective.

When documentation writers submit their drafts for review, any misunderstandings or gaps in communication become obvious. The writers' job is to narrate the system's behavior as a consecutive story and to translate its field names and menu choices and messages into a language in which the users already are fluent. If pieces of the story are missing or contradictory, or if the dialect is incomprehensible, the writers will notice. If the assumptions that have been made about the users' expertise, or education, or attention span, or sense of humor are way off the mark, they will point this out. Even more than the product manager, the writers should be closely attuned to the habits and expectations of all types of users.

Documentation created for technical support staff needs to fulfill an additional set of criteria. If your IT department employs a crew of service technicians who are dispatched to investigate problems when users complain that their computers are not working, the technicians will save your project team a lot of time if they know a few things about your product. They should be informed not only about what the users believe the product should be doing, but also about any circumstances or conditions that the developers and testers know will cause problems. One method of accomplishing this is to give the documentation writers access to the change management database and ask the developers and testers to flag any items the technicians will need to keep in mind while troubleshooting.

Training materials also can undergo a metamorphosis as a product grows and changes. On projects where the training materials are treated as a minor subset of user documentation, the first drafts are usually written at the eleventh hour just before roll-out. This approach works adequately, however, only for small-scale applications with paper-based classroom training led by a live instructor at a single location. In general, the more automated and electronic you want your training materials to be, the earlier in the development cycle you should start working on them, and the more revisions you should anticipate. Because training is inevitably task oriented, the design of training materials is particularly affected by alterations in the workflow. Training involves role playing, and good trainers have a pragmatic talent for imagining and acting out the behavior of their trainees in relation to the product. This skill makes them quite adept at identifying usability issues early in the development cycle.

At the beginning of a project, the developers, documentation writers, and trainers grab a copy of the product specifications and head off in different directions to tackle their individual challenges. Everyone recognizes that periodically they have to get together and synchronize their content, but in most organizations far less attention is paid to the coordination of style. The results can be rather jarring. Imagine a user interface with an ATM look and feel and terse, haiku-like messages, combined with documentation with a format that resembles an illuminated manuscript and prose that reads like an excerpt from a nineteenth-century novel, combined with a tutorial designed by someone who has obviously spent many, many hours playing real-time strategy war games and memorizing Monty Python jokes. This is not simply a question of aesthetics. From your users' point of view, your product consists of the programs that run on the computer plus all associated materials. Unless your IT department publishes a manual of style guidelines, you probably won't know very much about your team members' repertoire of styles before they produce a first draft or prototype. As soon as they do, you should get everyone together and agree on some basic guidelines. Ultimately, the software developers' taste should have the strongest influence because the users will spend the most time with their creation.

Dependency Review

It often happens during regularly scheduled, carefully planned team meetings that the most interesting and significant discussions are about items not included on the agenda. Such matters typically arise when one team member realizes that he or she can't accomplish a scheduled task before someone else does something first.

You may start your project with a meticulous plan that lists assignments and milestones and tasks broken down into 80-hour deliverables. As an act of collective imagination, it's an important exercise to go through—like getting all the instruments tuned up before the symphony orchestra starts to play. Software projects are more like jazz improvisation than anything played strictly from a score. Your original project plan will be out of date before the yogurt in your department's refrigerator expires. To a novice project manager, this can make the entire effort feel like ungovernable anarchy. But it doesn't have to be. Updating project plans so that they remain a useful medium of communication is essentially a matter of focusing on dependencies and making appropriate adjustments.

A dependency exists when one team member can't make progress on her task before another team member finishes his. To identify the dependencies, establish checkpoints in the product's development. A checkpoint is not a deliverable: it describes a general condition rather than indicating the completion of a specific task or function or document. A checkpoint enables you to ask two questions: Are we there yet, and what will it take to get us there? As the team discusses what needs to be done to reach a checkpoint, you will learn about dependencies on a much smaller scale than a project plan usually captures, including unforeseen dependencies on people outside your group.

The links between the various components of a product inevitably create the most complex and problematic dependencies. The larger your team and the more people you have working on the different pieces, the greater your challenge will be to ensure that the parts plug into each other and are ready for assembly on a schedule that doesn't leave anything hanging for too long. Developers and testers sometimes prefer to work on a particular area of the program or one type of task all at once. Perhaps it takes time to set up the environment and it's easier to keep going than to switch to something else. Or perhaps they like to follow a train of thought until they run out of ideas. It's good to let your team members set their own priorities as much as possible, but now and then you may need to intervene—for example, to suggest that the database developer put aside work on query parameters and finalize the design of a certain table so that the user interface developer can build a particular screen.

As long as everyone on the team is aware of the checkpoints and is communicating openly about routine changes in the dependencies, there's no need to revise the entire project plan and distribute it to them. You may have to recalculate schedules and create new versions for your client or for IT management, but you can do this on your own, without consuming your team's valuable meeting time. If you find yourself in a situation where someone is really stuck—where due to a design flaw or an unexpected technical limitation all progress in a certain area has ground to a halt—then some major adjustments are in order. Of course, you won't know how long it will take to resolve the problem, but you can rearrange development priorities to reduce dependencies on the component in trouble. Gather your team together, solicit their opinions, and give them an opportunity to review and sign off on the updated plan.

Tool Review

Once a month, even if nobody suggests it, add a tool review to the agenda of your team meeting.

Over time, tools can begin to show signs of wear and tear. They can turn out to be better suited to certain types of tasks than to others. It's easy to ignore the condition of your tools when you have so many priorities that more directly affect the product. Problems with tools, though, can soon lead to lapses in the development process if your team members neglect tasks or create their own workarounds. To maintain the quality of your information about the state of the project, you should expect to invest some time and effort in sharpening your tools and in adjusting the processes they support. At the top of the list for frequent inspections are these tools:

Project planning. You may need to recalibrate the project planning tool and reformat the reports. Your team, your client, and your IT management all have different perspectives on the project and different questions about how the resources are allocated. During the course of development, they will form new perceptions and opinions. They will want new measurements to be taken, new analyses to be performed, new estimates to be created. Often it's less a matter of learning the additional features provided by your tool than figuring out how to zoom in or out with statistics or how to combine data into varying sets, depending on the motive of the question.

Development toolkit. Before you begin coding, you selected your development tools (CASE, modeling language, code generator, programming language, and probably others). You made these decisions based on your project requirements and design specifications; your organization's standards may also have determined your choice. Once you actually started to use the tools and build the product, you may have discovered that they were not always suitable or optimal for the specific programming tasks you face. Unless you encounter a major roadblock, it's too late to change now. But you should keep detailed notes as you go along about time lost to fruitless tinkering and flimsy kludges hammered into place so that you can provide them as evidence when you reevaluate your selections after your first release.

Configuration management. The configuration management tool is both a database and a monitoring device. It should be able to tell you whether the machines in your test environment reflect your organization's standard image and audit your team members' machines for deviations from the standard. During development, machines often get moved around and reconfigured for experimental purposes. Now and then, it's a good idea to make sure all your project's equipment and user accounts are still connected to the configuration management system.

Version control. The version control tool should be an almost invisible utility. It should be available all the time from every platform and location. It should check files in and out quickly. It should not lose any files. If anyone reports problems in any of these areas, you should take the time to troubleshoot and fix them. On the human side of the equation, the developers using the tool should design their programs so that if different people need to work on different functions, the code should be in different files.

Automated testing. The automated testing tools will be very helpful at times, but at other times they will cause your testers to gnash their teeth and wail in frustration. If your tool is a basic model that compares bitmaps and table results, your testers will get fed up with the number of test cases they have to create to verify an adequate sampling of data. If your tool has a powerful programming language and is highly configurable, your testers may tinker endlessly with the code in an attempt to give the tool the correct instructions to run the tests they want. If your tool does performance testing, there will be many arguments about whether the tests are set up properly to simulate real-world conditions. You can listen sympathetically to their complaints for a limited amount of meeting time, and you can provide guidance in focusing the resources on the most critical and widely used functions of the product. You should make it clear to the QA manager, however, that the project cannot by delayed because of problems with the automated testing tool. Every automated test should have a corresponding document that lists the steps followed, the data employed, and the results anticipated. If you're approaching a deadline and the automated tool is unreliable, you ought to be able to bring in a squadron of warm bodies, hand them copies of the document, and execute the test manually. The exception to this rule is automated performance testing: there is really no way to accomplish this manually. For some products it might be worthwhile to delay a release not only until the automated performance test functions properly, but also until all critics are satisfied that the design reproduced conditions in the production environment as closely as possible.

Change management. The change management database reflects the workflow of your team, and therefore it is the tool most likely to require constant adjustment. Depending on the phase of the project or the parts of the product that cause the most headaches for the developers, you may need to alter the rules encoded in the system that determine who can do what and when. Because it also serves as the primary means of communication among members of the team—and as the historical record of their discussions—you should expect an ongoing debate about the ideal content and style of forms and reports. Listen closely to the issues raised: sometimes a team member might need more training, and sometimes a field might need to be lengthened or a classification scheme reworked, but often such disagreements point to other sorts of communication gaps. In addition, the longer people use the database, the more they're going to want to be able to create their own customized queries, reports, and graphs. Generally, it's a good idea to give everyone as much access and creative freedom as you can without endangering either the data or the system's performance. Developers and testers can find patterns in reports that may help them trace multiple errors back to a single defective piece of code. Documentation writers and trainers can pay particular attention to elements of the product that generate many change requests and make sure that they explain those functions clearly. The most enthusiastic customizers may also be willing to serve as database administrators and assist the QA manager in coordinating audits and analyses of the data.

Documentation library. The documentation library is never of paramount importance in anyone's mind . . . until someone needs to find something. Most people feel virtuous enough for simply remembering to file their work in a repository; filling out the form that identifies what it is hardly seems worth the effort. Without monitoring, over time a repository can become like a closet into which everyone throws things and then slams the door. Even if everyone dutifully submits their files and fills out their forms, as the project progresses you may find it necessary to enhance a database by adding keywords and search capabilities. You may realize that a category should be subdivided and its entries reclassified. The members of your team might discover that the contents of the repository are not arranged in an intuitive manner based on their role in the project, and they might request a different organization or a new method of sorting. If you think this is just busywork, consider how long it might take you to gather the supporting documentation for a comprehensive report to senior management defending your decisions on various aspects of your project. Then imagine how your staff feels when they have to compile their reports for you.

Standards Review

As we discussed earlier in the chapter, a standard is a statement of shared expectations. When those expectations change, the team meeting is the best forum in which to create a new consensus.

Often the reevaluation of a standard is triggered by a problem reported in some area that is more directly related to the actual construction of the product. It might be a communication issue, or a delay in the schedule, or a difficulty with a tool. Whatever the original agenda item might be, an examination of the specific problem might indicate that a more general revision of the underlying standard would help prevent similar problems in the future.

For example, there might be a change request that was implemented by the developers and verified by the testers but rejected by the users. An investigation reveals that the test cases were incomplete because they did not include certain undocumented boundary conditions. To avoid such gaps in testing other functions, the team might decide that the standard for system documentation should be modified to provide more use cases and that the standard for test documentation should be modified to place a greater emphasis on boundary data.

In practice, it is difficult to obtain a unanimous agreement about any standard. Furthermore, at a staff meeting the loudest and most insistent voices are not always the wisest. In cases where you have a clear majority and a few vocal dissenters, you can adopt a let's-try-it-and-see approach and schedule a reassessment a month later. In situations where there is an even split and passionate conviction on both sides, or where a large number of true believers are too shy to speak up in front of the group, don't attempt to resolve the matter at the meeting. Tell everyone that the issue requires further consideration, and then meet with team members individually and privately to better understand their positions and explore the alternatives for a compromise.

Consultant Product Review

To make sure your consultants obtain the information they need, you should invite them to most of your team meetings. To bolster staff morale and reduce risks to the project, you should periodically hold meetings without the consultants at which the entire team evaluates the consultants' performance.

Unless they are bound by a long-term contract with your organization, any consultants you hire for your project are going to spend a substantial amount of their time trying to line up their next engagement and trying to collect the money people owe them from their previous jobs. They also will be more inclined to perform tasks and use tools that keep their skills current and make their services more marketable. Most project managers understand these realities instinctively at the beginning of the development effort. As the weeks go by and the consultants labor side-by-side with staff members, and as their faces become familiar around the coffee machine, and as their work becomes linked to and interdependent with the rest of the team's work, it is easy to forget that they are independent subcontractors.

Nevertheless, even if they don't say anything about it, your staff will always have three things in mind whenever they deal with any consultant:

- Consultants can quit at any time, leaving the rest of the project team with much more work to do and probably some nasty technical messes to clear up.
- Consultants can finish a project and walk away from an organization without ever having to face the consequences of what they've done.
- Consultants usually earn a lot more per hour than staff members.

As a result, no matter how friendly they get with the consultant personally, when the time comes for a review of the consultant's work your staff will probably have little difficulty in recognizing their own interests and being objective.

The first issue to discuss is the consultant's competence. You as project manager might have been very impressed by the consultant's resume or references. Your staff, on the other hand, will have had the opportunity to interact with the person every day, to witness his methods, to probe her knowledge. It's not unusual to discover as your project moves through its development phases that your supposed jack-of-all-trades is stronger in some areas and weaker in others. If your staff unanimously expresses disappointment with a specific skill or subject matter expertise, bring this to the consultant's attention immediately and privately. Avoid mentioning the names of the complainers because they and the consultant will probably need to continue working together for a while; behave as though you yourself noticed the problem. You should be able to negotiate some financial compensation, particularly if you're obliged to hire additional consultants to fulfill your requirements.

Communication is another point about which your staff will have better insight than you. The consultant should be outgoing enough to solicit the information he or she needs to do the job. Frequently, this means that the consultant will be bothering the wrong people at the wrong time. Such detours and dead ends are unavoidable, and a cheerful, patient disposition will help improve the consultant's chances for eventual success. The consultant should refrain from lecturing staff members about how much better things are done by his other clients: occasional tactful suggestions are fine, but your staff will soon lose patience with a pompous, condescending blowhard. Most important, the consultant should be held to the highest standard of documentation without giving the person an excuse to inflate the bill. When the consultant leaves, you should be able to tell exactly what he or she accomplished. After reading the documentation, your staff should be able to understand every line of code and repeat every task—without making any desperate phone calls. Prior to the consultant's departure, bring the documentation to your team meeting and ask the staff members who will need to rely on it to evaluate its thoroughness and accuracy.

The productivity of a consultant is sometimes hard for a project manager to discern. Status reports and time sheets do not tell the whole story: anyone with a good imagination and a glib mastery of technical jargon can puff up a minuscule effort into a stirring account of continuous progress. Your staff should be able to tell you how much of what the consultant claims to be accomplishing is of actual value to the project. Although you would not want to encourage team members to spy on each other or act like tattletales, consultants are fair game, and your staff can alert you if your high-priced hourly subcontractor is spending too much time soliciting new assignments. On the other hand, because they get jobs based on their reputation, many consultants can be far more productive than an organization's full-time staff. In particular, they may be more experienced and more accurate at estimating how long a specific task might take, and they may be willing to give your staff some helpful tips. If the consultant's productivity is significantly below your expectations, and if the person seems to be working conscientiously and intelligently, you and your staff should reconsider your estimate of the amount of time necessary for orientation and training. Ask yourselves how long it really takes for an outsider to learn enough about your organization, your user community, and your tools to make an effective contribution.

Finally, there is the question of the quality of the consultant's work. Sometimes this is obvious and needs no discussion. If the consultant writes code in a programming language with which you're not personally familiar, and the code is invoked by a user interface designed by a staff member, and if it runs against a database schema created by another staff member . . . well, you get the idea. Again, your staff may have strong opinions and reasonable criteria for judging the work. Be on the lookout, though, for hidden motivations. Your staff may hesitate to second-guess your decision: they may figure that because you hired the person, you want to hear only good things. Or the consultant's work may be so much better than theirs that they'll do whatever it takes to get rid of the threat. These situations, however, are rare. If you've demonstrated to your staff that you can tolerate their criticism and can accurately access their talents and limitations, then their evaluation should be worth considering. Act quickly to replace consultants whose work your staff views as worthless or who are a liability to the project. If you are lucky enough to end up with a consultant whose work is truly outstanding, a person who may have been trained at organizations where the software development process followed much more rigorous standards than at yours, then by all means acknowledge his or her expertise. The methods, templates, and checklists the consultant employs are as much a part of the person's work as any code or test plan or user manual he or she may create for your project. You will emphasize to your staff that you care about the quality of your product if you advise them to learn whatever they can from the consultant's example.

Team meetings are an indispensable method of sharing information, but they are also a ritual and, at times, a form of improvisational theatre. The fact that you have to hold the meetings makes it important for you to keep these other aspects in mind and use them occasionally to break the monotony and relieve the pressure, particularly during the development phase. Rituals mark the passage of time and reinforce group iden-

Figure 6.1 The scales of justice.

tity; you might create your own version of a project time line and record funny or weird stuff that happens, or you might invent frivolous ceremonies to commemorate milestones. Improvisational theatre gives people a chance to act out roles; while conducting your reviews you might suggest that members of your team play the parts of your users or IT department colleagues. The type of games and amusements you invent for your meetings will be influenced largely by the personalities in the group. As team captain, you should remember that sharing information is as much about sharing as it is about information.

Deal with Conflicts

Techies have a certain image among the general population. We're supposed to be brainy, logical, introverted, and good at solving puzzles. People imagine us working together rationally and dispassionately, like the NASA Apollo mission control team in the movies.

In reality, the movie version of our professional lives would probably resemble one of those theatrical dramas in which the entire cast is eccentric but somehow manages to put on the show despite rivalries, tantrums, fits of despair, sneaky double-crossing schemes, personal tragedies, infatuations, religious conversions, overdoses, and broken hearts. It's just that we're not as noisy about it as thespians.

Software project managers who are new to the job generally expect that they will spend their days (and nights) worrying about problems that can be analyzed with a debugger. They are invariably surprised by how much time and emotional energy they need to invest in helping the members of their team get along—especially as work loads increase and deadlines loom.

Unless you have the personal charisma of a cult leader, you won't be able to compel your staff to act like one big happy family all the time. Conflicts are bound to occur. The important thing for you as a manager is to spot those conflicts while they're still at the ruffled-feather stage and deal with them before they erupt into squawking and pecking. Experienced managers have learned to anticipate trouble in several recurring guises.

Resource Balancing

One of the biggest challenges for new project managers is to accept that you are the one who keeps things moving. If the project were an assembly line, you would have to watch out for backups that cause the process to slow down and for idle machinery kept waiting too long. In software development, the assembly line itself may be invisible, and it may contain loops or follow different paths at different stages of the project, but the principles of constant, evenly distributed productivity remain the same.

From the project manager's point of view, it would be nice if you could attach dials and gauges to people to monitor how backed up or how idle they were in their work assignments, but so far nobody has figured out how to do this. (Stay tuned for further research in bioengineering.) Inevitably during the course of the project, as dependencies change and schedules are adjusted, there are times when some team members are totally overwhelmed and others are left without much to do. This can cause conflict in a number of ways. Too-busy people get peevish, lose perspective on what's important, and assume an air of self-importance. Too-idle people become insecure about their skills, feel neglected and left out, and start criticizing other team members' work (including the project manager's) without being asked. Everyone resents everyone else and feels the situation is unfair.

The status reports you receive from your staff should alert you to any major imbalances. If you ask everyone to describe briefly their completed tasks and their resolved and open problems during the specified time period, you should get a good sense of who is tackling complex, substantive issues and who is coasting. Now and then you should review a series of reports from each person; you will learn who is capable of following through independently on long-term goals, who tends to get distracted easily, and who can be trusted only with simple, short-term tasks.

Too-busy people may, in fact, simply have many more assignments than they can handle on a reasonable work schedule. If that's the case, then you as project manager have three choices. You can redistribute some of the tasks to other team members, you can hire a consultant to help, or you can prioritize the tasks clearly and readjust the project dates to let the person work at a less demanding pace. Sometimes people are busier than they need to be—they enjoy feeling powerful and in control and indispensable to the project. Some very talented, creative people behave this way, and if you try to reduce their workload by redistributing some of their tasks they act as though you are attempting to kidnap their child. If you find you have one of these brilliant dynamos on your team, you should be appreciative and sympathetic but firm about dividing up the tasks more fairly—or else you will end up in a tug-of-war over management of the project. Finally, there are people who appear too busy but, in reality, are struggling to achieve goals that are beyond their capabilities. Realizing that your project is stuck with an underachiever is always a disappointment for a manager. Realistically, though, if your project is already well underway, your best bet is probably to keep the person on the team and assign only those tasks on which you are confident he or she can succeed. Unless you have a very long-term project or very flexible deadlines, the distraction and disruption caused by removing a team member whose only offense is being less skilled than you originally thought is hardly ever worth it.

Too-idle people require closer supervision. Their temperament or education may have conditioned them to wait to be told what to do rather than aggressively seek out activities. If so, you should explicitly instruct them to come and see you as soon as they have finished each task on their lists. They may be preoccupied by personal problems; you may need to be flexible about their schedule or work location. They may actually be much busier than they seem and have difficulty communicating what they're doing. In such cases, you can give them advice about preparing status reports and walk them through the process once or twice. If they are frequently obliged to wait for other team members to give them the material they need to work on, they might devote their free time to tasks such as performing maintenance on the change management database, auditing system documentation, or participating in peer reviews. Too-idle people who turn out to be chronically lazy—the sort of slackers who respond to nothing but threats—should be quickly and unsentimentally removed from the team.

As you work individually with your team members to balance your resources, you'll keep your finger on the pulse of the group as a whole. You won't be able to prevent deadline crunches, but you will let everyone know you care about fairness—and that will help avoid conflict. Another preventive measure you can take is to plan an occasional group expense account lunch or afternoon of recreation. A few hours of bowling or Frisbee can do wonders to restore the collective tolerance and team spirit.

Health and Environment

You know from your own experience that people work best when they feel good: healthy, alert, and comfortable. Aside from being less productive, people who are exhausted and stressed get into more fights with each other. Once in a while you should put the project plan away and go take a close look at your team and their workspace.

Obviously you're not running a spa, and it's none of your business if members of your staff stay up all night for recreational purposes. But watch out for signs of collective chronic fatigue. If, as a whole, the group appears unwashed, disheveled, and listless, you've got a problem.

Trash in the work area is another warning signal, especially empty food containers. If you notice a lot of cardboard pizza boxes, wadded-up candy wrappers, and unrecycled soda cans, then the people who work for you are not taking good enough care of themselves, and they have lost the motivation to keep the environment pleasant for others.

As the project progresses, you may encounter piles of unsorted, unfiled documents sprouting up on exposed surfaces or tangles of wires and keyboards and other miscellaneous hardware piling up in obscure corners. This sort of clutter and disorganization gradually and subliminally makes people feel as though the project is out of control—and it can cause a great deal of annoyance when somebody can't find something important. Even if in your personal life your significant other calls you a slob and your preferred style of home decor is Earthquake Aftermath, when it comes to your team's shared space in the office, you should act like a neatnik.

Tackling any of these issues requires diplomacy and a sense of humor. You certainly don't want to come right out and tell your staff that they need to do their laundry more often or that they've turned their cubicles into pigsties. A more constructive approach is to acknowledge that everyone has been working really, really hard lately . . . and in their dedication to the project they have perhaps become a bit less attentive to their own personal needs and their surroundings. And be sure to give them the time they need to clean up their act.

Human Passions

Long hours, close quarters, creative visions, fussy clients, technical breakdowns, unpredictable failures—under constant pressure, sometimes even the coolest of heads can give in to emotion and behave disruptively.

There's no need to pay much attention to the ordinary antipathies and alliances among your team. Everyone will resent it if you're too nosy. A long-running feud or an amorous liaison, though, can create severe tensions. At first, you will probably sense the strain before you have any clue about what is causing it. Direct questioning rarely helps illuminate the situation. The parties involved will not want to talk about it. The other members of the team will be reluctant to gossip about their colleagues. The Human Resources department's policies may impose strict rules about the kinds of personal matters you can discuss with your staff. As a manager, your wisest course of action is to treat the participants as adults and respect their privacy while insisting on professional behavior. Whether they're brawling in the parking lot or trysting at a nearby motel, in the office they must keep their feelings under wraps. They should avoid being alone together, treat each other strictly as teammates, and do their share of the work. If they can do all this, the project should not suffer. If they cannot, then one or both of the parties will have to go.

Cultural misunderstandings can also lead unintentionally to strife and factionalism within a team. During the past decade information technology has become a truly multicultural endeavor. The melting pot that exists only in theory in residential neighborhoods or in educational institutions is now a fact of life in many organizations where people of different races, religions, nationalities, ethnicities, and sexual orientations collaborate every day. To facilitate communication among the various groups, many organizations have instituted diversity training programs. Critics have claimed, however, that such initiatives often tend to deal in broad stereotypes and merely reinforce people's existing prejudices, offering little guidance to managers who must cope with the perceptions and habits of complex, unique human beings.

You do not have to be an anthropologist to recognize that people from different cultures possess widely varying ideals about what constitutes "good behavior." In a work environment, the variations are most evident in a few predictable areas:

- Acceptance of authority/skepticism toward authority
- Control over subordinates/empowerment of subordinates
- Observance of hierarchy/egalitarian outlook
- Assertiveness within a group/shyness within a group
- Tolerance for conflict/emphasis on harmony
- Frankness/evasiveness
- Punctuality/indifference to clock time
- Flirtatiousness/asexuality
- Mingling of genders/separation of genders
- Equality between genders/superiority of one gender
- Equality between age groups/superiority of elders or youth
- Devotion to organization/devotion to personal goals

For example, some highly confident and articulate professionals never offer an idea or contradict an opinion at a group meeting, while others regard meetings as a convenient soapbox. Some men collaborate comfortably with women, while others have great difficulty sharing information or engaging in open-minded discussions. Some young team members unconsciously defer to their older colleagues, while others unconsciously regard their elders as less productive and creative.

Inevitably, some of these differences are a matter of individual character—but character and culture are closely intertwined. If a conflict arises among the members of your team that you believe is rooted in culture, you must proceed with caution. First, reflect on your own cultural biases and preconceptions: what are your own ideals of good behavior under the circumstances in question? Then analyze what you believe to be the opponents' ideals and try to identify the variances between them. Avoid thinking in terms of labels—for example, "Because Joan is a Taiwanese Buddhist grandmother, she does X" or "Because Lev is a Ukrainian Orthodox Jewish widower, he thinks Y." Instead, focus on the specific behaviors that seem to be causing the problem. When you meet with the people, do not mention or allow to be discussed either team member's race, religion, sexual orientation, or any other element of their personal identities. Without taking sides, describe what you perceive each one is doing and tell them specifically how you would like them to change their actions.

When it comes to cultural standards, there are often no right or wrong answers. In a global, multicultural organization, the ideals prevailing in the organization's home office are usually advocated worldwide. Discerning how much of a staff member's conduct is determined by character and how much by culture is not easy, and the task becomes especially challenging when the person's job performance is unsatisfactory. If your organization's standards are unclear, or if you sense even the remote possibility of a discrimination lawsuit, you should seek advice from the Human Resources department or from experts outside the organization.

On rare occasions, a team experiences conflicts because of one member who is really a troublemaker. Typically, it takes a while for the problem to be noticed and acknowledged, and new managers are hesitant to take drastic steps that could disrupt the project. There are several types of destructive behavior that you should not tolerate:

- Compulsive lying
- Substance abuse
- Sexual harassment
- Violent temper tantrums
- Free-lancing or running an outside business during work hours
- Gambling during work hours (including day trading)

If you notice an incident or receive a complaint from another team member, don't act hastily. Gather enough evidence to make sure you know what's really going on. Once you're certain a problem exists you should resist the temptation to play psychologist. The rest of your staff will benefit more from your firmness than the benighted soul will from your ministrations. Issue two warnings, and after the third incident go to Human Resources and ask that the person be transferred or dismissed. Your team will admire and appreciate your leadership. After you have explained the situation to your client and to senior management, they should respect your judgment and your decisiveness.

Nobody enjoys conflict, especially not among people from whom there is no escape without quitting your job. Managers dread being stuck in the middle or being forced to take sides. Novice project managers often try to ignore conflicts among their team members, hoping that the storm will eventually blow over. Sooner or later, you'll encounter a situation that just keeps getting worse and worse until the project starts to suffer, and then you'll just have to hold your nose and dive in.

With experience, you can become a wise and patient adjudicator. In the process you'll learn a great deal about leadership and about yourself. Except in matters involving company policy or legal liability, Human Resources is usually not much help. Some organizations offer seminars or will send managers to classes in arbitration and mediation. For guidance you'll obtain a broader perspective and deeper insight if you consult a social worker, a psychotherapist, a spiritual advisor, or even a parent with several grown children whose judgment you trust.

Whenever you become involved in resolving a conflict, you need to be prepared for at least some temporary short-term negative vibes from one or both parties. It's one of the burdens of leadership: not everyone is going to like you all the time.

Milestone Marker

The role of Team Captain during the development phase requires enthusiasm and stamina. The beginning of the project is exciting because everything is new and everyone is full of high hopes. The product launch is exciting because—well, it's the launch. In contrast, the development phase in between is not exciting. You may have moments of creative breakthrough, or hair-raising crises, or an especially enjoyable group lunch now and then, but most of the time it's just work. And the team captain needs to keep the players motivated through those long stretches of sustained effort.

With athletes, it's the love of the game that carries them along. With techies, it's the love of the craftsmanship. In their hearts, beneath their cynicism, your developers and testers really want to build something terrific. You show them that you understand this when you insist that they maintain standards, share information, and resolve conflicts. You encourage and inspire them when you remind them of those four Cs: the collective commitment to craftsmanship and cooperation. Your leadership sometimes consists simply of making them believe they can do it.

Toward the end of the development phase, your product will seem to acquire a life of its own. Even as your team is still fixing the last bugs and running the regression tests, your attention will begin to shift to the rollout. After a certain point, you'll all feel like a father-to-be watching over your eight-months-pregnant wife. Then making arrangements for the deployment of the product will suddenly become rather urgent . . .

CHAPTER 7

Step Right Up, Ladies and Gentlemen . . .

Being the circus ringmaster isn't all about wearing a snazzy top hat and red frock coat and making flowery, amplified speeches—no, indeed. Behind the glamour and the thrill are lots of worries. Was the trapeze artists' net repaired in time? Will the immigration cops arrest the acrobat family whose visas have expired? Will the clowns' smoke machine explode today?

Software project managers may dress less flamboyantly, but at the time of a product launch you might very well feel like a ringmaster in many other ways. In your role as an Entrepreneur, you have to figure out how to promote your product, focus your users' attention, and perform damage control all at the same time. You'll need to manage your users' expectations so that their only surprises are pleasant ones. You'll want to arrange enough publicity to make the users curious, but not so much that you're perceived as squandering resources or making too big a deal out of a routine event. You'll try your best to ensure that every user receives appropriate training so that you're playing to a full house.

Showmanship is not a character trait generally associated with technology professionals, but deep down there's a little P.T. Barnum in all of us. Get ready to unleash your inner impresario.

Figure 7.1 The ringmaster.

Manage Expectations

The larger your project, the greater the chances that when the final, ultimate, nonnegotiable deadline arrives you won't have finished coding and testing all the features you originally promised. Despite everyone's best efforts, you're simply not ready.

In many cases, this situation is really not the project team's fault. Here are some examples of circumstances beyond your control:

- Your product required new servers, and senior management didn't approve the purchase until four months after you expected they would.
- A major component of your system architecture isn't working properly yet—maybe it's losing records when it replicates data tables—and although you've been working closely with the component's vendor to figure out why, you still don't have an answer.
- Your users couldn't agree on the design specifications for certain functions in time for you to implement them.
- There was a reorganization in your user community that drastically changed the product's workflow.
- A law was passed mandating that certain types of data should be gathered—or should not be gathered—and the design specifications for your product needed to be altered for compliance.

- Performance testing revealed that when you finally integrated all the components into the production environment response time was unacceptably slow.
- An important member of your team quit unexpectedly.

While it's certainly preferable to keep one's commitments, you should bear in mind that this sort of crisis occurs quite often in the software development industry—it has probably happened to your client in the past. Don't get depressed or take it out on your team. Experienced project managers have learned that there are strategies for dealing with meeting impossible deadlines.

Triage

Everyone on your team sees how much work is left to be done before the deadline. Spurred by their professional pride, your developers are going to want to cram in as much functionality as they can. They will try to persuade you to let them keep on coding until the very last second before they have to move the product into the production environment.

Although this may be fine for college term papers, in software development it causes more harm than good. Your role as a project manager under these circumstances is to remind your developers that they are a part of a team and their efforts are a part of a process.

The time for you and your team to acknowledge that you are not going to be able to deliver everything you promised is before the last cycle of integration testing. You should make it clear that your client will not want to accept a slapped-together hodge-podge of untested algorithms; nor will your developers want to maintain and enhance a rickety code base. It is far better for everyone concerned if you build a smaller product that actually works.

Scaling back, though, is not a matter of crossing items off a list. Disabling partially implemented functions requires analysis and redesign. The data flow might change. So might the user interface or report layouts. Even graying out an inactive field on a screen or printing "NA" in a column on an exported spreadsheet takes some effort. When large sections of code get commented out, there is an increased risk of memory leaks and system crashes.

Inevitably, these kinds of changes make testers unhappy. Just as the developers have to modify their system design and revise their code, your testers need to update their test plans, test cases, and test data. They feel much more pressure to locate errors and weaknesses in a product whose altered characteristics they're given very little time to understand.

Therefore, the triage process should have two steps. The first step begins with a meeting at which the entire team reviews the condition of the product to date and the amount of time left in the schedule. The developers identify the missing features that can be eliminated or reduced with the least impact on the main purpose of the product. They discuss the technical details of how they think they would modify the user interface, the reports, and the code to stitch the patient back together after the organs have been removed. Of course, they will want to undo as little of their work as possible, but you should press them to come up with more cutbacks than are absolutely necessary to meet the deadline and alternative sets of interrelated functions to excise.

Once the developers have run out of ideas, it's the testers' turn to take the floor. For each of the revisions the developers proposed, the testers estimate the impact on quality assurance efforts. Often there are different methods of disabling program functions and rerouting data, and if developers understand the issues each one raises for testing they may be able to choose the approach that minimizes the effort for the team overall.

At the end of step 1, you should emerge from the meeting with a prioritized list of changes. Yet this list was distilled out of nothing more than a brainstorming session. Step 2 involves confirming your guesstimates.

As everyone leaves the meeting, emphasize to the developers that you don't want anyone changing any code until they have thoroughly investigated the consequences of their suggestions. Any experiments they wish to perform for the investigation should be conducted using a separate, temporary copy of the code—and likewise for the test-ware. The time allotted for the investigation shouldn't be too long (how could it be, with that fire-breathing deadline galloping toward you?), but it should be at least overnight so that the members of your team have a chance to sleep on it and contemplate the wisdom of their ideas outside the office environment.

At the follow-up meeting, your developers and testers finalize the technical details, time estimates, and priorities for the abridgement plan. To this meeting you should also invite your documentation writer and training developer because changes to the product's workflow and user interface will inevitably affect their efforts. Although the screen images, hyperlinks, and text in the user documentation and training materials have to be updated to reflect the changes, the interdependencies are not as complex as with program code and test cases, and the time estimates should be far less than for development and testing.

The triage process should provide you with several viable product designs and alternative strategies for delivering them on or near the immovable deadline. In practice, this exercise in collective problem solving often improves the team's morale dramatically and puts fresh wind into everyone's sails. Yet, once again, as project manager you may have to restrain the staff from immediately rushing out and acting on the group's recommendations. Up to this point, an important participant has been left out of the discussions: your client.

Types of Launch

If you've been communicating regularly with your client, the necessity of making a few trade-offs to meet the deadline should come as no surprise. When you break the news, there will still be some time before the actual rollout date. Your team will need that time for final coding, testing, and creating the production version. As a precaution, you should be prepared to explain to your client in detail why it's not feasible to keep on coding until an hour before the launch. In your desire to please or placate your client, do not compromise your process. If you do, both your team and your users will regret it later. If you're forced to, write a level-headed and even-tempered memo about the risks you foresee, distribute it to your client, and store it with the project documentation.

After your client has finished throwing a tantrum, you should present three alternatives:

Full launch. You can deliver a buggy, incomplete product on time, or you can push back the deadline and deliver a product that meets the requirements.

"Soft" launch. You can deliver a buggy, incomplete product on time, but make sure that nobody actually uses it. If there is an old product that your product is meant to replace, delay the cutover of the live data. If your product is brand new, display a message on the main menu or home page that indicates that this is a trial version. The decision to go ahead with a soft launch is often made for political reasons; for example, if the client knows his or her bonus depends on the on-time release of the complete product, but also knows that senior management won't read the fine print closely or pay much attention to how long it takes for the cutover to finally occur.

Phased launch. You can deliver a reliable but abridged version of the product on time and incorporate the missing features into the next release.

Experience eventually teaches most clients and project managers that a phased launch is the least of the available evils, so you should strongly recommend this strategy. Show your client the alternative designs and schedules your team has prepared. Faced with the prospect of eliminating features, your client may have different priorities than you anticipated. If this is the case, go back to your team and ask them to research the implications for the code, the testware, the user documentation, and training materials before you make any final commitments to your client.

Disclosure

You may be months behind schedule, and the product you're about to launch may not have all the wonderful features your team first dreamed of (at least not yet). Your client may have ignored your advice and chosen the full launch or the "soft" launch. Nevertheless, you want your team to feel proud of the work they've done. You also want your users to know exactly what they're getting.

Once you and your client have determined the final contents of version 1.0, no matter how you feel about it personally, you should act as though it's a great product. In all your announcements and communications you should adopt a positive, enthusiastic tone. List the features and describe how they work as though they all perfectly meet the original design specifications.

You should also explain matter of factly what the product doesn't do. If the code hasn't been written yet to handle certain exceptions to the rules or infrequent use cases, or if there are errors and problems you already know about, alert your user community and senior management to these situations before they find out themselves. Don't hide the information in eight-point type in a footnote to the user documentation. Simply tell people what they should expect.

The way to acknowledge that the product isn't done yet is to simultaneously publish your plans for enhancing it. If major features are missing, list them as scheduled for release in the next version. Be careful about specifying the version number or the projected release date. Although you and your client may have come to a private understanding about the development schedule for the next release during your negotiations over the features to be included in version 1.0, these plans almost always change after the product is actually in the hands of the users. No matter how carefully you've analyzed the workflow and the requirements, once the product is a fact of your users' lives they will surprise you with new inspirations, needs, and priorities. If you commit yourself in writing to a rigid timetable of deliverables and dates, you'll probably just have to retract it later. Be as vague as you can without seeming evasive: if you're questioned aggressively, tell people that you're deliberately keeping your plans flexible to better respond to users' needs.

Above all, as you manage expectations you and your team should bear in mind that reactions to your product will be mixed, no matter what you deliver. Focusing on what the product does well and what you all have accomplished together helps to provide the momentum and the *esprit de corps* to carry you through the rollout.

Create a Buzz

The launch of a new software product is hardly the sort of event people get excited about these days—not unless you're a hard-core gamer breathlessly awaiting the latest creation from a master of a genre. Truly revolutionary products like Linux or Napster tend to creep up slowly and take the world by surprise. In a work environment, new software often ranks lower in human interest scores than a new coffee machine.

From the project manager's point of view, marketing and publicity may seem unnecessary. Why bother selling the product to the users if they're going to have to use it anyway? Besides, if it's any good won't people appreciate it for its own qualities, not because they've been manipulated by a media campaign?

Ironically, the main reason you should devote some effort and resources to the promotion of your product is that your users have no choice. Most people dislike change (even though studies have shown something new in the environment causes us to become more engaged in our work and temporarily more productive). Except for the select groups who have been collaborating with your project team, your users are probably disposed to regard the rollout of your product more as an annoyance than a joyous event. Yes, they may have to use it, but they may not be inclined to use it correctly or appropriately. The intrinsic qualities of your product may be as imperceptible as the beauties of a landscape surrounding a conference center where the visitors are attending an obligatory sales meeting.

Promoting your product is a way of acknowledging your users' contribution to making the rollout a success. It lets them know that you are aware of their reluctance to change their habits and that you care about their opinions. Think of it as a form of recruitment.

Timing

Movie producers learned long ago that the best way to get people talking about a soon-to-be-released film is to show brief glimpses if it a few weeks in advance. Of course, your previews probably won't feature loud explosions or beautiful people locked in a passionate embrace, but you can pique your users' curiosity with demos and posters

Figure 7.2   Excess ruckus?

that show a couple of vivid screen shots alongside some well-crafted quotes from your beta testers, your client, perhaps even some humorous, made-up critics.

Several days before the rollout, you'll want to remind your users of what's in store for them. This gives them a chance to plan ahead and set aside time to become familiar with the product and any new workflow they may need to learn. If the launch involves any conversion of old data, the warning reminds them that they should finish any incomplete data entry tasks before the old system is shut down.

On the day of the launch you're entitled to a fanfare. Be as creative and entertaining as you can within the norms of your organization's culture. But don't overdo it—senior management may not be pleased if the juggler you hire to show how many new tasks your product enables your users to juggle instead distracts people from their work for more than 15 minutes. In addition to being clever, your announcement should describe the major features of your product and the improvements it will bring to your users' lives. Be sure to thank your client, your product manager, all the users who helped you, and your project team individually and by name.

A week or two after your product has been rolled out, contact your user community again. Acknowledge any major problems that have occurred, and thank everyone for their patience while your team resolved them. Emphasize that you are very interested in users' comments, complaints, and suggestions. Describe the communications procedures you have set up for reporting problems and making change requests. By the time your users receive this message, most of them will probably be just at the point of deciding what they like and what they don't like about your product, and it will establish the relationship for active, ongoing dialogue.

Media

Circus acts aren't the only way to get your users' attention. In any event, no matter how much fun they may be to plan and stage, wacky publicity stunts need to be reserved for very special occasions.

Here are a few lower-voltage (and lower-budget) methods of announcing your intentions:

Posters. Hang big, colorful posters with enlarged screen shots and minimal text on bulletin boards in your users' work areas. Put them up a week before your launch, and take them down a week afterward. In terms of content, they can be more decorative and eye-catching than informative because at the time of the rollout you will provide detailed explanations and instructions.

Trinkets. Hats, T-shirts, key chains, mugs—all that junk they give away at trade shows is relatively inexpensive to order in bulk. Have it delivered to your users the day before the rollout.

Handouts. Assign someone to stand at the entrance to the cafeteria or parking lot on launch day and distribute fliers. The page can provide some basic information about your product, but people will consider it less of a nuisance if you present your message in the form of a puzzle, word game, or other diversion. The idea is to give your users something entertaining to pass the time in the cafeteria or toll-booth line or to work on with their kids when they get home.

Many of the more serious forms of publicity cost nothing at all:

E-mail messages. E-mail does not have to consist of single-spaced text with bullet points. Of course, when you're sending your users the official announcement that describes the product's functions, answers the Frequently Asked Questions, and lists all known bugs, your format ought to be sober and straightforward. Advance notices and follow-up messages, however, can display more creativity. The dancing musical dragon that pops up every Chinese New Year in mailboxes around the world is a good example of balancing cleverness and dignity. Constructing these messages is a worthwhile task for your developers when you notice they're starting to get cranky and frazzled from working too hard on serious deliverables.

System messages. No matter what platform your product will run on, you probably have the ability (with the help of the database or system administrator) to display a message anytime on your user's screens. The best time for any message regarding your product to appear is when the user logs on to the network, a database server, an application, or the organization's internal Web site home page. The message should be short and relatively urgent; for example, it could be a reminder that your product is going to be launched the following day. Avoid the temptation to send any kind of instant messages that distract your users while they are working. If you communicate with your users via instant messaging, they will soon hold you and your project team in the same low esteem as telephone solicitors who interrupt their dinners, their showers, and other intimate moments at home.

Voice mail messages. A broadcast voice mail message from your client on the day of the rollout is like the bottle of champagne breaking over the ship's bow as it glides into the water. It acknowledges that your team has created something new that is worth noticing and emphasizes your client's support.

Every organization has its own traditions. After a couple of months, even start-up companies develop their own quirky customs. Balloons, relay races, barbershop quartets—from a distance they may all look silly, but they serve an important purpose in forging a group identity and making workers feel appreciated as human beings. Most computer software in the workplace is not intrinsically fun to use, but if you can make your product launch an occasion when your users indulge in some of your organization's favorite recreational pastimes—and take home souvenirs—you'll build up a reservoir of good will you can draw on during any crises you may encounter.

Coordination

"This all sounds great," says the novice project manager, "but it's really *not my job*." Compared to writing project plans and refereeing disputes between developers and testers, publicizing the product and ordering toys for your users are unquestionably lower priorities.

If you have an idea of what you want to do and you present it to your client early enough, you may be surprised by the amount of support and assistance you receive. Good managers are always on the lookout for opportunities to strengthen their teams and boost morale. The rollout of your product is a group event in your user community that provides an excellent reminder of their identity and purpose. Because the funds for the publicity will come out of the project's budget, you'll have to ask your client for approval of any noteworthy expenditures. Even if you're opting for the lowest-cost alternatives, you should discuss your plans with your client and product manager to ensure that they like the content and tone.

Delegate as much of the creative and administrative work and the event planning as you can to your product manager. In the period between the end of beta testing and the beginning of the rollout, product managers often have little to do except worry. Focusing on publicity will help keep him or her occupied with useful tasks while you deal with the technical details.

In many organizations the marketing department or the internal communications staff can serve as consultants in this area. Don't hesitate to ask their advice: they're the pros. They can give you cost estimates. They may already have contracts that will save you money with vendors of promotional trinkets, printers who make posters, T-shirt outlets, caterers, or skywriters. They also can help you design your materials and write your text so that you get your message across quickly, succinctly, and memorably.

Schedule Training

During development, you analyzed your users' training needs. You created scripts based on the activities of each user type. You evaluated the advantages and drawbacks of demos, classes, and tutorials, and you decided to what extent each medium would be appropriate for your project. You produced the training materials and made arrangements to train the trainers. Now it's not just your product that's ready for deployment—it's your training plan, too.

"Do I Have to Go?"

Why is it that no matter how far in advance you schedule training, something more urgent always comes up at the last minute? Even users who understand that they do need training and are eager to attend often find themselves torn between long-term educational goals and short-term problem solving. You can't be personally offended or hold it against them if they don't show up; you would do (and may even have done) the same.

The only way you're going to be sure your trainers won't be playing to an empty house is to have your client make it absolutely clear to the entire user community that attendance is required. This means that your client must compile a list of all the people who should receive training. It also means that your trainers need to take attendance and forward the list of participants to you and the product manager. You can enforce this procedure by activating each user's logon only after he or she has completed training. If your product is a more open system that does not employ security logons, you can achieve the same result by coding a first-time access key into the setup script.

In some organizations an edict from on high is still not enough to compel users to put their work aside and go for training. Rightly or wrongly, some people just assume they can figure things out faster by themselves. When pressed for an explanation, these folks always have a well-reasoned, compelling excuse for why the ship would sink if they left their post at that particular moment.

Ultimately, whether the users receive training is your client's problem, not yours. On the other hand, poorly trained users make too many support calls and submit too many unnecessary problem reports, thereby creating difficulties for your product manager and your project team. If attendance at your training sessions is consistently low, you might suggest that your client consider offering incentives. For software products that support an organization's essential functions, attending training is often incorporated into the user's job requirements and reviewed during their performance evaluation.

Even with your client's full support and your users' enthusiastic cooperation, some of the best-laid plans go awry. People get sick, including the trainers; legitimate crises arise; equipment fails; scheduling mix-ups occur. To plan for adequate coverage, over-budget by at least 25 percent. If you think you can train all your users in four classes, plan five. If you expect to give ten demos, allocate time and resources for another three. Then when users call up with their excuses and sob stories you won't panic or lose your temper; instead you can just shrug and cheerfully reschedule them.

There will always be some users who, despite your best efforts, will not be able to attend a training class that coincides with your product launch. This may happen because of the following reasons:

- They are on a long-term expedition to a remote area of the globe.
- They spend most of their lives on airplanes traveling between sales calls.
- They are taking parental or family leave.
- They are receiving medical treatment on long-term disability.

For these folks, your tutorial will have to suffice to get them started. In the first week following the release or following their return to the job, your product manager should personally call them to make sure that they have done the tutorial and that they have learned what they need to know.

Logistics

Planning, scheduling, and delivering training can be a major effort. To save time and reduce costs, consider alternative ways to subdivide your user community:

Location. How widely dispersed are your users? Does it make more sense to bring them all to one place for training or to send a trainer to each separate location? If you send your trainer on tour, how much work will need to be done to set up the training facilities at each location? Do users perform different tasks at different locations, and if so, is your trainer aware of the variations?

Security level. How many levels of security are there? Is it advisable for each security level to be trained separately, or is the risk insignificant if users with lower-level access are given a tour of the higher-level functions? Does the trainer know how much information can be disclosed to each group during question-and-answer sessions? Will participants in the training be required to display a photo ID so that only authorized users are allowed in the room?

Roles. How many different roles do users play within the system? Would it be more effective to train all the data entry clerks, or all the sales agents, or all the warehouse inventory inspectors at once—or should you mix users with different roles together so that they have a better understanding of the workflow? If you choose to train one role at a time, does the data need to be prepared in advance so that the users can perform the same tasks they will be doing with the production system?

Arranging the training environment in advance can prevent delays and frustration. As anyone knows who has ever given a presentation using any technology more complex than a whiteboard, the process of setting up the equipment can sometimes turn even the most experienced public speaker into a sweaty, foul-tempered wreck by the time the first audience member walks in. For software demos and classes, the potential problems can be compounded by the complexities of the system architecture. Not only does the trainer need to make the projector work, the computer turn on, and the program run, he or she may also have to connect to the network, and/or the Internet, and/or a remote server. For classroom training, these variables are multiplied by the number of machines in the room; in addition, the machines all have to be configured the same way. Just when the trainer thinks everything is going to work fine, when the entire class has been able to start the program and log in to the application and display the Web page and connect to the server, the queries and exercises can suddenly fail because an administrator forgot to grant permissions to the student user IDs in the training database.

Whether your organization boasts an official training department and well-equipped classroom facilities or resorts to commandeering conference rooms and borrowing users' machines, you'll probably have to supervise the logistics if you want the job done right. Ideally, your product manager should take on as much of the actual work as possible, with you issuing instructions, providing guidance, and checking results. For example, the product manager could do the following:

- Create the schedule
- Select the participants
- Review the choice of training materials
- Reserve the space
- Devise the sign-in procedures and ID verification
- Brief the trainer on the plans
- Order the projector and screen or other equipment
- Confirm the proper setup and connectivity of the training machines

Even if you are lucky enough to have a product manager who can handle all these tasks effortlessly, your project team should still expect to assume some responsibility for the back-end environment. You may need to create a setup script that alters the computer's registry or resets system options to point to a special training server and database. Your permissions repository might have to be expanded to include reusable student names, logon IDs, and passwords. A few hours before the first training session it is a good idea to schedule a quick rehearsal involving the trainer, the project manager, and yourself, plus your team on standby alert. Immediately after the first training session it is very helpful to jot down a checklist documenting all the preparations you discovered were necessary.

Phases

Training evolves. Like a performer honing a nightclub act, you will find out through experience that what you think you should say to your users isn't always what they want or need to hear.

By the time you're ready to roll out your product, most of the basic decisions about the content and format of your training will already have been made, and it will be too late for major changes. Even though the manual may have been printed, the CD cut, and the tutorial coded, you can still fine-tune your presentation.

The first phase of training is the previews. Take a hint from the movie industry: schedule your early coming-attraction demos in out-of-the-way places and invite junior staff. Observe where they start to doze off, where they perk up and pay attention, where they seem confused. Interview some of the audience members afterward, and probe their reactions. Gradually work your way up the organization chart and in toward headquarters, modifying the presentation as you go.

The next phase is your full-scale training initiative. These demos or classes should be scheduled intensively as close as possible to the release date, given the limitations of human trainers who occasionally need to eat and sleep and recover from jet lag. The goal of "just-in-time" training is that students should be able to begin applying what they have learned as soon as they return to their desks; if they are obliged to wait a week, they will have forgotten too much. This type of training assumes that everyone is starting out together as beginners, so it is comprehensive and exhaustive (and sometimes exhausting for both trainees and trainers alike). Though there is rarely time for structured observations and interviews, trainers do make many modifications in the curriculum as they go along, especially if they notice consistent patterns of response among their audiences. Because their changes tend to be recorded as scribbled notes in the margins of their manual or script, ask your trainers to document them and recommend revisions after the blitz is over.

The last phase is the routine you adopt once your users are accustomed to your product. Training becomes necessary then only when new people are hired and when you roll out new versions with significant changes. The scope of the training can be much narrower because new users will have experienced colleagues to help them and new features will be extensions of a well-understood model. At this stage, the evolutionary changes you make will consist of determining the amount of information you should include and updating the scripts to reflect new user behavior.

A final word of advice about training: no matter how busy you get during the product launch, make sure you get a chance to watch each of your trainers in action. It should take only about 10 minutes for you to evaluate how the person performs and how the audience is responding. An inept trainer can leave your users more confused than no trainer at all. A skillful trainer is a valuable addition to your team and a good will ambassador for your product.

Milestone Marker

A software project manager's first product launch is a time of high anxiety. A circus ringmaster can take consolation in the fact that whatever happens under the tent or in the arena, the audience will go home afterward and the performers will get another chance the following day. Your audience, however, will be with you for a long, long time.

During the rollout phase the project manager's entrepreneurial role focuses on the users' initial impressions. When you shape their expectations, create publicity, and arrange their training, you establish a favorable environment for your product to enter their work lives. Initial impressions are, of course, only the beginning. Whereas circus acts are short and disconnected and evanescent, your deployment is a complex process with many interdependent functions—and it delivers something far more lasting. If you feel a panic attack coming on the night before your launch, remember this: you have much longer than a ringmaster does to win your audience over.

How well you coordinate the process and integrate the functions of the rollout will determine your users' opinion of your product after those brief initial impressions. The next chapter will provide advice on methods you can employ to evoke a bravura performance from all participants.

CHAPTER 8

The Conductor Taps the Baton

Your project team is like a jazz band. It's small enough that all the members know each other well. During the development phase you've become attuned to each other's styles, and you can improvise. As project manager, you're in charge of the schedule and the repertoire; you lead the band in composing new pieces, and perhaps you even keep the beat. You're a creative ensemble. You're *tight*.

For a product launch the stage is larger and the group is more like an orchestra. The score is set, divided into parts for different instruments. The database administrators and the network operations staff aren't assigned the same tasks, but they have to come in at the right moment and execute their functions harmoniously according to the plan. In your Technology Partner role, you determine that during the deployment the program will feature three works: coordinating the environment changes, testing the production system, and tracking your users' problems and questions. Although the participants know what to do as individuals, they all look to the conductor for cues and for tempo. That, of course, would be the project manager. Your podium and spotlight await.

Coordinate Environment Changes

The launch of your first software product is undoubtedly a big day for you and your team, but for the rest of the IT department it's business as usual. Like your users, your technology colleagues are hoping for as little disruption as possible. They're also keep-

Figure 8.1 Maestro!

ing their eye on you, evaluating your capabilities and management style under stress. To obtain their cooperation and establish yourself as a worthy peer, take their requirements and schedules into account when you introduce your product into the existing environment.

Impact on the Environment

Throughout development, your team should have been keeping track of changes in the technology infrastructure of your organization. You should have rehearsed your deployment so that everyone on your team and elsewhere in the IT department knows what to expect. The final phase of any project just prior to rollout is typically a very hectic time, and it can cause a project team to develop a temporary case of tunnel vision. While preparing your user acceptance test, it's a good idea to take one last look around at your environment before you send your product out to fend for itself. Your checklist might include these items:

- Review the operations procedures
- Find out the schedules for backup and maintenance tasks
- Make sure the server space is still available
- Verify that the database software version is still the same as yours
- Check the available bandwidth on your network
- Determine the current standard configuration for desktop and laptop computers and other user interface devices
- Confirm the amount of free space on your average user's machine

Next inspect the upstream and downstream systems to which your product will link. Contact the appropriate project managers and determine whether there have been any changes in data feeds. Perhaps the file format might have been altered, or new fields added, the database moved to a different server, or different configuration settings applied. If your users plan to export data from your product to document templates, spreadsheets, or other applications, do a quick survey to ascertain that they haven't upgraded their versions while you weren't watching.

If you will be depending on a Help Desk to field any support calls, reacquaint yourself with their methods and any software they might use for tracking call data. Obtain the names of any service technicians who are assigned to support your user community.

Finally, update your contact list. Considering the high turnover in the IT departments of most organizations, it's a good bet that more than one of the people who were managing the environment at the beginning of your project have now left. If you're lucky, their positions will have already been filled, and their replacements will have learned enough about their new jobs to be helpful and reliable.

In the event that your environmental impact study reveals a change potentially affecting your product, you'll need to put the brakes on your deployment until you determine the actual consequences. First summon the team member you designated as configuration coordinator and ask for an explanation of why he or she failed to bring the matter to your attention earlier. Then call an emergency team meeting to review whether your product must be modified—and if so, how. Contact the project or service manager responsible for the product or function causing the conflict and attempt to work out a solution. The worst-case scenario is that you'll have to delay the rollout, update your project plan, and schedule another round of coding and system testing.

Expansion of the Project Team

All of the people on your contact list are now on your project team, at least temporarily for the duration of the rollout. They, however, may not know it—and the regular members of your team probably don't know all of them. Everyone may have seen each other once or twice when you rehearsed the deployment, but during the rollout you'll need to work closely together, especially if any problems arise.

You can facilitate this process by publishing and distributing a Who's Who directory. It should contain everyone on your project team and everyone who will have anything to do with the product launch: their names, numbers, locations, phone numbers, e-mail addresses, beeper numbers, and work schedules. For every job function, it should list backup contacts and indicate the escalation procedures if the designated technician encounters a situation that he or she cannot or should not handle. E-mail the file to every participant, and place a copy in your documentation library.

After you've compiled the directory, it helps if you can get everyone together once for an orientation and final walk-through. In some organizations you might encounter resistance from the IT infrastructure managers. Even if they don't say it in so many words, their attitude can be, "Don't bother us. What are you worried about? We do this all the time." Well, they may, but your team doesn't, at least not yet. Emphasize that you're new at this, and try to get them at least to send a representative.

At the orientation, review the plans you prepared earlier during the development phase when your project team rehearsed the deployment. Ask all of your colleagues to confirm their roles, tasks, and availability. What comes out of these meetings are usually issues of scheduling and control. Not everyone may be aware, for example, that your projected rollout date may be Ocean Day in Japan or All Saints Day in Spain and those offices will be closed. Or that a new security patch is being installed on the remote access server then. Or that the entire Help Desk staff was planning a team-building retreat, leaving the phones in the hands of a college intern. If there are conflicts over priorities, the walk-through meeting is the place to resolve them calmly and rationally—rather than during a conference call in the middle of the night while deployment is in progress.

Special Documentation

Based on the information you gather from the discussions during the orientation, create a procedures guide. Don't assume that everyone knows what he or she is supposed to do and in what order. Even after people sit around a table together and review the tasks they perform on a regular basis, they may neglect to leave adequate instructions for their backup if they are absent unexpectedly. You as project manager should understand all the steps involved in building, installing, or reconfiguring the environment so that your product can reach your users. If a problem occurs and you're trying to figure out how much your schedule is going to slip, you will certainly want to know whether the failure interrupted a process at the very beginning or when it was almost done.

As the clock counts down to rollout, probably the last thing anyone wants to do is spend time reviewing the contents of yet another document. Yet the activity is valuable for an important reason besides the information conveyed. By insisting that they put the details in writing, you are in effect obtaining a commitment from your technology partners that they will perform certain services for your project. Your operations staff, your database administrators, your network technicians, your system administrators, your technical support staff, and your Help Desk coordinator may not be accustomed to thinking in those terms—and many organizations take a dim view of formal interdepartmental service agreements as an impediment to teamwork. Even if they know you're not going to file a lawsuit or hire a thug to smash their car windows or do anything beyond complain to senior management if they let you down, people do take written commitments more seriously that verbal promises. As a novice project manager, chances are you need all the clout you can get.

If any portion of your environment is managed by an outside vendor such as an Internet Service Provider (ISP), the rollout procedures guide is not merely a nice-to-have document: it's a must. In fact, the vendor should already possess a standard template, and it should expect your project team to collaborate with it on customizing the guide. If it turns out that the vendor does not regard this deliverable as part of its basic service to you, make sure you put it on your list of demands for your next round of contract negotiations.

Deployment Project Plan

From the information in the procedures guide, prepare a special project plan for the deployment. It need not show every single task listed in the procedures guide, but it should break down the processes to a level of detail at which every dependency is clear. It should indicate not only who is responsible for performing each task, but also where the checkpoints are and who is assigned to verify compliance before the next task can proceed. While your regular project plan measures time in days and weeks, the deployment project plan will normally have a timetable scheduled down to hours.

It's probably not necessary for you to arrange another interdepartmental meeting to distribute and discuss the deployment project plan, but if you send it to everyone via e-mail it's a good idea to turn on the confirmation feature that informs you whether the recipient opened the message—and call the folks who don't. Simultaneously, you should announce that you are going to deputize one of your developers or testers to serve as distribution coordinator. Explain to everyone that the coordinator will assume responsibility for maintaining and updating the Who's Who directory, the rollout procedures guide, and the deployment project plan. He or she will be in charge of the actual logistics of the launch, supervising the execution of the tasks on the project plan and the verification of the results. Following the rollout, the coordinator will become the team's designated troubleshooter for any problems involving the delivery of the product or the users' access to it.

A few days before the launch, review the final version of the deployment project plan at a team meeting. Most of the names in the Verified By column will belong to members of your team, and some of them may be surprised by the amount of involvement they have in the process. There's also an almost ceremonial aspect to the presentation of this final project plan. Members of the group tend to glance around at each other and take a deep breath, as in, "Yikes, this is really happening!" It's a bit like the moment when one first sees one's own wedding invitations or receives the actual tickets for a long-dreamed-of adventurous trip. If you watch carefully, you'll see a current of psychic energy pass through your team. This is good: It will help keep everyone powered up for the challenges ahead.

Test the Production System

After all the files have been copied and the configurations set, the last step of the deployment is to make sure everything works before you let the users have a go at it. By the time you reach this stage everyone will be eager to declare victory and head home. It will be tempting to log on, add a couple of records, print something, and give the product a thumbs-up. But hold on—you're not quite done yet.

Test Plan

Don't trust your memory or your instincts at a time like this. A reliable test needs a test plan, with test cases and test data. It doesn't have to be a complete regression test, but neither should it be your "smoke test" that you use on new builds to determine whether they're robust enough to be worth testing.

The test plan should include at least one iteration of end-to-end data flow. If your users are in multiple locations, and especially if they are in different offices around the world, some data should be input at each location. If your product is a new system but is using data that has been converted from a legacy system you're replacing, make sure you create some test cases that input entirely new records, some of which manipulate converted records and some of which combine new and legacy data elements.

As you construct the test plan, remember to incorporate tasks that are performed by users with different levels of security access—from the lowest read-only user right up through the super-administrator who can create and modify other users' permissions. Pay particular attention to steps in the workflow where another user's electronic approval is required before the data can keep moving (such as a publishing system where an editor must review a document before it is posted on a Web site), or else in a day or two you may get a frantic phone call from a manager reporting a backlog of records in someone's queue.

Because you're now on the production system, it's preferable to run your final tests using real data. If you have a well-designed test plan, this probably means you can't just grab the first piece of paper off a user's input pile and start keyboarding. Show your test cases to your product manager, and ask the users to provide you with real data that fits your specifications. In the event this turns out to be impossible, be absolutely certain that you understand the consequences of entering invalid data into the production database. Someone with adequate security access will be obliged to go into the database at the end of your test and delete it; otherwise, you might see some rather peculiar entries on your public Web site!

Participants

Remember the story about painting a fence told by Mark Twain in *Tom Sawyer*? For those who may have forgotten or may not have had the pleasure of reading this American classic, the scene takes place when Tom's stern Aunt Polly asks the mischievous adolescent to spend a beautiful summer Saturday afternoon whitewashing her fence. At first Tom is very unhappy. But then, showing great promise as a future project manager, he has an inspiration. He begins to act as though he really enjoys the work, and he pretends that skill in fence painting is a talent bestowed on only the very few. Before long, the other boys in his town are lining up to trade him their valuable possessions (marbles, firecrackers, tadpoles) in exchange for a turn with the brush.

Your users are not likely to be as gullible as Tom's playmates. Their participation in the final test is highly desirable, if not essential. You don't want them trying to bribe you with their paperweights and staple removers, but you might present the opportunity to be involved in the final test to a few of them as an honor attainable only via recommendation. This results in a much more agreeable and enthusiastic bunch than if they have been recruited involuntarily and told they must make themselves available on Sunday night between 2 and 4 a.m.

The most qualified users for this procedure are beta testers who have demonstrated that they possess a predator's eye for defects, a drone's compliant attitude about following instructions, and a homicide detective's attention to detail in describing observed results. Before you approach them, check with Human Resources to make sure their presence won't raise any insurmountable issues of security, overtime pay, or union rules. If any of your users will be testing the production system from remote offices in other countries, remember to ask about the logistics and restrictions in each location.

If you decide you don't want your users around at this stage, or if their participation will cost a lot or require impossibly complex special arrangements, your developers and testers can take their place. This will probably be necessary if any of the permission levels or tasks in the workflow are reserved for management. But your product manager should certainly be at your side throughout the final tests, and so should any users who will play the role of system administrator.

Down Time

Perhaps your product is a new, standalone database and has no upstream or downstream connections. If it is, your rollout will be relatively simple with regard to infrastructure—once you've confirmed the files are loaded, the configurations are set, and the final test executes as planned you can turn out the lights and call it quits.

With many products, however, the environment is more complex. You might have incoming data feeds to plug into the correct fields in your database. You might be introducing a new piece of hardware to the network. You might be replacing an online 24×7 system. In all of these instances, your rollout will inevitably cause down time for somebody, somewhere.

Down time is a technological fact of life within most organizations: users take it for granted that now and then a system will be unavailable due to scheduled maintenance. Consumers, on the other hand, are not nearly so patient and understanding. A customer who is unable to perform a search or complete a transaction within a reasonable period may take his or her business elsewhere.

If you anticipate down time for any system as a consequence of your deployment, try to estimate how long it will be. Take into account not only the technical logistics involved in distributing and setting up your product and converting any legacy data, but also the execution of your final test. Multiply that figure by the number of iterations you think it may require to get everything set up correctly and to run the tests without any errors—to be safe, a minimum of three. Add in any special arrangements that need to be made to prevent breakdowns in linked systems, such as building temporary storage for incoming live data or turning off replication from other databases.

Find out whether your organization has any standard procedures for notifying users about down time. There should be separate procedures for IT staff and for end users because each group requires different information on a different schedule. Your technology colleagues may want to be informed several weeks in advance that your project will affect a certain server or database or OS user group or IP subnet on a particular day in case it might affect their own projects. On the other hand, if you send this information to your users, they will probably scratch their heads and say, "Huh?" Instead they will want to know what products and applications they won't be able to use or what tasks they won't be able to perform and for how long. For users, you should include a reminder about down time with the promotional materials you distribute immediately before your product launch.

One final warning about international offices: When scheduling down time and drafting your notifications, make sure you've got the time zones right. At first this may sound almost idiotically simple. In practice it's usually not, especially when it comes to factoring in daylight savings time. If you need proof of this, try arranging a conference call involving people in Boston, San Francisco, Sydney, Tokyo, Delhi, Frankfurt, and London. Say the call is scheduled for a Monday in late October at 2 p.m. Pacific Daylight Time; figure out the local date and time for every other participant. Attempt to perform this activity as a group exercise with your colleague. You'll be amazed at how many different opinions they offer.*

Rollback Procedures

It's unthinkable. Your team has worked so hard, the users are ready and waiting . . . but something has gone badly wrong. You've chewed off all your fingernails and now you're wondering if the consequences of proceeding with the deployment could possibly be worse than calling it off and trying again later after the problem has been fixed.

This scenario is rare, but it does happen. Just as your IT department as a whole needs to have plans for disaster recovery, you as a project manager should be prepared to take appropriate action if your launch turns into a meltdown.

To avoid irrational, panic-stricken, sinking-of-the-Titanic behavior, you'll need to have a plan. Before you give the word to set the deployment process in motion, meet privately with your client and product manager to discuss this possibility. Don't worry about undermining their confidence in your team's work or creating an impression of indecisiveness. They too have their own private fears about the outcome of the project, and it will help set their minds at rest to be able to articulate them. They will appreciate your professionalism in raising the issue.

With your client and product manager, consider the criteria by which you might decide whether to go ahead or turn back. What functions of the product absolutely have to work from the very first moment? What elements of data absolutely have to be correct? For the less critical items, what workarounds could be created? How long could the users live with the workarounds until it made more sense to postpone the rollout?

Even after you've had such a strategy meeting, pulling the emergency brake in the midst of a deployment is a tough decision, and you shouldn't have to make it alone. Try to persuade your client to collaborate with you on reviewing the situation during a crisis and approving the strategy you recommend. If your client will not be available or is somewhat slippery when it comes to issues of accountability, insist that the product manager play this role.

And, of course, there's the rest of your team to consider—both your regulars and the IT colleagues who have joined you temporarily. You'll need their advice to determine the scope of any problem and estimate the time and effort required to fix it. You'll need their help to keep the down time on the production systems to a minimum while you sort things out so that your users will experience as little disruption as possible. There's no need to call a special meeting to emphasize this, but you should mention it often enough during your regular planning sessions that they understand what you expect of them.

Because a system rollback involves restoring the environment to whatever condition it was in before you started your deployment, it's important to have adequate documentation of and backups from its previous state. Your product's setup script should

---

*[Answer: Boston—5 p.m. Monday; San Francisco—2 p.m. Monday; Sydney—7 a.m. Tuesday; Tokyo—6 a.m. Tuesday; Delhi—2:30 a.m. Tuesday; Frankfurt—11 p.m. Monday; London—10 p.m. Monday.]

provide an Install feature that records the changes it makes on your users' computers and an UnInstall feature that can delete files and reconfigure settings. If you are planning to convert data from a legacy system into a new format to be compatible with your product, one of the earliest tasks in your rollout project plan should be to create backup copies of all the databases and test that they can be restored easily. This much, at least, is relatively simple because it's under your team's control.

A more challenging task is to ensure that your IT colleagues and any participants outside your organization are equally prepared for a rollback. When documenting a change, most people know they need to record the expected *new* state; it's less obvious why they should bother to record the *old* one. Furthermore, when making routine environment changes as part of a standard deployment, many administrators can't resist tweaking the system to improve performance or clearing out old files to increase disk space—alterations to the base state that they may consider too insignificant at the time to record in a change log but that can cause problems for a rollback if they don't remember exactly what they've done. Therefore, in your meetings and in your rollout procedures guide, you should highlight the importance of updating change logs carefully and documenting both the base state and any alterations, no matter how minor.

When they begin to consider the complexities of a rollback, novice project managers sometimes decide that it would be helpful to develop a separate set of written procedures for everyone to follow. This approach usually turns out to be a waste of effort: while rollouts are generally predictable sequences of tasks, rollbacks are not. Every crisis is unique, and every one calls for a different response. If everyone makes backups of the data and configurations, keeps detailed change logs, understands their roles, and is aware of your expectations, your team should be able to cope with the unexpected and make sound decisions.

Maintaining communication is the key ingredient for a smooth rollback (and rollout, for that matter). As Yogi Berra once so eloquently stated, "It ain't over 'til it's over." Especially when there are difficulties and things drag on, it's tempting for network and database administrators or technicians in remote offices to finish their own tasks, switch off their beepers, shut down their PCs, and go to bed. Four hours later when you're frantically trying to contact them to ask them to undo what they did earlier, they're unreachable in dreamland—and meanwhile, you're watching your project degenerate from Three Mile Island to Chernobyl. The entire crew should know that nobody goes off watch until the ship is anchored in a safe harbor and the captain (i.e., you) dismisses them.

Track Problems and Questions

Rollouts are always exhilarating. You're launching something new into the world, and the outcome of any birth is unpredictable. You want everything to go well, so as soon as an issue crops up you rush to resolve it. After the deployment is all over you know you've lived through a big event, but almost immediately the details begin to fade.

In the heat of the moment it can seem like an unnecessary bother to stop and record what you're doing. The cost of a few seconds' delay, however, produces benefits you will notice before long.

Unforeseen Events

After a product has been in production for a while and is deploying only routine maintenance releases, the rollouts may become more humdrum. This is never the case with version 1.0. No matter how thoroughly you've discussed and planned and documented, stuff will happen. If it doesn't happen during the actual rollout, it will happen during the first week when your users are getting acquainted with the system.

Confronted with unexpected incidents and reactions, novice project managers sometimes assume that these things are happening because they've done a bad job. They imagine that if they'd handled the project better, the deployment would have proceeded like clockwork and the users would all be happy and productive. Even some managers of highly successful software development projects occasionally experience a kind of post-partum depression that can make them susceptible to feelings of inadequacy and self-doubt. Gathering data on the unpleasant surprises enables you to be more realistic about both the difficulties you encounter and your product's performance in comparison with other products' deployments.

Before the rollout begins, explain your goals to your team and devise your reporting procedures. Be sure to include your product manager because he or she should be the first contact for users with problems or questions. The ideal template for issue tracking is a subset of the input form for your change management system: issues that turn out to be defects or design changes or enhancement requests can enter the development process without having to be retyped or copied-and-pasted. Yet a simple paper or word processing document form, similar to Template 8.1, will serve the purpose.

For each issue, you should identify the following:

- Who reported the problem or asked the question
- Who submitted the item, if it was someone other than the person who reported the problem or asked the question
- The date and time of the incident
- The date and time of the submission
- How the item was submitted (phone call, e-mail, fax report, interoffice mail, meeting, database entry)
- A summary of the incident
- A longer description of the incident, including steps to reproduce it
- Who on your team is assigned to resolve the issue
- Who responded to the person reporting the problem or asking the question
- The date and time of the response
- The nature of the response (researched the question, investigated the problem, submitted a change request)
- A description of the response
- The date and time of the resolution
- The nature of the resolution (question answered, operational problem fixed, product change implemented, change request rejected)

During the rollout you should review the issues submitted every day to ensure that your team is collecting the data and that items are being addressed expeditiously. If you're storing the information in a database, it's important to emphasize to everyone that they are responsible for resolving items assigned to them. If they don't, all the sta-

Change Request for Users

PRODUCT: _____ CHANGE ID: _____

CHANGE REQUEST FOR USERS	
Summary:	Priority:
	Urgent
	High
Date submitted:	Medium
	Low
Reported by:	Category:
Name:	System crash
Title:	Application error
Department/Location:	Data error
Phone:	Usability issue
Fax:	
E-mail:	

Description (with steps to reproduce):

Template 8.1   Change Request Form for Users

tistics in your reports will be wrong, and it will seem as though people are not doing their jobs. After the deployment is complete, your client will be pleased to receive a summary report showing that your team handled unexpected problems and user issues in such a methodical and organized way.

Resource Monitoring

As you make the transition from building your product to maintaining and enhancing it, your issue tracking reports will help you measure the amount of effort your team members expend on troubleshooting and user support during different phases of the project.

Help Desk staff are accustomed to having their phone calls and e-mail messages monitored. They're paid to deal with as many user complaints and problems as they can during their shift. The constant surveillance and constant pressure to maintain volume make it a relatively low-level, high-stress job. The staff members on your project team, on the other hand, probably are used to a great deal more freedom, flexibility, and privacy. In most organizations, custom dictates that professional staff can use the phone and e-mail without being watched (unless they're in trouble for some reason).

When it comes to resource monitoring, this situation can put managers in an awkward position. You don't want to make your staff feel as though you're spying on them, but you do want to find out if they're spending all day creating workarounds to bypass program limitations or performing batch updates to production data that got overlooked in the conversion. It may take some persuading or some carrot-and-stick management techniques, but you should impress on your team the desirability of logging every incoming and outgoing phone call and e-mail message directly related to answering users' questions or resolving their problems. This means they'll have to keep copies of the paper form on their desks or leave the database input form open on their computer desktops. They'll need to become more conscious of what they're doing hour by hour and how they organize their workdays. Rather than opening up the code in an exploratory frame of mind and tinkering with any function that looks suspicious, they'll be obliged to focus more on troubleshooting individual problems in sequence and recording the effort involved.

In the beginning, this process inevitably seems burdensome, especially compared to the more free-flowing creative atmosphere of the design and building phases of version 1.0. When your team members complain, reassure them that the most intense phase of issue tracking occurs during and immediately after a rollout. In the meantime, the procedures they are becoming accustomed to following will serve the project well later on as the cycles of routine maintenance and enhancement evolve into a regular pattern.

There are more immediate benefits as well. If problems occur as a result of gaps in the services you depend on from your IT colleagues, you'll need evidence to demonstrate that neither your product nor your project management was at fault. If the resolution of the problems is outside the control of your project team, you might have to prove how serious the situation is before the responsible parties will bestir themselves to take action. If an outside vendor is the source of the trouble, your data may provide the grounds for demanding a rebate or filing a lawsuit.

A flurry of calls from your users about a specific program feature may alert you to a flaw in the system design or a missing element in the training and documentation.

Early recognition and acknowledgment of the issue can enable you to respond quickly, by distributing special instructions or arranging ad hoc demos, before too many complaints reach the ears of senior management.

Tracking questions and problems and monitoring the resources you need to address them can also help prevent staff burnout. Even though it's irrational and defies all logic and prior experience, deep in their hearts your team members are all hoping they've created the perfect software product. It's always difficult when the first complaints start coming in—even if they turn out to be unfounded and based on clueless users' misunderstandings. And there always will be legitimate criticism because no design fits all users equally well. It's only natural for your team to want to make your users happy, to clear up any confusion, to sweep away any obstacles that prevent the users from appreciating the wonderful product your team delivered. During a rollout, developers and testers can get so caught up in answering questions and troubleshooting problems that their time just evaporates. Eventually they collapse in exhaustion and despair without any clear idea of what they've done or how much they've accomplished. As project manager, you may not be able to eliminate your team's inevitable disappointment when reality intrudes on their vision of their ideal product. You can lift their spirits and show them you appreciate their efforts if you point out that the reason they feel so worn down is that they've investigated and resolved 68 reported issues during the 2 days since the product was launched.

Nobody can predict with any accuracy exactly how long a rollout will take from the moment the first files begin to move into the production environment to the moment the last user logs on to the new system and does whatever the product was designed to do. Even for the same product, different releases encounter different obstacles. Yet they do all come to an end eventually, and often there are patterns of issues or user behavior that remain relatively constant from one deployment to the next. By monitoring your resources, you'll be better prepared to forecast how long the most stressful phases will last for your team and to cope with the tactical and psychological demands of the siege.

Knowledge Base

The information you gather during a rollout about problems and questions forms the core of the knowledge base you will compile for your product throughout its life cycle. In some organizations, this knowledge base exists solely in the heads of the project team members, and therefore it is drastically depleted whenever anyone leaves. By setting up the tools and procedures to create a record of deployment issues, you can instead preserve the accumulated expertise of your team—and mine useful raw materials for other important functions. For example, you can improve the following:

Change management. If your users or your product manager input the deployment issues directly into the database, all you need to do to identify the items you will address by making changes in your product is to update their classification and create a filter. If your issue reports exist only on paper, in a set of word processing documents, or in a separate discussion database, someone on your team will have to copy the items submitted for development into the change management database. This can seem tedious, but in practice you'll find that many of the original issue reports lack important details that a developer or tester would be obliged to research anyway, such as specific data elements, the exact steps to reproduce the issue, or information about the user's hardware configuration.

Test plan. With their vivid imaginations, testers can conjure up a lot of scenarios in which the product might fail. Their repertoire is limited, though, by the knowledge they possess during development. During a rollout, the number of variables is so large that no tester could ever envision all potential disasters and glitches. After they've been through one deployment, they have enough information to create more comprehensive test plans for future releases. As your developers begin to design version 1.1, your testers should study the issue reports from the rollout of version 1.0 and add new cases to the installation and regression test plans.

Defect diagnostics. During the first two weeks after a rollout, user feedback will come flying at you thick and fast. You'll know right away about errors in particular functions, or problems with the workflow, or ambiguities in the user interface. Unless you have a record of specific incidents, however, all of your information will be vague and anecdotal. Deciding which issues to tackle first will become a matter of listening to those users who yell the loudest or have the most political clout. A far more effective approach is to analyze the data from your issue reports and determine whether certain modules of code or program interfaces are generating a disproportionate number of complaints and to make them your top priority. If your issue reports are stored in your change management database, you should be able to search and sort and filter the information by any criteria you choose; the database should also permit you to export the information to a spreadsheet, where you can perform further statistical calculations. Otherwise, the searching, sorting, and filtering will have to be a manual operation, but you can still benefit from classifying the items and recording information about them in a spreadsheet for analysis.

User documentation. A product launch is the ultimate usability test for your documentation. Your user manual, your tutorial, your Help files, your training materials, your technical support manual, your deployment procedures guide—all of them are ready and available for consultation. Your documentation writers and training developers have been waiting as anxiously as your software developers to find out if they've done a good job. Your rollout issue reports provide evidence of where they've succeeded and where they've missed the target. If they're consultants or if they don't have an opportunity to interact with certain groups of users in faraway offices, the issue reports may be their only evidence. As project manager, you'll know sooner whether revisions are necessary, and you'll know better the type of changes you should request.

You can create a very powerful knowledge repository using only your change management database and your documentation library. The principal feature you need to implement is a linkage between items in each system. For example, if you have a field called "Program Function" on your change request input form with a pick list attached to it, and if you add the same field with the same pick list to your documentation library input form, you'll be able to catalog and cross-reference all the material on any function you specify.

Tracking problems and questions in the midst of a rollout demands a great deal of self-discipline. To some, it may feel like petty bureaucracy—like a hospital clerk in the emergency room refusing to treat a desperately ill patient before all the insurance payment data has been recorded. Certainly everyone who develops software has encountered a few users who behaved as though they were in a life-threatening situation whenever their computer did something unexpected. In reality, the person who takes the time to gather and record the information is less like the callous bureaucrat than like the responsible doctor who wants to understand as much as possible about the patient's condition and circumstances before prescribing anything. Even though it may be difficult on your first project, stand your ground and insist that everyone on your team keep good records. Ask your support coordinator to inspect the records every day until you're sure the team has gotten the idea and they realize you're serious about it.

Milestone Marker

Like an orchestra conductor, a project manager at the time of a product launch is both very powerful and utterly powerless. In your Technology Partner role all eyes are focused on you, watching you for cues. You can speed up or slow down the tempo, or you can bring the entire performance to a halt at any moment. What you cannot do is play the musicians' instruments for them—and therein lies your helplessness. Inevitably you will hear an occasional sour note or missed beat. Yet if the overall performance is good, an audience rarely recalls the minor flaws. When you coordinate the environment changes, test the production system, and track problems and questions during your deployment, you increase the chances that on the whole your team members and your IT department colleagues will do their jobs well as an ensemble.

A successful conductor knows how to wield his or her baton under the scrutiny of a large and often critical audience. Similarly, a software project manager orchestrating a product launch puts on a very public show for the user community. But during the rollout a project manager also demonstrates a more intimate form of leadership behind the scenes among the project team. In the next chapter, we'll consider how you can help your team work more efficiently, productively, and harmoniously under mounting pressures.

All Hands on Deck!

If you've effectively cultivated team spirit up to now, you shouldn't have to announce that you expect everyone to pitch in during the rollout. They'll all *want* to be around. They'll want to find out what happens, to make sure everything goes well with their components, and to give each other moral support.

A project manager may not be able to control events, but in your Team Captain role you can provide coordination and guidance. You can set an example of how you expect your team members to behave. You can make them feel that their contributions are essential and valued. To accomplish all this, you'll need to devise some methods for pulling the team together—and for pulling yourself together as well.

Pull the Team Together

At long last, the moment arrives. The product is ready. The environment and infrastructure have been prepared for the launch. Your team and your IT department colleagues are standing by. Task #1 on the deployment project plan awaits. It's up to you to say the word, and everything will start happening. As the seconds pass and you take a deep breath before speaking, you wonder: is my rollout going to look more like a Keystone Kops movie or like an exquisitely choreographed action sequence in a James Bond thriller?

Your anarchy quotient can be reduced if you figure out in advance how you plan to deal with several important communication issues. First and foremost, your team members should have a place where they can communicate with each other. They should feel that they can communicate with you about whatever is on their minds. They should be confident that if they run into trouble, you will take the lead and make decisions and not burden them by communicating your own ambivalence or anxiety.

War Room

Coordinating the actions of many people simultaneously is possible only if there a central place where everyone can come to receive instructions and report information. You've seen it in the movies: it's the War Room.

Your War Room can be anywhere. It can be in your office, in a conference room, in the test lab, or any place your office layout provides appropriate space. No matter where it's located, it should provide the following:

- Enough chairs for the members of your project team to sit around comfortably while you're waiting for other participants to finish their tasks
- Enough privacy so that outsiders can't drop in and distract you and so that the members of your team can joke around or argue with each other without being overheard
- Enough uncluttered, washable surface area so that everyone can eat and drink without endangering equipment or papers
- Enough telephone lines so that you can be on several calls simultaneously and can arrange a conference call
- Enough computers so that you can simultaneously send and receive e-mails, connect to remote servers and shared drives on the network, access the Internet, install the production version of your product and reproduce its behavior, connect to the version control system, and load a second copy of the software for testing and debugging purposes
- Enough writing tools for collective brainstorming, such as a whiteboard with an eraser and/or a flip chart and plenty of markers

To enhance the atmosphere, some project managers like to decorate the walls of their War Room with printouts of the project plan and the requirements list, charts and graphs from the change management system that show declining error rates, or maps that identify locations around the world where the product will be deployed. If you decide to do this, invite members of your project team to contribute their own (tasteful, project-related) items rather than selecting all of them yourself. And don't even think about hanging up motivational posters unless you have the sort of team members who would enjoy defacing them as a form of officially sanctioned entertainment. Music can also be problematic because people's tastes vary so widely, and project-related stress can easily erupt into conflict over ska versus opera.

Even more important than the layout, equipment, and decorations of your War Room is its accessibility. Your team members must be able to work there 24×7 from the moment the rollout begins to the moment your client confirms that the deployment has been completed successfully. Depending on the scope of your project (as well as your management abilities and a small element of luck), this could be hours, days, or weeks. Plan ahead: make sure that the space will have adequate heat or air conditioning during the nights and weekends, and find out if your team members will need special

Figure 9.1 The War Room.

building passes. If privacy or security may be an issue, try to obtain a room with a door you can lock and distribute keys only to your team members.

Finally, in addition to your physical War Room, you will need a place where people who are off-site can exchange information. Of course, they can always call you on the phone or send you an e-mail, but then you are obliged to act as transmitter and filter if the information needs to be passed to others. This situation both increases the risk of garbled or incomplete communication and creates delays if you happen to be unavailable when the call or e-mail comes in. One possible solution is to set up a groupware discussion database through which everyone participating in the rollout can ask questions and comment on problems. A public e-mail folder combined with a group distribution list can serve a similar purpose, although less efficiently because the message threads can get tangled. Some telephone systems enable you to establish a temporary voice mailbox and send broadcast messages to your team members. This phone arrangement can be very helpful if your deployment involves a complex data migration that takes a long time over a weekend, especially if you have many team members off-site who are supposed to call in and find out if they're needed yet.

Opening-Night Jitters

Before you became a manager, you used to finish an assignment and turn it in, then move on to the next task. Perhaps sometimes you were worried about your boss's reaction, but eventually you got to know him or her well enough to understand what was expected of you.

Now that you are in charge, you'll notice that there's another dimension to your relationship with your subordinates. During the course of the project, you've become aware of how your behavior sets the tone for the meetings and how your praise or criticism can affect the morale or productivity of your team. At the time of a product launch, emotions run very high. Under pressure, people succumb to their weaknesses much more easily than they normally do. Good managers realize this—they expect it—and prepare themselves to stand by with the psychic glue whenever someone on their team starts to crack. This is a subtle skill, but if you think back on critical moments of group efforts you've participated in during your own career, you may remember occasions when your spirits were sagging or you were about to lose your temper and a word or action from your manager made a big difference.

It helps to understand the nature of people's fears. You're all afraid of failure, but each person sees the bogeyman in different form. As project manager, you can imagine your client and your senior IT managers telling you how badly your team messed up and how stupidly you've blown the opportunity you were given. Your product manager envisions hordes of enraged users demanding to know how she could have let them down—or colleagues treating him like a pariah because he is associated with your team. Your developers naturally fear that some bad code will cause the product to malfunction; they fear this the way athletes at the beginning of a match worry that their bodies will get broken. Your testers are more like new homeowners in a crime-ridden neighborhood: they've tried to figure out every possible way that evil-doers could break into their house and have installed locks and alarm systems to keep everyone safe, but they lie awake at night wondering if they've overlooked some weak point. Your trainers are anxious about the possibility that users who dislike the product will take it out on the person running the demo or class. Even your documentation writers dread the thought of having to do yet another draft if revisions become necessary.

Remembering what kind of nightmares each person probably is having will enable you to choose the right words of reassurance when panic strikes. You should also keep in mind that unlike you and the product manager, the other members of your project team may not really care what the client or IT senior management thinks of them. They want everything to go well because if it doesn't they will have to bear the disappointment and criticism of their peers.

Besides intervening with a kind or temperate remark or sending someone on a cooling-off errand to defuse a confrontation, you can do a lot of good simply by paying attention to a team member who is teetering on the edge. Don't hover over the person or ask intrusive questions; usually all it takes is an appraising glance and a smile every few hours, plus an occasional friendly, "How's it going?" (or "Wazzup?" or whatever your team's vernacular greeting might be).

Another surprise in store for new project managers during a project launch is the sudden need of certain team members to express their inner feelings. This phenomenon can manifest itself in different ways—from the normally reticent middle-aged guy inexplicably needing to tell you about the triumphs and travails of his kids' soccer teams, to the normally cheerful young woman corralling you in your office to cry on your shoulder about her boyfriend's transgressions. The first time this happens to you, you will probably be astonished and at a loss for words. After a while, you will come to expect it as normal and predictable, and you will be glad that your staff members trust you enough to confide in you.

The appropriate response to such outpourings is simply to listen. Don't offer advice, don't pass judgment on anyone's behavior, and don't take sides. Make noncommittal but supportive remarks like "I can understand how you'd feel that way" or "That must have been hard for you." If you suspect that the person is actually upset about something concerning the project, you can try a comment like "Yes, we've all been under a lot of stress lately around here" and see if the true complaint surfaces. Give the person 10 or 15 minutes of your undivided attention; usually the tirade will wind down, and the speaker will be very grateful for your patience and compassion. If not, you can smile and gently usher the person out as you plead an important deadline.

Acting as an emergency psychotherapist during a crunch time doesn't mean that you have to permanently adopt this role in your team members' lives. There are people who will misinterpret your emotional support as *carte blanche* to complain about their troubles to you all the time. Be tactful but firm with these folks: they're grownups, and you're a busy manager. If they persist in imposing on you or if they seem to have authentically serious problems, politely provide them with a reference to your organization's employee assistance program or a qualified therapist.

Your Finest Hour

Leading your team through a product launch can test your mettle in ways you never expected. It can also draw on skills you never knew you had, or at least never had to use at work.

For instance, there's the ability to make decisions quickly and resolutely under fire. If you're especially lucky, every task in your deployment will go smoothly. If you're more like the rest of us (on a later project, if not your first), something unexpected will happen and you'll have to change course abruptly. All faces will turn to you for instructions; all off-site participants will call or e-mail you at once in a state of confusion. When you find yourself on the spot like this, you need to be able to appear calm and controlled, even though you really have no idea what to do and you'd prefer to go hide under a desk until the crisis has passed. It's not easy, and you can't practice the skill deliberately. Parents who have been responsible for groups of children when calamity strikes will understand the type of bravery that's called for—but in a work environment you just have to live through it once to know how it feels and how you'll handle it. The challenge is even greater if the problem is caused by something one of your team members did or failed to do.

Figure 9.2 HMS Project.

Imagine that you're playing a game of chess with fate, and you've just been put in check. You need to figure out your next move in a hurry. Don't crack jokes. Don't rant and rave. Don't think out loud. Ask for your colleagues' advice it you want, but don't expect a consensus from them or a clear indication of what you should do. Walk away from those upturned faces if you need time to think. When you reach a decision, give instructions without going into much detail about your reasons—you can explain why later. Above all, make it clear that you are taking responsibility for the outcome.

Less dramatic than a sudden crisis but equally challenging to your management skills is a long, drawn-out, frustrating siege of endless setbacks. You're reasonably sure that everything will eventually work out in the end, but the end is not yet in sight, and with each new "progress" report it seems to recede farther and farther into the distance. Everyone around you is miserable. You would like to vent your foul mood at somebody—and you probably could, too, and get away with it because, after all, you're the boss.

For moments like this, you should practice giving pep talks. Nothing can lift a project manager's spirits faster than standing up in front of the team and trying to persuade them that they're champs who just have to get a grip on themselves and push themselves a little harder to win the game. Of course, your opponents are entropy, disorganization, and mechanical failure rather than a rival team, and nobody's going to take home big bucks in prize money. Yet the basic script of your speech can be borrowed from the sports coaches' textbook and will serve your purpose. Here's how it goes: You acknowledge the toughness of the fight and the discouragement of your players; then you remind your team of how talented they are and how well they've done so far; and finally you describe how they're going to overcome their fatigue and sense of futility and get out there and do whatever is necessary to achieve their goal. When delivering this speech don't overanalyze the situation, criticize anyone, or be sarcastic—play the part straight. Even the most skeptical, curmudgeonly team members will appreciate the gesture.

Pull Yourself Together

Managing your first software development project is a milestone in your career. The product launch is the moment of truth for you and your team. It's a stressful time, one during which you need to keep your wits about you.

No doubt you remember Mom's advice before the big test: get plenty of sleep and eat a good breakfast. Sleeping regularly and eating well, however, tend to be the first items to get dropped from the project plan as rollout nears, along with all the other activities of a normal, well-balanced life. It's wise to remember that your health and sanity are as crucial to the success of the project as any program function. Try to monitor your behavior, or ask someone you trust to do it, and acknowledge the problem when you cross over the red zone (which you inevitably will do at some point). Everyone has his or her own methods of depressurizing—a swim, a walk in the park, a motorcycle ride. If you need it, go do it. Your absence won't wreak nearly as much havoc as you dread. In addition to making you feel better, it will enable you to exercise greater self-control and react more thoughtfully and deliberately. You will provide stronger support for your team by helping them maintain their equilibrium, stamina, and perspective.

Equilibrium

Team dynamics are based on an interplay of roles and personalities. Ideally there should be a good balance—UI talent versus database expertise, outgoing social types versus taciturn loners—but in reality there usually isn't. Every real-world team is tilted in one direction or another, and over the course of the project they work out their own point of balance, like a group of kids arranging themselves on a seesaw. The manager is the fulcrum: you shift your position to keep everything stable.

During a product rollout, the forces tend to shift more wildly than usual. Emotions can run high; tempers can flare; fights can break out. As manager you can do a great deal to maintain the balance.

A few days before the rollout, set aside half an hour to think about your team's interpersonal relationships. By now you've worked with most of these folks for a while, so you should know them fairly well—at least in terms of their social behavior. Consider their strengths and weaknesses and any traits they may have that irritate others. Imagine you were all a group of scientists who were going to spend a long, dark winter together at a research station in Antarctica. Ask yourself these questions:

- Who will probably get on whose nerves, and why?
- Over the course of the project so far, what conflicts have already occurred? What friendships have evolved?
- Which team members enjoy working together, and which can't stand each other?
- Is there anyone on your team who is so irascible that he or she ought to be isolated behind a fence with a large "Beware of Geek" sign?
- Is there anyone who has the gift of being a natural peacemaker, whose mere presence calms everyone down?

A famous self-help book once claimed that a person learns everything he or she needs to know about life in kindergarten. While there may be some exceptions (romance, IRS audits), there's a great deal of truth to this statement when it comes to team dynamics. Your status as project manager puts you in the position of the teacher. It is not demeaning to the adults to work for you to compare them to schoolchildren because, under pressure, everyone tends to default to the behavior they learned when they were very young. And it can help you to approach your team's interaction over an extended period of time together in the War Room as an exercise in classroom management.

Simply viewing the situation from this perspective can give you insight into the appropriate actions you should take when relations within the group become fractious. Think about the good teachers you had and the techniques they used to maintain focus and civility. Talk to the teachers among your family and friends and ask them about their classroom experiences. The early childhood education section of a bookstore will also have many books containing anecdotes and advice; reading them may make you smile in recognition of the fact that human beings don't change much as we get older.

Stamina

Athletes know that stamina is part physical and part psychological. You don't get it from eating special foods, although diet can certainly help; you don't get it from drugs, at least not without serious long-term risks. The ability to find strength within yourself to keep going when your forces are completely spent can't be taught or learned from a book. But good managers have it.

By the time your product is ready to be deployed, your team is probably exhausted. They've done the best they could do to build the best system they knew how within the limits of time and resources. The creative part of their work is over, but they know the job isn't done yet—not by a long shot. In software development utopia, after the production build had been created the entire project team would get to take a few days off and rest before the actual rollout. But in the real world? Not a chance.

The role of the project manager is to lead your weary, footsore expedition in the final ascent to the summit. You're the one who must provide the motivation and the energy to keep them moving. You have to know when to push them and when to ease off. Most important, you need to set an example.

Demanding that everyone keep on working when they're obviously worn out can seem terribly callous and cold-hearted to a novice project manager. Unless you're sadistic by nature, it makes you feel like the cruel overseer on a slave plantation. But sometimes you just have to: there's a problem that must be solved before the rollout can continue, and if it isn't you'll be obliged to abort the whole process. If you find yourself in this situation, think about how you've coped with those moments in life when luck has turned against you. Maybe you've gone for a hike, gotten lost, and then it started to rain while you were bushwhacking your way back to the car. Maybe you're taken what you had hoped would be a great vacation, but instead your companion got sick and you spent most of it in a hospital room far from home. Mention those experiences to your team, and invite them to talk about theirs. The essential fact for everyone to acknowledge is that it's not you personally who is forcing them to keep going because you're a mean, heartless brute—it's the adverse circumstances you all face together.

Conversely, in the midst of a deployment you should always be on the lookout for opportunities to lighten up. You will have intervals when nothing much is happening, and your first impulse may be to shed your responsibilities for a while and spend some quiet time alone. Unless you really need to get away, your team will often benefit more from your instigation of some thoroughly mindless, time-wasting, yet entertaining group activity, such as one of these:

- Hallway bowling
- Coat rack ring toss
- Target practice with rubber bands and paper clips
- Paper airplane flying contest
- Sponge dart war
- Building things with blocks, Legos, or K'nex
- Scrabble
- Hangman

- Battleship
- Charades
- Card tricks
- Networked computer games

If you leave them alone for long enough, your team members will probably start doing some of these things independently to amuse themselves and relieve the pressure. But they'll stop as soon as you return, and they'll feel a bit sneaky about getting away with something behind your back. Furthermore, the group may split up into cliques as soon as you're out of sight. So stick around and lead the recreational activities once in a while. Playing together energizes the entire team.

Your own behavior during the most grueling episodes of the rollout will have a major effect on your team's stamina. None of your team members will feel entitled to take any better care of himself or herself than you do of your own person. If you forget to eat, they'll be reluctant to admit they're hungry. If you pull an all-nighter, they'll believe you expect them to stick with you until their heads drop onto their keyboards. If you keep on working without a break long past the time when your analytical powers, common sense, and courtesy have been depleted, they'll follow your lead.

A product launch is not an endurance test. Most of your team members don't have as large an emotional or professional investment in the project as you do. They may not be as young as you, nor as carefree and unencumbered, nor in as robust physical health. In the long run, all of you will do a better job and get along better with each other afterward if you set an example of self-awareness and moderation. No matter what problems you encounter during the deployment, try to keep as close as possible to your normal routine. Eat regular meals (or at least go through the motions of ordering or preparing them). Sleep a few hours every night (or at least lie down in a darkened room). While you're working, set your watch timer to beep every two hours to remind you to take a break—get up, stretch, walk around, read a magazine, talk to someone about movies or sports—and do whatever it takes to refresh yourself and restore your stamina.

If you absolutely cannot resist the urge to go on a work binge and drive yourself full-speed ahead until you hit the wall, before the rollout begins you should gather your team together and make a short confessional speech. Explain to them that you are a hopelessly neurotic workaholic, and for the sake of the project you don't want any of them to act like you.

Perspective

What is the point of your project? Of course, it has a purpose: you're building a tool that will enable your users to perform some activity they can't do now. But you and your team members all know very well the purpose is not the same thing as the point.

When you come right down to it, most software projects are essentially pointless. Many of them get cancelled before they're deployed. Even the successful ones only last a few years. It's the high-tech equivalent of sand painting.

So why bother? Why are you all knocking yourselves out like this? Maybe you'll get rewarded: a nice bonus, a promotion. Maybe your entire team has lots of stock options and hopes to get rich. For most software professionals, though, it's really just a job.

Most people like to do good work. We like to be respected by our peers. We like to make things that other people find useful and attractive. In the end, that's what it all comes down to.

Ironically, your team will perform better if you don't work yourself into a frenzy and act as though your product launch is the equivalent of D-Day. They're not dumb. They know it's not. You will have more credibility, more authority, and more honest communication with your team if you can share their perspective on the project. It will help everyone maintain a sense of humor.

Milestone Marker

Your product launch is unlike any other phase of your project. It's shorter. It's more intense. It throws people together in close quarters under stressful conditions. As a result, the Team Captain role is far more demanding—and more crucial to the immediate success of the endeavor. During your career as a project manager every rollout you participate in will be different, with unique technical crises and personality quirks to deal with. Yet the advice presented here on pulling the team together and pulling yourself together should stand you in good stead regardless of the system architecture or cast of characters involved. As time goes by, you'll build up a repertoire of funny, horrific, and absurd deployment war stories that you can tell your future team members as you're waiting for the database administrators to copy your indexes over to the production server.

Although it may seem endless while it's happening, your rollout will eventually conclude. You'll reach the last item on your deployment project plan, and everyone will stare at each other in disbelief. There will be no fanfares, no fireworks—just an immense, collective sense of relief. And foreboding because now your product is *in the hands of the users*. What will happen? Only time will tell. Stay tuned for the final project phase.

CHAPTER 10

Battlefield Reconnaissance

The deployment is complete. Your team delivered a product, and your users are becoming familiar with it. After the fast-paced action of the rollout, there is a lull.

But long-term peace is not necessarily at hand. You'll have to work at it. Like the general of a conquering army, you'll need to maintain surveillance of the territory where you've established your domain. You'll want to find out whether any rebellions are brewing. You'll strive to create alliances with local leaders so that you can stay in touch with the people's opinions. When you report back to the potentates who put you in charge of the campaign, you'd like to be able to tell them that the casualties were minor and the benefits are solid and enduring.

Your reconnaissance efforts will draw on skills you've already honed in your Entrepreneur role. During the previous phases of the project you took pains to establish good relationships with your user community and with senior management. The channels of communication you have opened will enable your team to help the users assimilate your product into their work processes. You can begin by finding out the users' honest opinions of the software you have given them. To foster long-term collaboration between your project team and your user community, you can form a grassroots network of expert users. Finally, you should write reports on the outcome of the project in your frank but upbeat entrepreneurial style.

Monitor Acceptance

Unless there was a major problem with the launch, your client and your product manager are probably going to tell you that, all in all, they're satisfied with the way things have turned out. Primarily, of course, they're relieved that version 1.0 is done and they can go back to focusing on their usual responsibilities. But an element of pride may also be involved. They put a lot of effort into the creation of the product; they want to feel good about it and get credit for their contribution.

Among the end users, the situation is often more complex than it appears. Important issues may exist, but the client and product manager may not be hearing about them. Because the client and product manager have collaborated so intensely with your project team, users in a close-knit community might not want to hurt their feelings by complaining. In a more authoritarian environment, users might be unwilling to speak up because they're afraid to criticize their superiors implicitly or to raise doubts about their own competence.

After a while, however, user dissatisfaction may emerge. The more repressed it has been, the louder the bang will be when it finally does erupt. Therefore, it is in the best interests of your project for you not to rely solely on your client's and product manager's reports, but to conduct your own independent research. There's not much you can do about the culture or the communication issues within your user community, but you can use your research to identify problems affecting your product so that your client can figure out the appropriate remedies.

Initial Resistance

It has been said before, but it bears repeating: people don't like change. Even if they are aware that your product does good things for them, the transition between old ways and new ways creates discomfort for your users. Don't underestimate these growing pains, and don't blame the human beings who suffer them. Experienced project managers anticipate resistance, and over time they develop insight into the causes. Some typical sources of trouble might include the following:

Work processes. Certain users react strongly to changes in their work processes. If they are accustomed to keeping everything in paper-based files, and your product replaces their tangible repository with an electronic system, they will be disoriented for a while. If they are accustomed to discussing their work face to face with colleagues before committing themselves to a final draft, and if your product replaces their personal interactions with an electronic workflow, they will have writer's block for a while. If they are accustomed to walking up and down stairs to pass documents around, and your product replaces their legwork with an electronic routing, they will gain weight and blame the software for a while.

Social patterns. Changes in social patterns upset some users, and occasionally with good reason. Software engineers tend to view work as a flow of abstract data from one point to the next. In reality, for most people work is a series of human interactions: you say hello to the cashier in the cafeteria when you buy your morning coffee, you make comments about the weather to the receptionist on your floor, you eavesdrop on the colleagues whose workspaces are adjacent to yours, you trade complaints about your favorite sports teams with the mail room clerk on his daily rounds, you exchange news with the attendees at your various meetings, you talk about your vacation plans with the technician you call when the copier gets jammed, and so on until you say goodbye and leave at the end of your work day. Sometimes people in an organization who are friends have a chance to get together only when their work processes bring them into contact with each other. If your product alters your users' social patterns—disrupting friendships, creating dependencies among previously self-sufficient groups, isolating people who used to work in teams—then you can expect muffled but palpable resentment.

Status. New software can also lead to changes in status among your users. It often happens that over time a person will become an expert in how things get done. This individual might not occupy a very exalted position on the official organizational chart: it might be a middle manager's administrative assistant or a junior-level professional who started out many years ago stacking boxes in the warehouse alongside the current CFO. Nevertheless, the person plays an acknowledged though informal leadership role in the group. If your product radically changes the way things are done, the leader suddenly no longer has any followers—and under such circumstances, insecure and unscrupulous spoilsports may engage in covert acts of sabotage.

Sometimes after the inauguration of a new software product a senior manager who knows very little about computers finds himself or herself at the mercy of a very young, brash, arrogant, techno-whiz geek. Diplomatic problems of this nature typically come to light indirectly, through an intermediary. Seeing other users getting along fine, the senior manager might not discuss the issue with the client or the product manager because this would call attention to his or her technical backwardness. Yet at, say, an off-site meeting of senior management peers, he or she might make some derogatory remarks about your product to a senior IT manager while they were working out together at the health club. If criticism of your product is conveyed second- or third-hand through irregular channels, consider offering private one-on-one training for senior managers.

Workload. The most common change introduced by a new software product is a redistribution of your users' workloads. Over time, your users have gotten accustomed to the rhythm of busy and slack periods in their jobs, and they have arranged their personal lives accordingly. By automating certain tasks and creating new workflow queues, your product may have created unanticipated bottlenecks in their processes. Even worse, there might be some minor but annoying errors. For example, your users will grumble if they have to recalculate a field your formula gets wrong or if they have to go look up a date your program imports incorrectly from another system. Usually it takes a while for all the flaws in a new product to reveal themselves. If your organization is a school, it might take one semester; if it's a business, it could take one revenue cycle. Until your users have lived through the entire phase, they are constantly discovering new quirks in the system and having to make adjustments. Their lives are unpredictable, and they become anxious about it.

Knowing the sort of changes your users are struggling with helps a project manager understand the motives for their resistance. To learn which users are most affected, and to what degree, you can employ both objective and subjective methods of research: data gathering and personal reports.

Data Gathering

Several weeks after your rollout, prepare a survey for your users. It can be a paper form distributed by your product manger, or it can be an electronic form distributed by e-mail. If you use an electronic form, you'll need to figure out a way for your users to return it to you anonymously. Explain the mechanics to your users in detail, so that they know how their privacy is being protected.

In the survey you can ask your users to rate the product's performance, design, and appropriateness for their needs. You can inquire what they like the most and the least and provide space for comments, complaints, and suggestions. You can also include questions about the documentation, training, and support that they've received so far.

Although survey data can be quantified and analyzed, it is enlightening only up to a point. Even if your client insists that all users are required to participate, not everyone is going to fill it out, and you cannot credibly guarantee anonymity if you go after the slackers. There is also no reliable method of compensating for people's individual temperaments. A new hire who is just thrilled to be at your organization may give your product high marks simply because the honeymoon glow has not worn off, while a grumpy, overworked veteran may rate everything merely OK even though he or she really has no complaints.

What surveys do provide is an unscientific, imprecise reading of where you stand overall—plus an opportunity for people who are truly furious to tell you off without risking a personal confrontation. If a lot of your users participate willingly, that in itself is a good sign. The fact that you care enough about their opinions to conduct a survey should make a deposit in the good will bank of your user community.

Examining your product's database logs can yield other types of information about your users' behavior. You can determine who spends all day entering data or sending queries and who rarely signs on. In some instances the disparity may be a result of different roles, but in other cases it may indicate a problem. For example, a technophobic senior manager who is supposed to be using the product may be delegating the work to someone else. Or a flaw in the design of the product may be forcing some users to create workarounds, bypassing the system altogether.

Items entered into your change management database are another reliable indicator of users' discomfort, particularly when you notice many duplicates. If your users input items directly into the database, you or your product manager may need to read through them carefully to identify the duplicates because users can be very creative in describing diverse and multifarious symptoms that are all attributable to the same issue.

Depending on how your organization handles user support, Help Desk logs and statistics can furnish additional data on the approval ratings of your product. During the deployment, your project team probably dealt with support issues directly, keeping track of any problems and questions that arose. After the product was launched, the first-level user support may have been transferred to a Help Desk. If your organization follows this pattern, your support coordinator should inspect the Help Desk's logs and statistics periodically to find out what sort of problems your users are experiencing. Verify that appropriate issues are, in fact, being passed along to your project team. Ask your product manager to speak with a couple of your users whose problems the Help Desk claims to have resolved, and make sure that the action taken or advice given was correct.

Personal Reports

Your product manager is still your most important ambassador to your users. But the position of the product manager changes perceptibly after the launch of version 1.0. While the product was under development, he or she was a member of the inner circle of your project team. The person represented the users' ideas and interests and coordinated meetings and usability reviews, but the users themselves went about their business and left the product manager alone. Now, however, the users are in the product manager's face constantly. With the product a reality of their daily lives, the product manager is a lighting rod for their frustrations. This alters the product manager's relationship with your team. Over time, it can acquire a slightly adversarial edge, at least on some occasions. Whereas the product manager's attitude during development was, "Hey, let's make this the best product we can!" after release it's often, "Damn it, why can't you fix that bug right now!"

If you and your team show some understanding of the pressures your product manager must contend with, the adversarial tone will not come to dominate the relationship. Day in, day out, the product manager walks a thin psychological line. On the one hand, he wants peace and contentment in the user community—and therefore is inclined to minimize the severity of problems when dealing with users. On the other hand, she wants action as soon as possible—and therefore is inclined to maximize the severity of problems when dealing with the project team. If the product manager feels besieged or ignored, this contradiction can make it difficult for him or her to research the true state of affairs among the users and to report information impartially. The more effort you invest in maintaining a collaborative, supportive relationship with your product manager, the more objective the accounts you receive will be.

Direct personal contact between your project team and your user community helps clear up misunderstandings and prevent an us-versus-them mentality. Tone of voice and body language convey subtle messages not easily perceived from e-mails and database entries. You can schedule regular meetings and select the participants, but a more spontaneous gathering can also be effective. At least once, try to arrange an early-morning open house—a "Doughnuts with the Developers" in the users' conference room where anyone can walk in and talk about anything on his or her mind.

The members of your project team should occasionally go visit the users' work areas. They can make appointments to meet with particular people, or they can just stroll around and say hello. Sooner or later, the users will say hello back and start to chat. If your team member steers the conversation in the right direction, before long he or she will get an earful of issues. Moreover, these spontaneous encounters remind your users of the human beings behind the product and keep the users' characteristics uppermost in your team members' minds.

You will be able to resolve some user acceptance issues by altering your product. In the next version you release, you might modify the user interface, the workflow, or the program rules to address urgent problems. Some, however, will be beyond your control—especially those arising from changes in your users' social patterns or status. Once you've identified the problem and the cause, your client may be able to think of an appropriate solution. For example, if your users are more isolated in their work than they were before, activities could be planned that bring them together. If a former leader has lost authority, a new task or responsibility could be assigned that reinforces his or her prestige. By focusing your client's attention on these people-oriented concerns, you demonstrate that your project management skills extend beyond technology.

Empower Your Users

As your product becomes integrated into your users' daily routines and work habits, a different kind of communication will evolve between them and your team. Your product manager will remain their primary liaison, and from time to time you will hold training classes or demos when new hires join or when you release a new version. Yet plenty of minor issues will arise—not problems, not enhancement requests, simply questions about the system's rules or the correlation between the actual work practices and the data model. To deal with these issues, you should develop a cadre of local

Figure 10.1 Point Person Council.

"power user" experts. The larger your user community and the more widely dispersed they are, the more you will benefit from this network of point people.

Users who serve as point people should not necessarily be the same users who have been usability consultants and beta testers, although the two sets will certainly overlap to some degree. Every location of your user community should be represented by at least one person; every department and user type should also have their own delegate. In general, a ratio of one point person to approximately a dozen users should provide adequate coverage without overcrowding your conference room. If you have a large user community, you can establish an advisory cabinet of up to 20 senior point people and empower them to create user groups with more junior point people in their own locations, departments, or functional areas.

Point Person Profile

The ideal point person is a technophile and tinkerer. He reads computer magazines and buys the latest gadgets. When a new version of an operating system, an office application, or a programming language becomes available, she wants to install it right away—perhaps months or years before your organization is ready. When things go wrong with his computer, he does not bother to call for technical support, at least not initially, and won't until he has tried all kinds of creative solutions himself. Friends ask her advice about new technology, and at family gatherings she often finds herself cornered by cousins with computer problems.

A point person is also an expert in the users' work processes and data. He should have been a member of your user community for at least a year. She should be aware of the activities upstream and downstream of her own tasks, and she should understand how your product helps the organization accomplish its goals. When inaccurate data appears in the system—either because it was input incorrectly, the conversion program made a mistake, or your product's calculations were incorrect—he should recognize it and be able to make an educated guess about what ought to be done to fix it. She should have lots of ideas about how to improve and enhance your product, even if many of them are impractical.

Communication skills are essential. Other users should naturally gravitate toward her. He should be sociable, eating lunch or going shopping with his colleagues frequently. In their free time coworkers should hang around her office to complain about their jobs and try out her new gadgets. He ought to be able to speak well at meetings and deliver coherent presentations. Her reports, memos, and e-mails should be grammatically correct and concise. He should know when to offer praise sincerely and how to criticize diplomatically. She should be attuned to the politics within the user community and be willing to provide advice about the feasibility of different strategies.

Most importantly, a point person should command the respect of his or her peers. He should be a problem solver. She should have a positive outlook that things can be changed for the better. Maturity and good judgment and fair-mindedness all contribute to the person's natural leadership role.

Of course, if you put all these characteristics together, you wind up with an excellent candidate for CEO of your organization! In reality, you're not going to find many users of your product who possess even most of these traits. But keep the profile in mind as you survey the available talent, and try to create a balance of skills and personalities among the network as a whole.

Recruitment

Unless you have a great deal of personal charisma, users are not going to leap at the opportunity to become a point person for your product. In all probability, you will need to recruit them actively. Before you divert substantial resources to canvassing your entire user community, however, consider who may be the most likely prospects.

Zealots. Every department in any organization is blessed with a couple of zealots who really, truly care about customer focus and/or process improvement. If you work in a hospital, they want to make sure every patient receives the best treatment available. If you work in a business, a decline in sales or a complaint about the quality of the merchandise personally upsets them. If you work in the Motor Vehicles Department, they are bothered by long lines and rude inspectors. They may be junior staff members eager to impress the authorities, or they may be veterans who have been with the organization so long that their own identities have merged into the group's mission statement. Whoever they are, whatever their motives or neuroses, they usually become excellent point people.

Whiners. At the other end of the spectrum are the whiners. Every department in any organization also has a few of these. They criticize your product relentlessly, complain about your project team, and submit lots of problem reports. Your product manager hates them, and you wouldn't want to be stuck in an elevator with them. But on occasion they do express concerns and spot defects that affect many other users. Within the user community they serve as the designated squeaky wheels. They, too, make good point people, and sometimes the responsibility of this role helps tone down their whininess. Just be careful not to recruit more than a quarter of your point people from this type, or their cumulative negative energy may cause everyone else to dread your meetings.

Star pupils. If you provided training classes for your users, your trainers will have encountered a few star pupils. These students asked more questions than the others. They assisted slower classmates in figuring out which tab to click on or what data to enter. They may have been so quick to learn the lessons that they got bored and ventured off into areas of the system not covered in the curriculum. As point people, they will be quite adept at explaining issues in terms your project team can easily understand.

Cultural issues can play a role in the recruitment of point people. In the United States, with our relatively egalitarian and informal customs, volunteering tends to come naturally. Regardless of our social position, we understand that we're expected to help out in our PTAs, in our community service organizations, in our amateur sports leagues, in our religious groups. In these environments, individuals from diverse backgrounds mingle, exchange ideas, take the initiative, and seek help from others. Unconsciously, such attitudes influence Americans' behavior in the workplace. But elsewhere in the world, or in U.S. offices where the majority of the staff were born and raised elsewhere, the situation is more complex. Societies where the hierarchies are more rigid and the boundaries between groups are more strict do not foster egalitarian, informal behavior. In the workplace, a junior staff member will not step out of line to volunteer to be a point person no matter how bright, dedicated, or ambitious he or she might be because the act of calling attention to oneself in this manner is considered offensive. Similarly, a senior staff member will not seek advice from a junior staff member, nor will a member of Team A spontaneously assist a member of Team B. In some environments a man will not ask for help from a woman, nor will an older person approve of an independent initiative undertaken by a younger individual. Therefore, if your user community encompasses offices around the world or many distinct subcultures, you will need to be sensitive to these attitudes and customs when you recruit point people. Generally it is most effective to adopt a top-down approach; ask the manager of the office or the leader of the particular user group to assign the point person role to an appropriate staff member.

Senior management should recognize that the contributions your point people make to your product are important and substantial. It is an added responsibility; it takes time and effort. Their work should be acknowledged publicly and rewarded financially. Before you begin recruiting, meet with your client and explain the benefits of cultivating a grassroots network of expertise. It will be far easier to persuade end users to become point people if as a result they can look forward to greater prestige and a bigger bonus.

Training

Your point people are going to be full of ideas about how you can improve the product and make users' lives easier. This will be helpful for your project team—but the help they provide should also go in the other direction. On behalf of the project team, you'd like your point people to explain to the users how the product works, what it can and cannot do, and why.

For example, you'd like them to understand the basic architecture of the system. They should know about the servers and databases and replication processes. They should be familiar with the structure of the tables, the flow of data, and the organization of the user interface. If any data is imported from other systems or delivered to other systems, they should be aware of the timing, the constraints, and the error tracking procedures. They should learn about the workflow rules encoded in the system. The various levels of access and permissions and the administrative functions for creating user profiles should be clear to them. For monitoring the data quality, it would be helpful if they were able to bypass the user interface and send queries directly to the database.

This is a lot of information to convey, and in the beginning it is usually most effective to do it in a classroom. Your trainer or your product manager can put together a special presentation with a demo and hands-on exercises. It's helpful to have at least one developer attend the class to provide more in-depth answers to technical questions. Gathering all the point people together in a classroom also helps to establish their identity as an elite SWAT team and to underscore the seriousness of their purpose. If you have point people in remote offices who can't fly in to participate you should try to arrange for them to be present via conference call and remote-controlled PC.

After the initial class, you should hold regularly scheduled meetings. To some extent, you can let the point people take the initiative in deciding how often they should convene, but the product manager should be the chairperson and should be the one who sends out the invitations. Immediately following the release of version 1.0 you should expect to meet at least once a month. As the product stabilizes and matures, a quarterly meeting is usually sufficient. Although most meetings will inevitably be scheduled at the convenience of the point people in your organization's headquarters, now and then you should make an effort to arrange a meeting during the business day of point people in remote offices and different time zones.

To help your point people remember the technical details, give them documentation written in a language they can understand. Your documentation library should contain all the core material: the system architecture schema, the data dictionary, the data model, the data flow diagram, the design specifications, the user type list, and the message list. If you provide them with a good map, your point people should be able to find their way through this maze of information. In practice this usually means annotating diagrams, adding footnotes to specifications, and compiling a glossary of technical terms. The point people themselves will also let you know during the training classes when the information you are presenting is unclear to them, and you can amend the documents accordingly. Maintaining and enhancing the documentation for point people eventually becomes an ongoing responsibility; sooner or later, you will need to ask your client for resources to support it. The task can be undertaken with equal success by one of the point people, by the product manager, or by a member of your QA staff.

Your product manager should always be treated as captain of the point people, but every individual point person should also be given direct access to your product's developers and testers—and to you. If anyone starts to abuse the privilege, you can gently steer him or her back to the product manager. Your ultimate goal in creating a network of experts is to strengthen the relationship between your project team and your user community. Achieving this goal is worth a few interruptions now and then.

Turnover

Users who make good point people possess a number of valuable skills. They will probably not remain with your organization until they retire. Even if they do stay, they'll probably be transferred or promoted out of your user community.

All too often, project managers put a great deal of effort into establishing a point person network and very little effort into sustaining it. For a while every thing goes well, but then attrition starts to take its toll. When one point person leaves, the effect is hardly noticed, especially because the person was no doubt responsible for many other, more mission-critical tasks. One by one, they quietly depart. Over time your meetings get smaller and smaller, and your communications from users get sparser and sparser. Suddenly you wake up and realize that your point person network has become nonexistent.

Sustaining the point person network should be established as a maintenance priority for your project. Realistically, though, it's not always easy to put these good intentions into practice. Your users have lots of other work to do, and after your product has been through several releases everyone may assume it can take care of itself. Your project team is far more interested in building new features and fixing bugs—efforts that produce tangible results—than in cultivating new relationships and repairing broken links in a human chain of communication. Yet if you plan ahead, enlist the support of your client, and make your intentions clear, you can foster a self-regenerating point person network.

First and foremost, your client and your user community need to recognize the point person role as a legitimate project or task in itself. If your organization follows a formal performance review process and documents each staff member's annual goals, the point person responsibilities should be included on the list along with estimates of the time commitment involved. When a point person leaves and the manager redistributes the person's responsibilities among the other staff members or assigns them to a new hire, the manager should know that the point person's responsibilities must be accounted for. At the end of a review cycle, the performance of the point person should be evaluated, with input from the project manager and the product manager or client.

Your client ought to make sure that your project team is informed about new hires, departures, transfers, and promotions within your user community. This is especially important if the user community is dispersed across remote offices or different departments. If your users' managers tend to be absent-minded about such details, you might arrange for Human Resources to add you and your product manager to their distribution list for staff change bulletins.

Orientation for a new point person is a requirement that can easily be overlooked or underestimated. Not only must the person learn about the inner workings of the product; he or she must also figure out how to cultivate an appropriate relationship with the user constituency and the project team. To obtain information about the product, the person can meet individually with you or one of your developers. Training in the point person role and in effective communication strategies is less straightforward, and often it is best accomplished by informal, peer-to-peer instruction. You can facilitate this type of knowledge transfer by assigning a veteran point person to be the buddy and mentor of the neophyte. This gives the new point person more confidence to begin to act like an expert, and it underscores the value placed on the network's ongoing vitality.

Report to Management

Your first release is history. Your project team has shed a lot of blood, sweat, and tears. You may not have delivered exactly what you originally promised, but you've overcome obstacles, persevered through adversities, and created a product.

You know all this, and so do your team members, your product manager, your client, and many of your users—but senior management probably does not. They've heard anecdotes in staff meetings and read blurbs in status reports, but their understanding is fragmentary.

To solidify your reputation as a project manager you should compile your own history of the project from conception through the first release. It doesn't have to be an epic: two or three single-spaced pages push the limits of most executives' attention span. But the effort is worthwhile for several reasons. First, it forces you to reflect on the events, organize your thoughts, and draw conclusions that will influence your future projects. It enables you to tell your version of the story coherently, creating a permanent record of events to refute potential critics who might try to distort the facts in retrospect. And it shows that you are capable of analyzing your own work in the context of the organization's goals.

As with the status updates you submitted regularly during the development phase, your history should actually comprise two separate documents that are customized for different audiences: one for your client and one for IT.

Client Report

For your client, the project history should focus on the product itself and the users involved in designing, testing, and supporting it. Describe your early discussions at which you created the initial requirements and schedule, and list the participants. If there were different points of view about what should be included in the product and some ideas were vetoed, explain what was rejected and why. Summarize the purpose of the product, the reasons for building it now, and the benefits it is expected to bring to your user community.

Without going into much technical detail, describe the development effort. If parts of your original design proved unworkable, discuss the changes you made. If problems arose that caused delays in your schedule, review the issues and the steps your team took to resolve them. Emphasize the frequency of your meetings with users. Outline the procedures you followed for usability reviews and beta testing, and list the participants. Give an overview of the documentation you created and the training you offered. Explain the processes you have established to facilitate ongoing communication between the product's users and your project team. Mention your point person network, and list the participants.

If any major setbacks occurred during the deployment, briefly explain what went wrong and how it was corrected. Discuss any outstanding issues that affected the product's design or workflow, and that need to be resolved before the product can evolve further. Summarize the priorities for future enhancements.

At the end, be sure to thank your client and your product manager for their contributions to the success of the project.

IT Report

For IT senior management, the project history should provide more technical background. It should review the product's initial requirements and explain why the design and architecture your team selected were most appropriate. List the languages and tools you used for development and testing. Summarize the meetings you attended and the processes you followed to ensure that your product would function properly within your organization's technology infrastructure. Similarly, if your organization recommends or enforces certain methodologies or standards, indicate the steps you took to mandate compliance. Give an overview of your development and test environments. Identify the location of your documentation library, your version control database, your change management database, and any other databases you employ.

If problems occurred during the rollout that were caused by the actions of your colleagues in other IT areas, present the facts as briefly and as diplomatically as possible and suggest process improvements for the future. Likewise, if your project was delayed because of environmental changes, scarcity of hardware resources, database administration bureaucracy, server or network performance issues, or lapses in configuration management, point out the consequences of these difficulties.

Explain the role of any consultants who participated in your project. Describe the tasks they performed and their relationship with the staff members on the project team. Confirm that the work for which they are billing you has been deposited in a central storage location such as the version control database or the documentation library. If any conflicts arose between the consultants and staff members over process, communication, priorities, or responsibility for certain deliverables, summarize the issues. Without blowing your own horn too loudly, explain how you dealt with the situation and mediated the dispute.

Looking ahead, describe any limitations of the system design, the architecture, the environment, or the tools that must be overcome before the product can achieve its long-term goals. Forecast the technology changes that you anticipate may affect your infrastructure or development strategy and discuss your options for adapting the product.

In conclusion, list the members of your project team and your IT colleagues who helped you out substantially, and thank them for their efforts.

Milestone Marker

Immediately after your product is launched, you may feel as though your user community is a battleground and you are the general of the occupying army. You may be surprised by the amount of resistance your product encounters or the degree of confusion it provokes. Up until then, in your entrepreneur role you regarded your product as a desirable commodity, a gift package your users would be glad to receive. Yet from your users' point of view getting new and improved software is not like acquiring a bigger and faster copy machine. Software takes control of their behavior in ways that no other product can. It may give them new powers, but it inevitably imposes new restrictions. Therefore, you have to expect an initial period of adjustment during which your users may not seem as grateful to you and your team as you would like after all the work you've done for them. When you monitor acceptance issues and create a point person network, you demonstrate your ongoing commitment to fulfilling their needs. When you report to management, you remind everyone of how hard you've tried and how much your team has actually accomplished. Before long the tide will turn, the adjustment period will be over, the product will be assimilated, and the users will start thinking about what else they want you to do for them. A new project cycle will begin, and you will feel like an entrepreneur again.

Making the transition from the development of a new product to the maintenance of an existing system has a profound effect on any project team. It alters the balance between creativity and analysis, the tempo of the work, and the roles of the participants. The next chapter will describe the final tasks you should perform for version 1.0 so that your team is ready to face their new challenges.

CHAPTER 11

At Cruising Altitude

Your product is launched. It's off the ground. The system is up and running.

Visitors from a preindustrial culture translating English slang might easily mistake software development for a type of aviation. The way we talk about our projects sometimes, you'd think it was gravity that caused our systems to crash.

Whether your product is a Cessna or an Airbus, it can't fly entirely on autopilot. In your Technology Partner role, you'll need to plan ongoing maintenance to keep it aloft. You'll compile statistics to help you determine how well all the components and processes are running and whether you should alter course. You'll evaluate the tools the team uses so that you can decide if any of them ought to be replaced. You'll update your documentation to ensure that everyone has a reliable reference guide they can consult before tinkering with any vital parts. Eventually you'll bring the aircraft in for a smooth landing (we hope).

Of course, some turbulence is to be expected. Here are a few tips from veteran pilots on how to avoid thunderstorms, keep the plane in good shape, and let the passengers enjoy the movie.

Plan Maintenance

Building a brand-new product is a creative, adventurous endeavor. Fixing and improving an existing product is another type of challenge altogether. The methods are different. The skills are different. In some cases, the people have to be different.

Novice project managers are often surprised by how much things change when version 1.0 of their product is rolled out and the project moves into the maintenance mode. After all, they come to work at the same office, they manage the same project team, they get phone calls and e-mail messages from the same users. Adjusting to the altered mood and pace and circumstances takes time, but it's easier if you understand what's happening and why.

Maturity and Entropy

Spontaneous interaction, unstructured communication, and collective inspiration are what make the development of a new product fun—and effective. As project manager, you try not to burden your staff with too many strict rules or too much documentation. Of course, you have to know enough about what they're doing to be able to track their progress, but you're aware that the best ideas emerge from the group being left alone as much as possible to play and brainstorm. At the end of the process, you get an architecture and a code base that may not be perfect but is at least coherent. It hangs together. It all makes sense to everyone on the team. Nearly everything in it is functional and serves some useful purpose.

As time passes, however, entropy sets in. New features are tacked on to the code base, new layers are added to the architecture. Detours are created in the data flow and branches grafted on to the logic, causing sections of the program to become unnecessary, redundant, vestigial. Members of the original project team leave and are replaced by newcomers who have no memory of the original system's coherence. Each new recruit brings a different sense of design to the project, and the changes he or she makes further distort the basic schema.

Many project managers shrug off this issue. They assume that unreliable, unparseable spaghetti code is an inevitable state that every mature product reaches sooner or later. Or they figure that by the time it happens they'll have moved on to another project or another organization and it will become somebody else's problem.

Yet such attitudes are changing. The wired world is getting smaller every day, and people's reputations tend to follow them around. If you walk out on a mess, the complaints of the developers and testers on your legacy system may eventually catch up with you when you least expect it—during a conference, during an expo, or during a job interview at an organization where a friend of your former staff member already works. Conversely, developers and testers who are hired to perform maintenance on a mature product can immediately spot the signs of careful project management, and they spread the word, too.

Entropy is a natural process, but mishmash architecture and spaghetti code are not the preordained result. In fact, you should already have in place the procedures and tools necessary for skillful ongoing maintenance. What will change will be the goals they support and the methods of using them.

During the maintenance phase of a product, it becomes increasingly important to track all the revisions to the system. Any alterations to the code or the production environment should be recorded, such as the following:

- User interface
- Stored procedures

- Database structure
- Server configuration
- Applets
- Program code
- User workflow
- Operations procedures
- User processes
- Hardware and network components

The goal is to enable your team to reconstruct the product and its operating conditions for any day of its existence.

Measuring the effort and cost associated with revisions to the system also assumes greater significance. When you're building a new product, most of the time you really don't know how long a particular feature will take to implement or how much of your budget it will consume—you've never done it before. Between version 1.0 and version 3.6 your team's ability to estimate and forecast should improve. This is valuable because most users tend to be a lot more generous when funding new projects than when paying for repairs and improvements. The goal is to enable your team to quantify the effects of any changes made in the past and predict the requirements of any changes proposed for the future.

To accomplish these goals, you'll rely on the same tools you've been using all along: the version control database, the change management database, the documentation library, the change control database, the configuration management system, the status reports, and the project plan. Although during the development phase you occasionally looked the other way or gave permission to cut corners in the interest of getting the job done, now you'll be stricter about enforcing the rules. You'll insist that the process be followed and the documentation be written and updated.

Expect a period of discontent among your developers. Of all your team members, the developers will most acutely feel the transition from creation to maintenance. In a way, their entire job has been transformed: whereas once they were the architects, now they are more like the superintendents. Different skills are necessary to do a good job. People who excel at designing and building are adept at seeing the big picture and translating abstract concepts into tangible models. In contrast, people who can make changes to an existing product without breaking it are usually better at focusing on details and formulating hypotheses. They have a great deal in common with detectives and archeologists because their work often consists of sifting through layers of accumulated material in search of the clues that matter.

Your developers aren't going to change their personalities to suit your product's life cycle. Your most talented designers will probably vent their frustrations by complaining loudly about your new emphasis on process and documentation. They may even quit: some developers just aren't happy if they're not conjuring up brand-new products out of the latest technology. It may be futile for you to try to prevent your coding cowboys from riding off into the sunset. On the other hand, there may be some developers on your staff who prefer starting from scratch but have the flexibility to morph into the maintenance role. There may be some developers who were mediocre at modeling user behavior but turn out to be forensic geniuses when it comes to tracking down that one line of ancient program code causing errors in a new function. Under the circumstances, the best you can do as project manager is to acknowledge and discuss the realities of the maintenance phase with your team, recognize your staff's varying talents and interests, and give whatever help and support you can to the people who choose to remain with the project so that they can make the transition.

Enhancements

Your list of enhancements began long before rollout on the day you froze the features for version 1.0. By the time you launched your product it was probably fairly large already, and in the weeks after deployment it kept on growing. You'd like to respond quickly and to please as many users as you can, but you know that for the sake of your team you ought to proceed in an organized, methodical way so that they don't feel like they're constantly fighting fires.

Your strategy for deploying enhancements will vary depending on whether your product runs in a client/server, Internet, or mainframe environment. Yet the management issues are similar regardless of your technology or platform. Among the issues you confront will be these:

Versioning. The first standard you'll need to establish is what constitutes a new version of your product. This usually entails defining and drawing an imaginary boundary line around all the elements of your system: the user interface, the Web page content, the stored procedures, the applets, the database structure, and anything else that is solely under the control of your project team. Any changes made to any element within that boundary will result in a new version of the product.

Scope. Changes to your product come in many different sizes. Correcting a spelling error on a Web page is a minor effort carrying little risk of unforeseen consequences. Adding a new data feed or a link to a different site is a somewhat larger task. You'll have modifications to the workflow and refinements of the user interface design—everything up to and including a reorganization of the database tables. Whenever you receive an enhancement request, a member of your project team should analyze the type of changes necessary to implement it and provide you with an estimate of the scope.

Grouping. Creating a new product version for every single change is not an effective use of your project resources. For a compiled program it would be absurd, but even for a Web site it raises issues of testing and user acceptance. Whenever you release a new version with any changes beyond cosmetic improvements or proofreading corrections, verify that the existing functionality has not been adversely affected. Some regression testing and some usability validation are advisable. To avoid burning out your testers and annoying the users who collaborate with your project team, group as many changes as possible into one new version.

Labels. Every new version of your product should have a unique label. The label could be as simple as a date stamp, or it could be a code with distinct parts incremented separately depending on which element of the system has changed.

Version release plan. After you've decided which changes are going to be included in a particular version and you've given the version a label, document the information in a release plan and distribute the plan to your project team and product manager. Because the plan may go through several drafts, include a change log section. Your plan might look like the sample in Template 11.1.

Test plan. For each change included in your new version, determine how much testing is appropriate. Although your quality assurance (QA) manager will (and should) object, there may be some low-risk changes that you can put into production without any testing at all; however, this is a slippery slope. Especially with Web sites, it is easy to acquire a false sense of confidence based on nothing more than dumb luck. When you go on vacation and don't want to be disturbed, it's tempting to give your developers permission to use their judgment about rolling out changes without testing. Just remember: ultimately, you're responsible. Be cautious and stay vigilant and insist on approving the test plan for every revision, no matter how minor. With regard to more profound changes, consult with your QA manager and decide on a strategy for regression testing. You might choose to verify only the changed feature by itself. Or you might want to check the entire workflow surrounding the change or the upstream and downstream data. Under certain circumstances you might conclude that you shouldn't implement the change without reconfirming the behavior of your product in relation to the supported operating systems, browsers, hardware configurations, and third-party applications. Bear in mind that the complexity of the change does not always correlate with or dictate the complexity of the testing required to verify it. Some simple code fixes demand tests that take days to set up and execute; the converse is also frequently true. After you create your test plan and figure out how much work is involved, meet with your product manager, review the changes proposed for the next version, and finalize your release plan.

Scheduling. Regular, predictable releases reassure users and give them a sense of progress. They also give your project team structure, routine, and attainable goals. They strike a balance between a reactive, management-by-crisis approach and a perfectionist, system-as-work-of-art mentality. Your challenge as project manager is to determine how often regular releases should occur and when you should make an exception. Don't assume that from your users' point of view a faster development cycle is always better. They want your product to meet their needs, but they don't want to have to learn new procedures or modify their behavior all the time. How adaptable your users really are is something you'll find out by listening to your product manager and point people, by keeping track of requests for more training and documentation, and by monitoring the items submitted to your change management database. Eventually you should strive for a release schedule that gives your users a chance to get comfortable with each version and enables your project team to address and resolve at least one major outstanding issue. If your project is operating on "Internet time"—for example, your users expect rapid change, short development cycles, and constant reengineering to take advantage of new technology—you may need to create multiple development tracks. Under this arrangement, you can give your users their new version every week, and it will contain something noticeably different. Inevitably, for most versions the changes will be relatively minor. Meanwhile, you'll schedule major changes far in advance, and your project team will work on them concurrently. To accomplish this without getting everyone hopelessly confused, you'll be obliged

Version Release Plan

PRODUCT: _____ VERSION: _____

CHANGE LOG				
	Date	Reason	Manager Name	Title
Submitted				
Approved				
Changed				
Changed				
Changed				
Changed				

MILESTONES

Analysis start _____

Design start _____

Coding start _____

Submitted to QA _____

QA approved _____

UAT approved _____

RELEASE ITEMS				
Item #	Priority	Test Plan	Description	Developer

Template 11.1   Version Release Plan

to set up an additional development environment and pay very close attention to version control, and probably invest more resources in automated testing. As the project progresses and you gain the confidence of your end users and senior management, negotiate for periodic cease-fires in the barrage of change requests. Educate them about your development processes, and demonstrate how much less risky and less expensive it is to work on only one version at a time.

Rollouts. The launch of a new software product brings people together who have never collaborated before and gives them tasks to accomplish that many of the participants have never practiced. Predictably, the result is a certain amount of chaos and confusion. From that point onward, though, everyone knows the drill. There are also usually fewer setup and conversion procedures involved. Nevertheless, include your IT colleagues in your discussions about your release plans for future versions. Just as your project benefits from bundling multiple changes into a single new version, your IT department may benefit from scheduling multiple product releases simultaneously. You'll win friends and accumulate good will by offering to cooperate voluntarily. While you're at it, establish some fast-track procedures for emergency releases of your product—to deal with those rare situations where somebody overlooked a minor detail and a patch is a better solution than a rollback.

Establishing the standards that work best for your project is a trial-and-error process. After every rollout, you'll discover something you could do better the next time. To ensure that you pay attention to these issues and reexamine your approach on a regular basis, your team should review your project procedures guide at a meeting following each release of your product and update the appropriate sections to reflect your improved practices.

Environment Changes

No matter how well your project team plans your releases and schedules your new versions, you'll still occasionally be thrown off track by changes in your technology environment. Sometimes you'll be told about these changes well in advance and have plenty of time to analyze their effect on your product, modify your code, create a test plan, execute the tests, and revise your modifications until the product functions as before. Sometimes you'll find out about these changes only when your system crashes, and you'll frantically scurry around hunting down the perpetrator. Nevertheless, even if you don't know exactly what they'll be or when they'll happen, you can count on environment changes as a recurring fact of life.

Factoring these types of changes into your project plan is a challenge, to say the least. There is no industry-wide, scientific equation on which you can base your calculations: every organization is different when it comes to managing technological dependencies among central IT functions, various departments, and particular projects. Experienced project managers often use an approach comparable to the way employees decide how much money to set aside every year in their flexible spending accounts to cover non-reimbursed health care expenses. For example, you could consult other project managers in your organization and ask them how their activities had been affected by environment changes during the past year or two. Inquire within your IT department about upcoming environment changes under consideration, such as upgrades to the database software, operating system, browser, e-mail, or office applications. Present the information you receive to your project team and solicit their opinions about the impact on their schedules and priorities. Explore the possibility of joining forces with other projects and jointly hiring a consultant to do the same type of remedial work on several products at once. And then, after doing all this research, using any innate talent you may have for intuition or fortunetelling, basically you guess. Pick a number, and add it to your project plan. Unlike with flexible spending accounts, your organization won't confiscate the time you don't use if you overestimate.

Your ability to cope with environment changes will be greatly enhanced if you create a standard manual regression test plan. Of course, every change will require unique test cases to verify the specific functionality affected: an upgrade to an ODBC driver will need a different kind of testing than a new format for e-mail addresses. But there will be many instances when you're not entirely sure about what might break in your product, and you'll want to put it through its essential paces. If you used an automated regression test, it might not be programmed to catch weird behavior, or the environment change might cause it to report failures so often that the results became meaningless. Instead, the most effective approach is to assemble a list of test cases and test data that verify the core functionality of your product and document them in a manner such that any member of your project team or any end user could perform the tests. When you are notified of an environment change, review the test plan and select the appropriate test cases. If necessary, design new test cases specifically for the environment change, and append them to the regression test plan. Before long, you will have constructed a very useful diagnostic tool that enables you rapidly to determine how much havoc any environment change might wreak on your product.

Because an environment change affects multiple projects within an organization, IT administrators usually can't afford to wait until a time that's convenient for everyone before deploying it. They may give you a deadline and tell you that your product must be tested, modified, and made compatible by that date. Or they may simply announce the deployment and leave it up to each project manager to handle the situation as he or she sees fit. From the vantage point of your project, however, if your product needs to be modified it makes more sense to group the environment change with other fixes and enhancements in a single release than to devote an entire new version to the environment change alone. Be sure that your modifications are backward-compatible, though. Otherwise, you may release your change as scheduled, only to find that other project managers who are less skillful and well organized than you have not met their deadline and the deployment has been postponed!

Decommissioning

You've just launched your product . . . surely it can't be time already to think about its demise?

Software by its nature is impermanent. Once in a while in an organization you'll come across a product that is so old, so technologically outdated, and nevertheless so well designed and so necessary that it's kept running on special machines set aside for the purpose. By and large, however, the average software product lasts for as long as the technology and the development tools are still mainstream. Even now as you read this, plenty of perfectly healthy Windows applications are being slowly drained of resources so that their browser-based successors might grow and thrive.

Being a talented and ambitious project manager, you're probably not going to want to continue to work on the same product at the same organization through its ongoing technological incarnations for the rest of your career. Still, change happens quickly— and it's often much easier to learn about a new technology by applying it to problems for which you already know the answers. Even though you don't need to worry about the obsolescence of your product immediately after the release of version 1.0, if you're still assigned to the same project a year later it makes sense to begin to look around at the evolutionary possibilities.

At the point when you start scanning the horizon for future trends, you should let your project team know about your curiosity. The brightest, most promising members will leap at the chance to explore new ideas and opportunities; you may be surprised at how many of them will do this on their own time without any specific instructions from you. Be conservative about approving R&D initiatives that divert resources from the primary mission of your project. Unlike startup companies, most established organizations are reluctant to fund projects based on "bleeding-edge" technology. Whatever new direction you ultimately choose, you may need to persuade your IT department senior management and your project manager colleagues that it's the right move at the right time.

Even if your team doesn't go trekking off into the wilderness and colonizing new technological frontiers, your explorations will influence your day-to-day project activities. Once your team is aware that they need to begin to plan for change, the small, incremental modifications they make to the architecture and design should facilitate a flexible, open-ended development path. During code reviews and at staff meetings where you discuss implementation issues, you should evaluate to what degree the fixes and enhancements you are incorporating into the product help or hinder your various long-term options.

It's also important to involve your users in your deliberations. For the most part, your client, your product manager, and your point people will stare at you blankly and mutter "whatever" when you lecture them about technology trends. Therefore, you'll have to focus your presentation on the implications the possible alternatives might have for their own tasks, relationships, and organizational goals. Usually even after you go to the trouble of spelling it all out in language that they understand, they'll still shrug and tell you that they'll leave those details to you—but sometimes something in your description will spark their imaginations and open up a new realm of opportunity. At the risk of boring them occasionally, it's a lot better if they hear about innovations from you than from their competitors. Furthermore, when your users feel as though they have helped determine the long-range technology strategy of the product, they are much more likely to cooperate with the inevitably tedious, labor-intensive details of the actual migration.

Compile Statistics

Management is all about measurement. Certainly understanding and motivating people plays an important role, but if that's all there was to it you might as well be a social worker or a salesperson. Managers count things, compare things, and assign value to things. The more they measure, the better their insight into how well they're doing their job. As they acquire more authority and responsibility within the organization, they learn what types of statistics are most informative for the decisions they need to make. When they reach the top of the organizational chart, they may have someone else crunch their numbers for them, but they still depend on the data.

Now that you've released the first version of your product, you can start to compile your own statistics. You've been collecting and analyzing data since the beginning of your project, but the end of the first complete development cycle serves as a boundary that encloses the effort and resources expended so far. Subsequently, the release-to-release time period will become the primary unit of measurement by which you categorize and benchmark other types of information.

Scientists know that it's possible to amass quantitative data on almost anything. Your organization may have its own requirements; you may decide it's worthwhile to count and graph the number of times per week your developers throw paper airplanes at each other over the walls of their cubicles in relation to the number of change requests they implement. There are, however, several kinds of statistics commonly used throughout the software development industry that may be helpful for your project.

Environmental Impact

As soon as your product is launched, it will have an impact on the people, services, and equipment of your organization. Although you may have foreseen many of these consequences during the initial design phase of your product, there are always some surprises. Your users may realize that a particular feature of your product provides them with an opportunity to do something they've never done before. To understand the nature and scope of these potential consequences, you should be able to answer specific questions concerning the usage of any resource your product directly or indirectly consumes. Among the resource-related questions you might be asked are these:

Server. How much space does your database occupy? Does usage of your product affect performance for other applications sharing the server? What are the peak times for usage of your product? If your product includes a Web site, how many hits and page views does it get per hour, per day, per week?

Database. What kind of maintenance does your database require? Are there any replication problems? How many of your users log on simultaneously? Are there recurring periods of particularly heavy transactions? Do your users submit complex queries to perform research on a predictable schedule?

Network. How much bandwidth does your product fill on the LAN and WAN? What does the usage pattern look like? Is your product creating performance problems for any other application?

Internet/intranet access. Does your product enable more users to access the Internet? Does it encourage your users to visit specific external Web sites? Does it run on the organization's intranet? How much traffic is your product generating? At what point will everyone's response time start to slow down? Does the usage of your product raise any concerns about data security, virus protection, or the firewall?

Upstream and downstream data. Has your product created a greater demand for information from external data feeds? Are licensing or copyright issues involved? If your product supplies data to other systems, is it functioning reliably? When it fails, are the notification and recovery procedures working as planned?

E-mail. Do your users send or receive more e-mail messages than before? If your product facilitates bulk mailings, how well are your messaging software and mail server handling the demand? At what point will they reach their limits?

Storage. Are your users saving more files or e-mail messages? Is everything they save necessary? If your product causes them to fill up all the disk space on their computers and servers, whose job is it to create procedures for getting rid of superfluous items?

Office equipment. Because of your product, do your users make or receive many more phone calls? Do they send or receive more faxes? Do they print more reports and consume more paper, or has your product enabled them to store more records electronically?

Monitoring these resources is typically not the job of a software project team. To obtain the information, you'll need the assistance of your IT department colleagues, particularly the service managers in areas such as operations, database administration, and network support. You'll also need help from your product manager to find out what your users are doing. You don't want to bother these busy people with requests for unnecessary information, but if overloads or shortages begin to occur in any resource you should know whom to contact to research the problem. You should also understand the techniques they employ for monitoring and data analysis, and you should be able to evaluate whether these methods provide you with reliable intelligence.

Confronted with a resource problem in the technology environment that is outside the product's own infrastructure but is indirectly caused by the product, many novice project managers shrug and say, "Hey, it's not my concern." As politics in most organizations go, it will soon become your concern, and you will probably be asked to help devise a solution. Because the solution often involves spending more money to buy more equipment, it helps to find out about these issues as soon as possible so that you can determine whether the expense could be charged to your project's budget.

Project Plan Variance

Without looking in your file folder, take a guess: how many times did you revise your project plan for version 1.0? It might be possible to create an equation to predict the answer that is based on the length of the development cycle, the number of people on your project team, the function points in your product, and a variable expressing the flakiness factor of your client—but so far no such formula has been proved. For most novice project managers, the response is "Don't ask."

Even if it brings back painful memories, reviewing your project plans can be a very enlightening exercise. It can tell you a great deal about your own assumptions, leaps of faith, and blind spots. If you do review your plans after every release you should notice an improvement in your own measurement and estimation skills. You'll also begin to understand how much of your project you can actually control versus how much is in the hands of fate. Get out your calculator or open up a new spreadsheet, and crunch numbers until you have a clear, quantitative picture of your project's performance in each of the following areas:

Overall effort. Add the total work hours of your entire team, and compare the total to your original estimate. Calculate the difference as a percentage. After each new version, compare the percentages. If your project management skills are improving, the percentages should get smaller. If they don't, try to determine whether for certain phases or activities your estimates are consistently wrong or if each version experienced its own unique difficulties.

Duration of each phase. Figure out how much longer each phase of the development cycle took than you expected. Compare the length of each phase with other phases. Identify where you cut corners or imposed arbitrary deadlines. Ask yourself what you would have done differently if you had known how the resource allocation and scheduling would turn out in the end. Decide whether you should change your assumptions about the relative length of each phase for the next version.

Resource balancing. Analyze the work hours for each member of your team. Find out if anyone has played the role of unsung hero or if anyone has been slaving away as the team's lackey. Evaluate each person's actual accomplishments in relation to the hours he or she has reported. If you suspect cheating or inflation, apply the manager's golden rule: how would you have behaved in that person's situation? Create a plan to reallocate roles and tasks for the next release, and schedule private meetings with any potential liars or slackers to investigate the situation.

External dependencies. Examine each version of the project plan in sequence, and determine when and where each major problem originated. Compile a list of the problems caused by people or circumstances outside your project team. Review the list, and note any recurring names or conditions. Consider whether it might be possible to eliminate the dependencies for the next release. If not, try to calculate an uncertainty factor for each dependency and include it as a variable in future project plans.

As you look back through your outdated project plans, you'll probably become aware of at least one positive improvement: you're spending a lot less time now trying to figure out how to use the project planning tool!

Development Metrics

People who work together to build a new software product evolve their own methods and procedures. Through trial and error, each team establishes a unique way of getting the job done—and your team is no exception. Yet if you ask the members to describe how it works, you'll hear only part of the story. Many of their collective habits are unconscious, and many of their individual decisions are reflexive. Development metrics can provide valuable feedback to sharpen professional skills and encourage process improvement. You will learn many valuable lessons by compiling statistics on the following subjects:

Code base expansion. Chart the growth of your product through the iterative development cycles. As units of measurement you could employ lines of code, function points, number of program objects, number of input and output fields, or any other criteria appropriate for your project. Analyze why the product grew more rapidly during certain phases than during others. Your conclusions will help you identify gaps and obstacles in your development methods, as well as factors that enhance your developers' productivity.

Redesign iterations. Count the number of times your team went back to the drawing board and made major revisions to the architecture, the database structure, the coding conventions, the workflow, or the user interface. Figure out why each attempt failed to incorporate the complete product requirements or design specifications: what was missing, and how did it get left out? The answers will point to deficiencies in your requirement gathering methods and system design techniques.

Build cycle. Count the builds your product accumulated in development before the final release version. If your product is not based on compiled programs, count the number of interim versions you tested. Review the testing efforts for each version, and determine whether your test resources were allocated effectively. The results of your inquiry will indicate whether your developers performed enough unit testing before they incorporated new features or bug fixes into a version. You should also have enough evidence to consider the effect on the team's productivity and the product's quality of increasing or decreasing the number of builds or interim versions.

Custom versus packaged components. Review the design of your product, and make a list of all the components in it that your team did not create. Include shrink-wrapped applications, third-party software, code licensed from a vendor, certified applets, downloaded shareware, reused modules from other products in your organization, and common DLLs. Based on your team's experience so far in building, deploying, and supporting version 1.0, reconsider your strategy. Evaluate whether your present mix of custom and packaged components provides the most effective long-term solution.

Change management compliance. Audit your change management database. Determine the correlation between items recorded in the database and modifications made in the product. Calculate the percentage variation. Ideally, this percentage should be zero. If it's not, emphasize that for future releases all modifications in the product should be recorded in the change management database—even if the source of the modification is the developer's brain rather than a tester's problem report or a user's suggestion.

After your project team has collaborated on several versions, your developers will become accustomed to gathering, analyzing, and discussing this type of data about their work. They will gain an understanding of the manager's perspective and feel that they have a greater influence on the project's policies and routines.

QA Metrics

Testing helps to identify errors and weaknesses in your product. To be effective, though, the testing process itself needs to be tested now and then. Following the release of version 1.0, your users' response probably gave you a general idea of whether your testing efforts had been thorough enough and had focused on the riskiest elements of the system. The statistics from your change management database and from your documentation library can provide detailed quality assurance metrics about both your product and your testing process:

Error rates. Create reports from your change management database that show only the problems, bugs, errors, defects—whatever you call the items that describe the product doing something wrong. Sort the reports in several different ways: by project phase, by build, by severity. Distribute the reports to your team and analyze the results. Figure out whether certain activities or stages in the development effort were more error-prone and why.

Error distribution. Create similar reports sorted by program function, architecture component, data type, and workflow sequence. Distribute the reports to your team. Ask the developers to investigate and explain patterns of errors in specific areas of the product. Ask the testers to evaluate whether the test cases adequately probe those troublesome areas.

Error perpetrators. Create a report showing not only the problems recorded but also the fixes submitted that were tested and that failed. Sort the report by developer. Do not distribute this report: review it yourself and evaluate your developers' performance. If it appears that someone's count of errors and failed fixes is relatively high, look for other explanations before you conclude that he or she is doing a lousy job. For example, consider whether the developer in question is working on a larger number of smaller tasks than the others. Find out whether there are communication issues between the developer and the tester. If you determine that the developer is in fact performing poorly, make arrangements for remedial training, and insist that he or she create, execute, and document more unit tests before incorporating code into a build.

Test documentation. Audit your documentation library. Find out how many test cases were created and how many will be reusable for the next versions. Evaluate the test data: did it include normal, error, and boundary conditions? Analyze the test plan coverage to determine how much of the system was verified. Discuss appropriate techniques for measuring coverage. For example, you might focus on program statements, task scenarios, data flow, or user interface objects. Review the proportion of manual to automated tests. For each automated test, assess whether the investment in development and maintenance has been worth the time saved during test execution. Based on your statistics, create a strategy for test case design, test plan coverage, and test automation for the next release.

The average developer dreads meetings at which QA metrics are on the agenda. In the euphoria following the release of version 1.0, many novice project managers are reluctant to throw cold water on the team by calling attention to such matters as error rates and test coverage. Yet your testers need to find out how effective their efforts have been. Reports generated from the change management database may indicate that improvements should be made in tracking issues or categorizing information. An inspection of test documentation may reveal that in the end large portions of the product were released without any testing—and although there were no problems with this release, next time you might not be so lucky. Furthermore, testers are always criticizing developers. This is an opportunity for developers to return the favor.

Compiling statistics about your project is like videotaping yourself when you're practicing your golf swing or public speaking style. Your flaws are revealed with humiliating clarity, but it's also easier to see exactly what you're doing wrong, what is holding you back, and what changes you should make. Consequently, the manner in which you present the project statistics to your team will have a strong influence on their attitude toward metrics in general. If you are upbeat, group oriented, and nonjudgmental, they will reflect on the evidence you submit and make an effort to improve. If you harass and harangue them with numbers, they will treat you like a dietician who is forcing them to count every calorie and taking all the fun out of eating.

Evaluate Tools

When you began your project, you selected a set of tools that at the time you believed were most appropriate for the job. During the development process, you may have discovered that they left something to be desired or new and improved versions may have become available. Switching tools in the midst of a development effort is usually considered too time-consuming and too disruptive to be worth the trouble. Now that version 1.0 is released, you should seize the opportunity to make any changes that would improve your team's productivity.

Project Planning

By now you've got to know the features of your project planning tool well enough to decide whether it permits you to do the kind of analysis you prefer. Even if your IT department or your client imposes a standard format, you probably realized at some point during the development cycle that there were certain questions it wasn't designed to answer and certain types of data it didn't present clearly.

The most common problem with project planning software is the level of detail. It's difficult to get the fit just right. Every project manager is different, every organization is different, and one size definitely does not fit all. Even if you're using a simple spreadsheet, the possibilities for data collection and format customization are virtually limitless. If you have a more powerful tool at your disposal that automatically generates PERT charts and GANTT charts and calendars and resource graphs, you've probably spent a few idle moments tinkering with its advanced features, pretending you're the manager of a huge factory that builds space shuttles or submarines. In any event, by now you probably have a much better idea of the degree of magnification you want for your microscope. Recalibrating your tool after a major release enables you to start planning the next version on a more suitable scale.

The reports you distribute to your team, your client, and your IT management might also be problematic. Most project planning tools provide several preformatted reports.

Novice project managers under pressure often just choose one and click on Print—then by default that format becomes the one everybody gets accustomed to using. If your reports contain a lot of unnecessary data or, more importantly, if they lack particular elements of data that you always end up scribbling in the margins, after the release of version 1.0 make it a priority to reconsider your needs and select or design the appropriate format.

Finally, there's the question of usability. Complex project planning tools can impose a structure and a process on you and your team that may be inappropriate for the way you actually behave. If you find yourself struggling to model your workflow and the rules encoded in the tool are so inflexible that you're wasting hours on the phone with the product's tech support people trying to program a solution, then it's time to jump ship. In the long run, the discomfort and inconvenience of starting over with a new tool will be less of a burden than enduring continuing frustration—even if the tool you're abandoning is the organization's standard and you're obliged to do some double entry. Your project management tool should serve as an extension of your thought processes and an abstraction of your team's activities: insist on nothing less.

Development and QA

Your developers and testers by now have formed strong opinions about the tools they've been using. In many cases, it may be a love/hate relationship because few tools provide all the features and conveniences your heart desires. To distinguish between inconsequential kvetching and serious complaints, and to determine whether you want to continue using the same tools for the next version, schedule a tool review for a team meeting a few weeks after the rollout. Discuss each tool, and ask everyone to voice an opinion on pertinent questions. For example:

CASE. Is the tool capable of modeling your architecture? Does it correctly map relationships between components? Will it be used much for future releases?

Modeling language. If you did not use a standard modeling language during the development of version 1.0, in retrospect do you think it would have been a good idea? For maintenance purposes does it now make sense to go back and model what you have built? If you evolved a modeling format of your own, were there any problems with consistency among developers? Should you create a guide so that future team members can decipher your work?

Code generator. How useful is the output from this tool? If your team has several developers, is the resource available to all? Is it effective for unit testing?

Programming languages. Have new versions of your current languages been introduced that offer new features you might take advantage of? Should some components of your product be rewritten in a different language to improve their flexibility or performance?

Configuration management. How easy is it for you to audit the files and settings on your team members' machines? Can the queries and reports be customized to focus on areas that were sources of trouble during your development? Has the tool been helpful in maintaining the integrity of your test environment?

Version control. Is the database organized intuitively to facilitate sharing code among developers? If your product comprises several tiers of architecture and several programming languages, is it easy to create a unique build out of the various components? Is your version labeling system still appropriate? Are there performance issues for developers on different platforms?

Monitoring. Are your team members being notified when your product has operational problems? How long does it take? What kind of problems are being tracked? Can the range be expanded? Can you generate graphs and reports describing the performance and availability of your product under normal conditions?

Automated functional testing. How intelligent is the tool about recognizing the program objects your developers create? Does the tool do a good job of validating data in the tables that populate the user interface? Is the test repository easily maintainable?

Automated performance testing. How easy is it to set up the tool to run on multiple machines? If you execute tests in remote locations, are the results reliable and meaningful? Are the statistics about virtual users' experience helpful, and do they accurately predict the experience of real users? When performance problems occur, does the tool capture enough information about the behavior of the product and the data and messages displayed?

Change management. Is every team member participating in the workflow who should be? Are the stages of the development cycle modeled accurately and the correct people associated with the different roles? Are the reports and graphs simple to create? Are the queries flexible enough? Does everyone who needs to have access to the data have it, and should some nosy armchair managers outside the project team have their permissions limited or revoked?

Documentation library. Are the data fields that identify the documentation detailed enough? Do they provide appropriate categories? Are there text fields that would be better as pick lists, or vice versa? Do your team members classify documents consistently, or are similar documents identified in many different ways? Does the application offer a Search function that is powerful and flexible enough to retrieve the documents your team members want, or must they bypass the user interface and write their own queries directly to the database? When they add documents that they have created on their own computers, does the database preserve their formatting? Which team member has the most imaginative excuse for not filing or updating documents?

User documentation. Is the tool well integrated enough to create both online and printable documentation from a single source without much reformatting? Can style changes be applied easily to multiple components all at once? How efficient is the indexing function?

The answers to many of these questions are going to be *No* or *Not as much as we'd like*. In theory, if you had an unlimited budget and unlimited time your team could acquire a set of tools that perfectly suited all their needs. In practice, you do the best you can with whatever you can afford. Yet the discussion will be helpful in other ways besides enabling everyone to vent their frustrations. You will be able to learn whether there is a particular tool your team now depends on that actively hinders their work or one that they do not possess that could greatly expedite it. If this is the case, you should be sure to allocate resources for a new tool in the budget and schedule for your next version.

Even if new tools won't solve all your problems or you're certain no purchases will be approved, your team's analysis of the situation will lead to ideas about making the best use of whatever you have. It's an opportunity for you to reexamine your processes, standards, and procedures and to learn from past experiences before you forge ahead.

Forms and Templates

The difference between obstructive bureaucracy and competent administration can often be traced back to the forms and templates people use. Gathering too much irrelevant information and storing it in too many different places decreases productivity and makes everyone annoyed. On the other hand, collecting just enough information and organizing it so that it can be easily retrieved and understood creates a powerful medium of communication and makes everyone confident the process is functioning reliably.

During the development of version 1.0, you learned by trial and error what worked well and what seemed awkward or unnecessary in your forms and templates. At the time you may have been reluctant to modify them: the data elements they contained may have been linked to fields in your project databases, or the procedures they guided may have been too deeply embedded in your team's workflow to meddle with them. After a major release you can sever links and break habits with fewer negative consequences. As with the development and QA tools, you should devote some time at a team meeting to reevaluating your forms and templates for the following:

Project planning and reporting. Can you streamline the status reports and time sheets your staff gives you? Should you add or modify data elements so that they integrate better with your project planning tool or your change management system? Are the categories provided for classifying tasks and development phases still up to date?

Change request. Does the change request form integrate well with your change management database? Does it provide the necessary fields for approvals and comments? Does it integrate well with the documentation library and the version control system? Is it effectively tracking the timeliness of responses to users?

User acceptance. Have your client and product manager cooperated with an acceptance process based on a form? If they have been reluctant, can data elements be added to or subtracted from the form to change their minds? Should the form be circulated among the point people as well to ensure adequate representation of various user perspectives?

System and test documentation. Is the format of your documentation clear enough so that a newcomer to your project team would be able to decipher it? Are all of your team members using the same naming conventions? Does everyone agree that the document templates provide an appropriate level of detail? Do the categories for classifying documents integrate well with your documentation library?

User documentation. Based on the initial response from your users, are the templates for the manual, the Help files, and the training materials well designed? Do they convey information clearly and in an attractive format? Can the templates be modified easily? Can the information be updated section by section without publishing an entire new edition?

Revising a form or template by committee can become a tedious, time-consuming, nit-picking chore. The best way to avoid getting bogged down in this endeavor is to have a general group discussion and then assign the task to a team member who excels in user interface design. Alternatively, you might assign it to a junior developer who wants to improve his or her skills in this area and offer the services of your UI expert as critic and mentor.

Amid all the competing pressures and priorities, it's often difficult for a project manager to focus on something as invisible to the users as your tool kit. It's even more difficult to justify investing time and resources in them—even in discussing them at length. As the proverb says, it's usually the cobbler's children who walk around barefoot. Yet these tools are essential for maintaining your product efficiently and managing your project intelligently. Treat your tool review as a housekeeping task: put it in the project plan after every major release, roll up your sleeves, do it all at once with everyone's help and cooperation, and then enjoy the results.

Finish Documentation

No museum curator has yet created an exhibit of office folk art. If anyone did, it would be sure to include a couple of timeless favorites—versions of which may one day be discovered in hieroglyphics adorning a pharaoh's tomb. There's the classic poster, "You want it WHEN???", which depicts several blobby creatures laughing hysterically. Another popular, flowery specimen urges Random Acts of Kindness. But the all-time winner of the copy machine manufacturers' Most Duplicated award has to be the cartoon figure sitting on a toilet underneath the slogan, "No Job Is Complete Until the Paperwork Is Done."

People document their lives in many ways, from handwritten journals where we record our thoughts and feelings to checkbook ledgers where we keep track of our income and expenses. If we do it for ourselves, it's a process that seems natural and sensible, and we take it for granted. If someone else asks us to do it, though, we tend to perceive the task as pointless, time-wasting paperwork.

Nowadays many technology professionals, including project managers, seem to feel that they can get along just fine without documentation. Whenever they're obliged to produce system or test documentation, they regard it as a sort of penance they have to endure as a consequence of any fun they had building the product—like doing an expense report or filling out a tax form.

This wasn't always the case in the computer industry, and it's certainly not the case in other professions. Imagine how confident you'd feel about flying if aerospace engineers had the same standard of documentation as your present software development colleagues. Certainly no one would ever voluntarily submit to an operation if the hospital organized its X-rays and patient records the way most IT departments maintain

Figure 11.1   Flight controls.

their project documentation, or if the internist, surgeon, and radiologist relied on oral communication to the degree that many software development team members do.

Project managers often protest that they are not building airplanes or running life-support systems and that creating "proper" documentation would stifle people's ingenuity and cause unacceptable delays. While this may be a valid argument for version 1.0 of a product, after that first release it no longer carries much weight. As soon as you begin maintaining what you've already built, you're going to need memory aids and reference materials.

But what do you document and in how much detail? If you consult any of the engineering standards, you might just abandon the whole idea because the scope and precision of their recommended approach may be beyond your project's resources. There are other less ambitious, more pragmatic solutions you might try.

The main principle to keep in mind is that the purpose of any project documentation is to serve as a communications medium for colleagues who work together. There may be other purposes—such as capitalizing on the organization's investment in software development or fulfilling regulatory requirements—but the principal goal is to share information. You want to have an authoritative source where the project team members can go to look things up.

When Julius Caesar returned from his trip to Gaul, he provided his management with a famously terse summary: "I came, I saw, I conquered." Of course, he then went on to elaborate at greater length about the route he took, the customs of the barbarians, and the exploits of his army. As you assemble your documentation, adapt Caesar's formula (although if you put a statue of him on a pedestal in your office, other project managers might get the wrong idea about your ambitions). Based on the information you record, any reader should be able to learn what your product is supposed to do, how it was constructed, how it was tested, and what happened during the development process. Explain to your team that rather than treating it as a chore like filling out expense reports, they should imagine themselves publishing a travel guide, so that any future colleagues who join them later will begin their journey equipped with a map, a guide to points of interest, and a brief history of the territory. Immediately after the rollout, begin this endeavor by taking inventory of your documentation for project planning, system development, testing, and user support.

Project Wrap-Up

The final days and weeks of a project are typically a blur of activity. No matter what methodology or process you follow, so many last-minute issues pop up that it's hard to dot all your *i*s and cross all your *t*s on anything but the product itself. Everyone pitches in and does whatever it takes during that final push to get the product out the door. Your follow-up reports and statistics are likely to be based as much on scribbled notes as on real documents.

Before you move on to the next development cycle, take the time to update your project documentation and put it in order. Revise the schedule and budget to show what actually occurred and how much you spent. Recalculate the resource time line. Ask your team members to take a fresh look at the project procedures guide and development standards and to recommend changes. Determine which documents should be archived in the version control database and the documentation library—and make sure everyone follows through and transfers their files. When you're satisfied that the task is complete, update the documentation index.

System Reconstruction

Imagining and building new programs is unquestionably more fun than stopping to write down what you've already done. Novice developers naturally think that they are always going to remember how their code works. It's up to the project manager to adopt a mature, long-range perspective and insist on diligent record keeping.

The type and amount of system documentation you'll need will vary depending on the standards of your organization and the scope and architecture of your product. Different IT departments refer to document types by different names. Wherever you work, whatever your product does, the purpose of system documentation remains the same. It helps you identify dependencies and predict consequences when you decide to change the code. It enables you to reconstruct the product in the event that Godzilla stomps on your server or your entire project team quits to seek enlightenment in Tibet. (Not to mention the more mundane disasters such as fire, flood, earthquakes, terrorist attacks, and mass defections to form a startup company.)

Impress on your developers that you are committed to producing adequate system documentation. Ask your documentation coordinator to audit the documentation library and inspect the revision date on each important document. Review the documents at a team meeting to make sure everyone agrees they're up to date before they begin working on the next version.

Test Arsenal

Testers often become more and more intuitive the longer they work on a project. They might start out keeping meticulous records, but as they get to know the product and the developers better they acquire a feel for where the bugs are lurking. Or at least they believe they do. As a result, when they're given a new build they ignore the documented testware and don't take notes while they proceed on a hunting and gathering expedition through the program.

Not all testers succumb to this behavior, of course, but the temptation is there. In the final phases before a release it's also not unusual for even the most methodical testers to bypass the formal change management procedures and pick up the phone to inform the developers immediately if they find a major bug.

All of this is just the way things get done. But once a product is deployed, you'll want to go back and finish building up your arsenal of tests. Your QA manager should make sure the scenarios those intuitive testers improvised get written down, especially the ones that revealed problems. Record those last-minute bugs in the change management database so that you remember to check for those problems in the next release and you account for the effort it took to find and fix them.

User Education

Soon after your product launch you will find out what's good about your user manual, Help files, tutorials, and training materials—and also what needs more work. The recurring questions asked by your users that appear in your call logs and trainers' notes will indicate the features of your product you should focus on first in order to provide further clarification.

The time for you to make those revisions is within a month after the release, while the issues are still fresh in everyone's minds. It's easy to overlook this step or to dismiss it as unimportant because the current members of your user community are at long last adequately trained and have assimilated your product into their work routines. Yet the demand for educational materials persists, and often it grows in unforeseen ways. There will always be staff turnover among your users; if your organization expands, your product may be deployed to additional groups in other locations. Furthermore, the educational materials developed for your users should be the first training documents you give to new recruits on your project team.

Whether they're staff members, consultants, or vendors, make it clear to whoever creates your user documentation for version 1.0 that you don't think their task is complete until they've produced a post-rollout edition.

Everyone can agree in principle that over the long term documentation saves effort and reduces risk. The practical questions project managers face every day are how much and what kind. What's good enough to get the job done without wasting resources?

There are no simple answers to these questions. No formula has ever been devised that tells project managers when they reach the point of diminishing returns. Yet there are more subjective, common-sense measures you can employ.

Suppose your users decide to change their requirements. Let's say they want to introduce a new service. This new service is conceptually different from any of their existing services, so incorporating it into your product is much more complicated than simply adding a row to a table. You can see right away that you'll have to restructure your data model, reconfigure your workflow, and modify many user interface components.

Here's the challenge: you have to identify every data field, procedure, file, UI component, program control, object, module of code, and test case affected by the proposed change—and you have to do it within a reasonable amount of time. The parameters of "reasonable" will depend on your organization's culture; at a stock brokerage it might be two days, while at a community college it might be two weeks.

If you can meet this challenge, then you can rest assured that your documentation is good enough.

Milestone Marker

One of the distinguishing characteristics of a skillful project manager is the amount of time, resources, and energy he or she invests in Technology Partner activities immediately after a rollout. If you neglect this phase, you're like a baseball or golf or tennis player who chokes your swing after making contact with the ball: you lose all the power of the follow-through. Planning maintenance, compiling statistics, evaluating tools, and finishing documentation all serve to increase the effectiveness of your team—and to get you into position for the next cycle of your project. In aviation terms, these tasks enable your aircraft to log as many flight hours as possible at cruising altitude, keeping close to its schedule of arrivals and departures and avoiding midair mechanical problems.

Another notable trait of an experienced project manager is follow-through with the people on the team. For many techies, this doesn't come naturally. All too often, the geek mentality regards people as if they were program components: when they're finished executing their tasks, you're done with them and need not give them another thought. Yet building something together is a creative, emotional human endeavor. In the final chapter we'll examine how your leadership culminates with an appreciation of those who brought your product into existence and made your project a reality.

CHAPTER 12

Back in Base Camp

It's easy to dismiss a software development project as no big deal, just all in a (long) day's work. Sometimes, for some participants, that may be true, but not always. Now and then, there's a project that somehow takes off: the team comes together, the ideas start flowing, and the product becomes a landmark in the organization's history. Years later, the participants still use it as an ideal by which they measure all others. At meetings they'll get a faraway look in their eyes and say, "Well, back on the XYZ Project, this is the way we handled it . . ." To have been a team member on such a project may become a highlight of a person's career. To have managed such a project is a personal adventure and a professional triumph.

Your first experience managing a software project won't be so glorious. But if you have aspirations, you should be aware that your behavior toward your team after the rollout of version 1.0—no matter what happened, no matter how things turned out—will set the stage for their future performance. In the midst of all the other post-deployment activities, you should make it a priority to recognize their accomplishments, schedule any training they may need or want, and arrange a celebration.

The guiding principle is that as Team Captain you should acknowledge you've all been through an important experience together. Imagine that you're part of a mountain climbing expedition in training for Everest. You've scaled K2, your first practice peak. Mistakes were made, equipment was damaged, climbers were injured, but you made it. Now you're back in base camp. It's time to review what went right, what went wrong, and what the team could do better in preparation for your next ascent.

Figure 12.1 A peak experience.

Recognize Accomplishments

Everyone responds to praise. One of the great pleasures of management is watching a smile break out on the face of a person whom you've just told (sincerely!) that you thought he or she did a good job. But even praise can be misused. Despite your good intentions, if you focus on the wrong thing or are insensitive about your delivery, you can end up leaving people feeling worse than if you hadn't said anything at all. Be mindful, and speak deliberately.

Team Focus

All teams have stronger players and weaker players, and your staff is no exception. But when it comes time to thank them for their efforts, address the group as a group. A message of inclusion and shared responsibility should prompt your choice of words. Don't single out individuals for special commendation or blame, and don't compare individuals' achievements or contributions. Narrate the story in the first person plural, as in: "After the database got corrupted we thought we'd never have time to build the Cost Center Report before code freeze, but we worked all night to restore the backup and input the changes, and we made it after all." The second person plural is also fine, such as "You put up with a lot of indecisiveness and contradictory requests from our users, and I'm proud of the tactful way you responded."

As you speak to your team and consider the actions or events you want to highlight, try to select incidents that illustrate team members cooperating with each other rather than feats of single-handed (or even multihanded) heroism. With small teams this can be challenging because each person's role may be different form the others, but it is worth the attempt if only to show that you value all of the roles and understand their interdependence.

Novice project managers who come from a military background or who have endured the verbal abuse of tough-as-nails sports coaches are sometimes suspicious of this egalitarian, collective approach to group praise. In their opinion, it seems at first more suited to a kindergarten playground than to an adult work environment. Your goal as project manager, however, is not to use your authority to publicly elevate or humiliate each member of your staff. On the contrary, you want to solidify the foundation of trust and good will your team has established as a result of surviving their first product launch together. Whatever rivalries or conflicts they may have struggled with during development, the brief post-rollout euphoria is an opportunity for letting bygones be bygones and strengthening the bonds within the team. If you help promote their group identity, they will find it easier to work together on future releases.

Individual Acknowledgments

Even though you won't mention individual team members' contributions when you're speaking to the group, you should make a point to acknowledge each one's efforts privately. To avoid the appearance of favoritism (because people do sometimes compare notes about what the boss has said), make a list of several accomplishments you can praise for every person who reports to you. Of course, the nature and the scope of these items will vary greatly according to the talent and seniority of the recipient. The objective, however, is to have something positive to say about and to everyone.

Conveying the message should be a spontaneous and informal task. You'll schedule an official meeting with each team member to evaluate his or her performance on the project, but this gesture of personal thanks should take place more on the spur of the moment. By the elevator, in the hallway, at the water cooler—you can do it anywhere as long as the two of you have a few spare moments to talk and don't have an audience. Experienced project managers soon learn how much these encounters can mean to staff members. Attention and appreciation build loyalty.

Publicity

Recognition from the project manager—collectively or individually—encourages and energizes your team. If recognition also comes from other parts of the organization, it shows your team that you are proud enough of their work to publicize it.

Many organizations publish a newsletter or maintain an intranet Web site that features articles about noteworthy projects and initiatives. Usually the editors are eager to receive announcements, ideas, and submissions (translation: they are always desperate for new material). Protocol often dictates that a project manager obtain approval from a senior IT executive before parading his or her team's accomplishments in the media. If you're given permission, don't hesitate to dramatize the comedies and tragedies of your project's story. If your documentation writer thinks only in bullet points, find someone more creative who will interview everyone on your team, plus selected characters from your user community, and distill some lively quotes. Arrange for a photographer to take group pictures. Enliven the layout with screen shots and graphics. Most important, make sure the article mentions your client, your product manager, and all the members of your project team, including you.

The photographs for the article can also be used to create a poster to commemorate your product's first release. You could display copies on bulletin boards in your user community's locations, in the IT department, in any places your organization designates for internal announcements, in your project team's common work area, and, of course, in your own office. When you choose the photographs for the poster, though, remember that they will be scrutinized much more closely than the ones accompanying the article.

Even if your organization doesn't customarily promote its own software products outside the user community, you can probably arrange for your project team's achievement to be acknowledged by senior management. Most senior managers are glad to send congratulatory messages if they know what to say and to whom to address it. Draft the message yourself, and submit it first to your client and to your IT manager for their consent. But keep it a secret: you don't want to spoil the pleasant surprise when your team members open their e-mail inbox and see the words of praise from the Olympian heights of the organizational chart.

Evaluate Performance

After the digital dust has settled, it's worthwhile to set aside some time to review the successes and failures of your first version while the memories are still fresh. Eventually you will probably have to write official performance evaluations of your staff, and if you employ consultants you will have to decide whether to renew their contracts. Both of these processes will be easier and fairer if you have notes on the planning, development, and rollout phases of the project for reference.

Team Members

For each staff member on your project team, schedule a private, one-on-one, hour-long meeting to discuss his or her efforts and accomplishments. Before the meeting, ask each person to prepare and submit to you a description of work he or she performed along with a self-evaluation. Because people's response to this assignment will vary considerably—some handing in a terse paragraph while others agonize over an introspective, philosophical essay of Dostoyevskian scope—you could tell everyone you expect approximately one double-spaced page. Some organizations provide official self-evaluation forms to be used in the course of an employee's job performance review, but these documents tend to provoke a lot of anxiety and carry too much Human Resources weight for your purposes, so it's better to let your team members employ whatever styles and formats they find most comfortable.

When you read the material before the meeting, you'll probably be surprised by both the content of the description and the tone of the self-evaluation. Even though you have had regular meetings with your team, a lot of work gets done without the project manager ever noticing—especially by the modest, quiet folks. Asked to criticize their own work, people tend to view themselves through the lens of their self-esteem, and what they see sometimes is invisible to an objective third party.

After you've read through the person's response, collect his or her status reports and compare the post-mortem summary with the notes made during the course of the project. Refer to the project plan to confirm the person's assignments and deadlines. If there are variations between what you expect from the person and what he or she actually achieved, think about your criteria for success. Be specific, and write down examples.

At the meeting, discuss the description and self-evaluation and explain why you agree or disagree. If there are any major discrepancies between the summary and the status reports, ask the person to elaborate. Offer praise as well as criticism, and give the person an opportunity to dissent. Outline your criteria for success in the past and in the future, and propose methods by which he or she can meet the goals you set. Inquire about the collaboration between the person and the other members of the project team: were there any issues or problems or conflicts that could have been handled better? Finally, convey to the person that you are truly interested in his or her suggestions for process improvements. Encourage the person to speak; listen without comment and take notes. Immediately following the meeting, or as soon as possible thereafter, write a brief account of your discussion. Include the person's objections and suggestions and your own recommendations. File it with the other material you keep that relates to your staff members. Months later, when it's time for you to write an official performance review on which the person's salary and bonus is based, you'll be glad you have it.

IT Colleagues

In your report to IT senior management, you've already documented any crises caused by your IT colleagues' errors. Yet during the course of the project there were probably occasions when processes were followed or decisions were made that weren't exactly problems, but that seemed inefficient or unproductive nonetheless. Because this was your debut as a project manager, in many instances you kept quiet and played along to learn how things were done. Now you have the wisdom of hindsight—plus you have the credibility of a real product. Now you can express your opinions, and your colleagues may actually listen to you.

You're still a relatively new kid on the block, so it won't do to send out e-mails thunderously denouncing the status quo. If you have grievances or suggestions, schedule one-on-one meetings with the managers in charge of whatever functions you'd like to change. Imagine you're a lawyer, and prepare the argument for your case thoroughly. If possible, give evidence of the negative effects of the current practice on your project. Make specific recommendations for improvements, and be realistic about the impact your innovations might have on the present staff or procedures. Maintain a cheerful, positive attitude, and be sure to thank your colleagues for the help and support they gave you on your first project (even if they didn't do much or you disapproved of the way they did it).

Organizational change often happens very, very slowly. The larger and older the organization, the more ponderous it becomes. But change does happen. Furthermore, senior management is usually on the lookout for bright newcomers who have a vision of a better way of doing things and the initiative to try to make it happen.

Consultants and Vendors

The release of your product can be a turning point in your relationship with your consultants and vendors. If things went well, they're your good buddies, and you can't imagine proceeding without them. If not, you're probably counting the days until you can cut them loose, and they know it, too.

Before you renew or cancel, review the terms of their contract and the work they actually produced for you. Document the variances from the schedule and the agreed-on deliverables. Take into consideration any extenuating circumstances—lack of appropriate equipment, delays in your providing materials or components on which they depended to accomplish their tasks, vague requirements that needed to be clarified. If you suspect that any of your staff members may be covering up shortcomings in their own work by blaming the outsiders, investigate the matter until you're sure you understand what really happened. Then, with all the information in front of you, put aside your good will or ill will and do a rigorous cost-benefit analysis. Ask yourself a few questions:

- Could this relationship have been managed better on either side or on both sides?
- Would another contractor have provided better service or the same service at a better price?
- What changes should be made to the contract to prevent future misunderstandings?

Once you've answered these questions, schedule a meeting with each consultant or vendor. If you have many consultants from a single firm, meet with the firm's representative for your organization. If you deal with a vendor who does business with other groups in your organization, include the person in your organization who coordinates the legal and financial arrangements with the vendor. Present your evaluation, accompanied by supporting documents. Even if you've decided to terminate the contract, give the other person a chance to respond, and listen to his or her side of the story. If you would prefer not to terminate the contract but are dissatisfied with the current personnel, procedures, or fees, summarize the goals you would like to achieve and the reasons why the present arrangements won't get you there. Avoid arguments: if you reach an impasse, tell the other person you want to consult with senior management or the legal department, then move on to the next issue. Schedule a later meeting to go over the unresolved items, and if necessary bring in the reinforcements to help with the negotiations.

Terminating a contract can be a difficult and complicated matter, but it doesn't have to be risky or disruptive. As soon as you're sure that this is the best course of action and have obtained the necessary approvals, begin to plan your exit strategy and recruit replacements. The language of your contract may be somewhat vague about the details of the work product or the tasks involved. The staff members on your project team may have become accustomed to informal communications with the consultant or vendor. When the time comes to end the relationship and transfer the responsibilities, the project manager needs to be confident that all relevant knowledge, tools, utilities, data, templates, and other supporting materials will be handed over by the departing contractor. Before you meet with the consultant or vendor, ask your staff members to prepare an inventory of what they will need from the contractor in order to keep everything running smoothly afterward—and withhold your final payment until you get it.

Self

A contemplative life is much more feasible for a lighthouse keeper than a software project manager. Thanks to e-mail, voice mail, laptops, PDAs, cell phones, and other instruments of technological progress, privacy and seclusion are no longer socially acceptable among the digerati. Nevertheless, there are occasions when your personal growth requires that you pause, take stock, and consider where you've been and where you're going. The release of your first software product is such a time. Think of it as an investment in your professional future.

If you're not accustomed to this sort of reflection, here are a few strategies you might try:

- Get away from the office. It's too busy there, and you can't completely be yourself.
- Get away from home if you have family or roommates under the same roof.
- Spend an entire day by yourself doing something you like.
- Sleep. A lot. Deep sleep helps your brain sort through your experiences and store long-term memories.

It also helps to talk in detail with colleagues about the project. They should be friends you trust, not potential rivals within the same organization, and they should have enough patience to listen while you tell them the whole story. Simply figuring out who among your acquaintances falls into this category will be the first step in cultivating a network of your own professional associates.

Finally, write down your thoughts. You don't have to be a great writer to keep a private journal. The act of writing will sort out your ideas and establish your personal priorities. In a few years you'll reread what you've written and be impressed by how much you've learned.

Schedule Training

Educators agree that learning by doing is the most effective way to become proficient at most tasks. Whether it's speaking a foreign language or parking a car, there's only so much you can absorb from your book or demo: it's not until you actually put yourself on the spot that you acquire the skill, the judgment, and the timing.

You and your team have collectively learned how to build and launch a software product. But part of learning anything is figuring out what it is you don't know yet. No doubt at many points during your project the areas in which you or your team members lacked expertise were quite obvious. In other words, you may have learned what you needed to know well enough to accomplish your goal, but now you've also learned what you need to know to do it better. During your evaluation meetings with the members of your team, you've identified specific criteria for improvement for each person; during your interlude of self-evaluation you probably thought of a few new personal goals. Before everyone gets caught up in the next product development cycle, make arrangements for training.

Project Direction

The first version of your product provided many features and functions your user community wanted. You had to draw the line somewhere, and many items on their wish list got left out. Over time, you've come to understand more about their work and their internal communications, and perhaps you've realized that the members of your team lack certain skills or information to model the users' long-term goals. For example, the developers or testers on your team might benefit from training in areas such as the following:

Domain knowledge. What may look like a generic process on the surface may turn out to be far more complex and idiosyncratic. For example, at first you may have thought you were building a simple, straightforward billing system, but when you began to write test cases, you discovered that every rule had 15 different exceptions. This can be an especially thorny thicket if your project involves customizing an off-the-shelf application or integrated enterprise-wide system. Often the best training strategy under such circumstances is to persuade your client to treat the members of your project team as new employees in the user community and give them the same orientation and mentoring that would typically be provided to actual new hires. Although this approach is time-consuming, creates delays in your project plan, and places a burden on your users, in the long run it is really the only way for your project team to comprehend both analytically and intuitively how the users are going to employ all the various features of the software tool you are building for them.

Alternative solutions. Sometimes it happens that when you've already built most of the product you suddenly suspect that to implement the last few features—or the enhancements you're saving for the next version—it would be better if you had used a different design or a different technology from the very beginning. Or you succeed in building a product that meets the users' requirements, but your performance testing indicates that you're going to have scalability problems before long. Or you purchase a shrink-wrapped product with plans to customize it, and then discover it can't provide all the functionality your users want. If you find yourself in any of these situations, the time immediately after your rollout is a good opportunity to investigate alternative solutions in depth. Now that you know the right questions to ask, research the issues thoroughly. Join user groups, talk to tech support, and attend classes.

Business analysis. Many highly skilled developers and testers have difficulty seeing a product from the users' point of view. If you are lucky enough to count professional business analysts among the members of your team, then this blind spot should not be a problem because you've got a seeing-eye dog to guide them. If you don't, though, you may have become frustrated by recurring communication issues. You're not going to able to teach your users to think more like programmers, but you can teach your project team to analyze a system from the human roles down rather than from the code base up. Before you enroll everyone in Unified Modeling Language training, however, discuss the situation with your client and product manager. Find out what sort of flow charts and use cases your users will actually be able to understand—and bother to read! A business analyst needs to act as a liaison and interpreter in both directions, translating the users' behavior into a system model and the systems design back into concepts and language with which the users are familiar.

Planning and estimating. The ability to analyze a large task, break it down into separate sequential activities, identify the dependencies, and estimate how long each activity will take is not rocket science. It's clairvoyance—and anyone who possesses this gift should head straight for Las Vegas instead of wasting his or her talents building software. Seriously, though, this ability does improve a great deal with experience. Clear requirements and good communication among the project team also help. Certain techniques can be taught, and certain methods can be practiced in a classroom environment. If members of your team are consistently way off in their forecasts, sending them for training is a better alternative than continuing to stew in frustration and uncertainty.

Depending on who in your organization finances the training budget, you may face a tough customer when you try to sell the idea of training for your staff in skills not directly related to coding or testing. If your client pays the bills, you'll have an easier time; if it's an IT department senior manager, you may need to enlist your client's support in furnishing testimony on why it would benefit your project. Sometimes the best way to obtain approval is to hire an expert to come in and provide the training on-site to your entire team.

Tools

Many development and quality assurance (QA) tools nowadays provide very sophisticated functionality—far more than most software development projects will ever need. When you began to work on your product, your team knew (or learned) enough about them to achieve certain initial goals. As the project progressed, they probably realized there were other features they could take advantage of to improve the product or the process. Unfortunately, at the time they were too busy meeting deadlines to figure out how to implement them.

For example, the languages you use for coding may have evolved and provided new opportunities for streamlining the architecture or program design. New utilities or add-on components may have been created that you could incorporate to enhance your user interface, hardware performance, or execution speed. On the other hand, if the limitations of your organization's infrastructure have forced your team to program in a relatively ancient, stable language, you might want to send them for training in a newer one. Based on their intimate knowledge of the system requirements, they may be able to present IT senior management with a feasible migration path to a more state-of-the-art solution.

The tools available for data modeling, prototyping, automated testing, and tracking program changes grow more complex and powerful every year. Training in any of these tools inevitably leads to discussions among your project team about standards, methods, and processes. Before you give your staff permission to implement anything they have learned about the newer or more advanced features of these tools during training, however, ask them to demonstrate the specific benefits to the project. But be open-minded. Over time, project managers who no longer do hands-on work gradually lose touch with the latest tools; listening to your team members' advice can help you update your own knowledge.

Training in database software can be another worthwhile investment. If your organization is planning to upgrade to a new version, it's a necessity so that you'll know how to test and modify your queries to keep your programs running. Even if you're master of your own fate when it comes to server and database administration, you may be able to alter your configuration settings and optimize your queries for better performance. Enhancements in database software are often not promoted as loudly or as splashily as those in programming languages and tools, so unless you read the appropriate magazines or have regular contact with the sales rep you might be even less aware of what's going on. Your developers and DBAs, though, should be keeping up with the news. When they tell you there are things they could be doing better if they had time to take a course and experiment with the code, give them a chance to prove it.

Professional Growth

Your project team has stayed focused for quite a while. To build the product and meet the deadline they put a lot of their personal priorities on hold. When they were bored or frustrated, they pictured themselves doing something else and sighed, "I wish I could . . ."

Well, now they can. Even the most loyal, dedicated staff member who would never dream of quitting in the midst of a project and letting the boss and/or the teammates down can sit back after a major rollout and say, "OK, I've done my share—now I'm going to do what I want for a while." The more demanding the project, the greater the sense of personal entitlement may be afterward.

Restlessness and distraction are predictable conditions among your team following version 1.0. With a few exceptions, you probably don't want people to quit. You've all invested a great deal of effort in communications and teamwork, and collectively you possess a great deal of undocumented organizational knowledge. Of course, some people will have personal priorities that are totally unrelated to their jobs. No matter what you do, they might quit because they're moving to another town or going back to school. Although you'll sorely miss them, you should cheerfully wish these folks goodbye and good luck. Other team members might want time off to get married, to go on a trip, to renovate their house. For their benefit you should help bend the organization's rules if necessary—because when they come back they'll be more grateful to you and more loyal and hard working than ever.

There is a third group, however, whose daydreams involve their professional life. While toiling away on the more tedious aspects of your product, they may have imagined themselves working on something bigger and better or just different. After finishing a major project, some people like to move on simply to seek a new challenge. This is a group that you really want to stay. Your odds improve if you can offer them training that promotes their professional growth.

For your most talented and creative team members, you may have to interpret the notion of "job related" rather loosely. When you ask a star performer what sort of training he or she would like, be prepared to hear about something that may have no discernible relevance to your current project. If the person can persuade you that there is a connection between his or her interests and any other project or technology currently in use or being considered anywhere in your organization, go ahead and approve the request. Eventually your protégée may become a mentor or resource for other software development initiatives. If that happens, you will receive credit and respect for having had the foresight to support unorthodox, visionary ideas and to promote innovation at the R&D stage.

The same principle holds true for team members who want training in advanced skills that have no immediate application to their project assignments. If what they hope to learn is an extension of what they are already doing, chances are, sooner or later, they'll find a way to draw on their knowledge constructively—to resolve an unforeseen problem or to suggest a better approach to a task. If your project takes off in another direction entirely and they never get an opportunity to put their new skills into practice, they still may be able to provide useful insight into or comparative evaluation of the designs, programming languages, tools, software, or methods you choose to adopt.

At the other end of the spectrum is remedial training. During every phase of your project you no doubt observed that certain team members were not accomplishing certain tasks as proficiently as you had hoped. Assuming you were communicating openly and clearly with your staff, these people were soon aware of the gap between your expectations and their results. At your performance evaluation meetings you should have discussed the situation and your criteria for future success. For many people, the achievement of the goals you set will require training. When you recommend this type of training, you should emphasize to the person that it is not punishment: it is a contribution to their professional growth.

Finally, for everyone on your team, consider the sort of training that will make them more well rounded and improve their long-term career prospects. Shy people sometimes need help with presentations and public speaking. Stubborn, emotional people often benefit from a course in negotiating skills. Absent-minded or overworked people may appreciate a seminar on time management. Developers who already design excellent Web sites might find their outlook broadened by a class in database design. Testers who have mastered their automated tools will learn a great deal from a conference on usability testing. When you first propose ideas of this nature, expect to receive some funny looks and skeptical shrugs. If you don't press the matter—if you give people time to think about it and you behave more like a laid-back, supportive sports coach than an overbearing high school guidance counselor—in the end many of your team members may see the wisdom of your suggestions. Even if they don't, or if they don't agree with your advice, they'll appreciate the fact that you're interested in their future success.

Providing appropriate training for your staff is a group effort, and it demands a sizable time commitment from everyone. The project manager investigates the organization's policies on paid leave and tuition reimbursement, lobbies senior management for as much as they're willing to give, evaluates people's requests, obtains official approvals, and supervises the scheduling so that everyone is not away from the office at once. Your team members research the courses or conferences they believe will provide them with the knowledge they seek, document for you how the choices they recommend will enable them to achieve their training goals, and, of course, attend the training itself. When they return they should also submit reports to you that describe what they learned, how effectively the courses or conferences were presented, and whether they would recommend these choices to their colleagues.

Occasionally, you may encounter a senior manager who does not believe in training. Why invest in training your staff, he or she will argue, when their new knowledge and skills increase their market value, prompting them to look for higher-paying jobs somewhere else? It's true that if your organization treats its employees as expendable, use-them-up-and-throw-them-away commodities, this outlook will probably be justified. Even in a more stable, nurturing environment some managers become bitter and paranoid after a few of their most valued team members, people they've trained and encouraged and trusted, unexpectedly quit. But most novice project managers soon realize that their success largely depends on the commitment and good will of the people who report to them. Whether your organization's culture is dog-eat-dog or touchy-feely, you should manage as though people matter. Expectations have a way of becoming self-fulfilling, so believe the best of your staff. Assume that every member on your team will stay with your project for a long time. Assume further that every member of your team wants to learn and grow and move ahead with his or her career. Let them know this is how you feel. Now and then you may be disappointed, but, on the other hand, you may at times experience the gratitude of a person who did not believe in his or her potential until you did. The best managers—the ones who inspire admiration and loyalty—understand that they must also be educators.

Celebrate

It's party time! You and your team have earned a break, a reward, a chance to pat each other on the back. Schedule your celebration as soon as possible after the release. Pick a date, make the arrangements, and publicize the event enough so that you would be embarrassed if you canceled it. If you don't, you'll find that at the last minute there will be all kinds of crises and excuses. In an effort to be considerate you'll postpone the festivities—and this will happen again and again until you're well into the development of version 2.0 and the triumphant mood has faded. So be firm! Act resolutely! Demonstrate your management priorities!

The event itself doesn't need to be a blow-out. It would be nice if your organization funded it, and you should certainly approach senior management with your hat in hand. But even if they won't give you a dime you should do something. Spend your own money if you have to. At a minimum, order a cake and some soda and have dessert together in the conference room.

If your budget permits more elaborate arrangements, consider the habits and taboos of your guests. Long-distance commuters and parents of young children won't be able to spend much time at a gathering after work; sales people who take clients out to lunch won't be available at midday. Any catered food should include good selections for vegetarians and people who observe religious dietary laws. Before you decide to make an

Figure 12.2   You deserve it!

open bar the main attraction, figure out how many people in your culturally and ethnically diverse group actually consume alcohol. On the other hand, if you work with a hard-drinking crowd, find a location where you won't be kicked out if they get rowdy after a while.

Then there's the matter of speeches. You'll have to make one, of course. Rehearse it beforehand, and edit it down to less than two minutes. Thank your client, your product manager, and all your team members. Relate one funny incident from the project. Ask your client if he or she wants to say a few words.

If you are shy about acting as the host, enlist the help of a more gregarious member (or members) of your team. Bring a camera, and ask someone else to take pictures. Keep in mind that your role is largely ceremonial, so comport yourself with dignity as befits a leader.

And enjoy yourself. Your personal and professional accomplishment is being honored. Savor the praise, the camaraderie. You're an experienced project manager now.

Congratulations!

Index